VANDALISING IRELAND

HOW THE GOVERNMENT, NGOS, ACADEMIA AND THE MEDIA ARE ENGINEERING A NEW GLOBALIST IRELAND

DR EOIN LENIHAN

Western Front
BOOKS

ISBN #s:
978-1-959666-85-1 (paperback)
978-1-959666-86-8 (hardcover)
978-1-959666-87-5 (ebook)

Western Front Books
12407 N Mopac Expy #250
Austin, TX 78758
www.WesternFrontBooks.com

Rev. 11-19-2025

CONTENTS

PREFACE

I grew up on the edge of the Burren. It is a barren, lonesome and uniquely beautiful karst landscape. When Edmund Ludlow, Cromwell's eventual commander in Ireland, brought bloody suppression to Co. Clare in 1651 he famously remarked, "After two days march, without anything remarkable but bad quarters, we entered into the barony of Burren, of which it is said, that it is a country where there is not water enough to drown a man, wood enough to hang one, nor earth enough to bury him."[1] It remains a striking and inhospitable place, incapable of supporting human life, to the outsider's eye. Yet, survive people have, their isolation in an austere landscape protecting them and their ancient culture from outside influences into the 21st century. In my youth, the Burren was yet one of the last great living oral cultures, a landscape interwoven with stories of fairies, death coaches, black dogs, banshees, giant serpents and other hidden entities who resided in lakes and fields and graveyards, in ancient monuments, above ground and below. These Burren fairies were not the twee renderings of the Hollywood and Victorian imagination, stories to excite and entertain children and sell books and movies. In the Burren, the fairies were supernatural figures who, when they showed themselves, were mostly indistinguishable from humans. They were treated with reverence. Where respect was not given to them and the places they inhabited, illness, death and ruin were certain to follow, but when locals stayed out of their way, respected their ancient dwellings and the places they were known to frequent, then all prospered.

These were not simple bedtime stories, they were integral communal building blocks known to all in the community, acting as cautionary tales that reinforced accepted norms. These stories regulated behaviour and interactions. Stories of drunken men who stayed out too late being trapped in a fairy field overnight were common, as were stories of the housewife who kept an untidy house only to be forewarned by a mysterious stranger that the fairies were en route to harm her unless she tidied up fast. These stories identified and protected ancient monuments, castles, earthworks and sacred places by warning of dire consequences for any farmer so stupid as to bulldoze or damage them. The story of the farmer who cut bushes in a fairy fort (fortified Bronze/Iron Age domestic settlement) only to get a splinter that turned into blood poisoning and resulted in death was a common motif as was the story of the farmer whose cows grew emaciated and produced no milk for his carelessness in allowing them to graze in a fairy fort. The regard in which these fairy stories were held accounts for the unusually high survival rate of Bronze and Iron Age earthworks and other archaeological monuments in the west of Ireland compared to other European nations.

Fairylore as a means of community regulation has been passed down orally in the Burren since pre-Christian times. For centuries, Burren communities accommodated both their Catholic faith and their Fairy faith equally, and a faith it was. What made the Burren storyteller so powerful and his stories so believable was that they were always delivered as personal eye-witness accounts or as the experiences of a neighbour or family member. In this way, each telling wasn't just a story, it was a profession of faith, a sworn statement of fact and those friends, neighbours and family gathered around the fireplace listening dared not question the veracity of events recounted. I never saw this world in its ascendancy. I was born approximately a half a century too late.

My father is a lifelong collector, archivist and relayer of Irish fairylore. From the 1970s until this very day, he has travelled the length and breadth of Co. Clare seeking out those who still believe, spending hours recording and preserving their testimonies. I was his apprentice. To step into the cabins of these old men was to transport back in time at least one hundred years. Rough flagstone flooring was a rare luxury with most having a bare poured concrete or compact dirt floor. The hearth was never cold, a black pot of spuds and a kettle of water for the tea always simmering amid the coals. In Celtic times the bard sat at the high table right of his king and stood venerated throughout centuries until electricity and television dealt him a fatal blow. For those who would listen, the impact of the words from these broken-down bards persisted into my youth. The routine was always the same. A few steps inside the three-roomed cabin I would be led to the hearth, the men in the two good chairs, I, the child, making do with whatever stool could be found. The old man, dressed in a suit pants and jacket that shone around the elbows and pockets from wear settled himself. Tea or something stronger was always extended by a giant, worn hand with creases and fingernails caked with earth or coal. It would be a grave offence to reject the kindness. Such hospitality was offered in a vessel that hadn't been thoroughly washed in a decade. They never needed to be clean. By the time I came to know these old bachelors they had few visitors and what they had to say was decidedly unfashionable in the early roar of the Celtic Tiger. The bards were old, dirty, impoverished and shameful. It was only after death that distant relatives would show up, squabble and glean what the land might be worth to a developer. I had the sad honour to witness the passing of worlds. I grew up in Celtic Tiger Ireland and took day trips to ancient Ireland in its feeble, humiliated and unwanted twilight.

Mikey Griffey was the one I knew best. I listened to his stories as a child and as a university student. I recorded him extensively for my own MA research. He taught me more about the power of community, tradition and place than any lecturer or book ever did. His stories wove people, landscape, the past and the present together to flesh out a comprehensive social and moral worldview. Mikey was 86 in 2004 when I took over my father's microphone and interviewed him myself for the first time. He told me about his personal experience with the Cóiste Marbha (the death coach).

"Did I ever hear of the Cóiste Marbha? I did and I heard him! I heard him and I met him. Well, I didn't meet him because I went in through a gap in the wall over there. He used to go in there to that graveyard once upon a time...I didn't see him, only heard rattling and rattling and it like five or six tractors all rattling. I was coming home from my Cuaird (night visiting) at half ten or eleven and I heard him coming in the road and I went in through a wall of bushes and my face was all cut. It passed in to the graveyard. There was a funeral a few days later. There was, there was."[2] The insinuation was clear. The fairies had taken the soul of someone in the locality off. The death coach, much like the banshee's wail, announced to the community that a death was imminent. Not long after, examining the folklore archives of Clare County Library in Ennis, I came across remarkably similar testimonies which had been collected by the antiquarian and archaeologist Thomas Westropp, who had conducted a survey of the folklore of the Burren between 1910 and 1913.

Though physically diminished and nearing the end of his life at 86, it was impossible not to feel the wisdom and warnings of my ancestors echo powerfully through Mikey Griffey's words. When he pointed to place after place in the landscape with a depth of knowledge only farmers possess and painted an intimate picture of practical, earthy wisdom dressed up in ancient morality tales, I understood how life in my small part of the world unfolded for centuries and how critically endangered it was. What Mikey Griffey taught me is that Ireland was once a collection of little villages and places unseen to conquering and outside eyes. There was a secret Ireland that survived every invading force, land clearance, murderous famine and emigration. It was this hidden Ireland and its broken-down bards that fortified the roots of the more celebrated aspects of Irish national identity that emerged in the later 20th century—the language, litera-ture, GAA revivals. The bards and their oral customs were living culture in its purest and most ancient form. They connected the Irish to their landscape, their history, culture and to their ancestors. The death of every bard represented a devastating break between the past and the present.

The Celtic Tiger brought mass immigration, massive foreign direct investment, wealth and unprecedented greed to Ireland. In pursuit of shiny things the Irish grew ashamed of the likes of Mikey Griffey, seeing only poverty and backwardness. By the time that orgy of material overindulgence ended with a violent economic crash, those who began searching for a way forward found little of their pre-Celtic Tiger identity still intact. The Celtic Tiger claimed all of the traditional voices of guidance. The likes of Mikey Griffey were dead. So were religion, tradition, self-assured identity. By the time the historic 33rd Dáil coalition of Fianna Fáil, Fine Gael and The Greens took control in 2020, Ireland was a nation in which almost a quarter of its occupants were born overseas, with little more than the pursuit of money to unite them. Ireland was a country without traditional community leaders to help shape a coherent and meaningful sense of self. Into this gap has stepped a coalition of NGO, academic, media and political activists with the express intention of changing Ireland into a faceless post-culture, post-history, post-nation, globalist experi-ment. Ireland teeters on the brink.

1

A NATION ON FIRE

Nine days before Christmas, 2023, fire services are scrambled to Killaguile House in the tiny Connemara village of Roscahill. Built in c.1863[1] by the Anglo-Irish landlord James Jackson, the historic house, better known locally as Ross Lake House Hotel, was set ablaze after more than a week of protests which saw locals barricade the roadway to the house with felled trees, vehicles and other debris. Word had spread throughout the close-knit community of 300-odd people that 70 immigrants of unknown origin were to be placed in the disused hotel under the government's International Protection Accommodation Scheme[2] (IPAS). The next day, Tánaiste Micheál Martin denounced the burning, tweeting, "There is never any excuse or place for violence, hatred or intimidation. Those responsible for this criminal act do not speak for their community or this country."[3] Taoiseach Leo Varadkar added, "There is no justification for violence, arson or vandalism in our Republic. Ever."[4] As defiant as Martin and Varadkar were in the wake of the Killaguile House fire, a simple fact remained. Killaguile House had survived the ravages of the revolutionary period (1920-1923) which saw 300 landlord houses or 'Big Houses' burned to the ground but it could not survive the very first Fianna Fáil and Fine Gael coalition government.

The ruins of the burned-out Big Houses loom large in the memory of the Irish. They are icons of revolutionary mythology and are skeletal trophies of an independence from colonialism hard won.[5] From 1920-1923, 24 Anglo-Irish Big Houses were burned-out in Co. Galway.[6] A stone's throw away from Killaguile House, across Lough Corrib, the ruin of Ower House is a sobering reminder that the people of Galway barricaded the Norman usurpers inside the walls of Galway City, kept Cromwell's plantations across the Shannon and defied the Famine to ultimately take their country back from a colonising force. And yet, almost exactly 100 years later, again amidst whispers of plantation and a government at war with its own people, the big houses are once more burning. And not only in Galway.

As of August 2024, there were at least 31 fires at properties of proposed or rumoured IPAS centres across Ireland.[7] Most—14—occurred in Dublin with the majority of fires reported between the end of 2023 and mid-2024, an escalation matched by the state in its use of violence to put down demonstrations outside of proposed IPAS centres.

By January 2024, Ireland had welcomed more than one hundred thousand Ukrainian refugees fleeing the Russian invasion of their country. In the twelve months prior to September 2023,[8] Ireland had accepted these refugees at a rate ten times the EU average. There had been an increase of 72.1% of Ukrainian arrivals in Ireland at a time when arrivals in other nations including France, Luxembourg, Czechia and Austria dropped and the average percentage increase in Ukrainians seeking refuge across the EU was 7.2%. Why the dramatic increase in asylum applications in Ireland, a tiny island speck of rock on the very periphery of Europe?

In February 2022, a month before the European Council adopted a Temporary Protection Directive which granted Ukrainian refugees residency protection and associated benefits across the EU,[9] Justice Minister Helen McEntee announced the immediate lifting of visa requirements between Ireland and Ukraine, stating, "This will apply to all Ukrainians who want to travel to Ireland."[10] Ireland was not obliged to take in any Ukrainian refugees as it retained an opt-in or opt-out clause on any EU proposals in the areas of freedom, security and justice through the EU Treaty of Lisbon. The decision to take unlimited numbers of Ukrainian refugees was made without international obligation. As late as May 2023, Taoiseach Leo Varadkar, while attending the Council of Europe summit in Reykjavik, stated, "there are no proposals to cap the number of Ukrainians coming to Ireland."[11] For the first year of the Russian conflict, tiny Ireland, with a population of 5 million, threw open the door and invited up to 41 million Ukrainians to come on in.

The government, woefully unprepared to deal with the largest wave of refugees in the history of the state chose to enter into lucrative contracts with private hoteliers, guesthouse owners and other private rentals normally used for tourism. On top of being put up in holiday accommodation in some of the world's most visited beauty spots, refugees were given a weekly stipend of €232 which was the same as the jobseeker's rate for unemployed Irish people. The figure was, by some distance, the largest payment made to Ukrainian refugees anywhere in the EU—the lowest being Hungary at €13.79 per week. France (€99), Luxembourg (€63), Czechia (€42) and Austria (€41), those nations which saw a drop in Ukrainian refugees as Ireland's numbers surged in late 2023, provided decidedly less generous incentives than Ireland.[12] And the incentives were also generous for Irish hoteliers.

Placing refugees in hotels had a dramatic effect on communities along the western seaboard who are disproportionately dependent on tourism for economic survival. As of February 2024, all of the top ten towns or villages with the most Ukrainian refugees by local electoral district were located on the western seaboard. They include Ennistymon—which took in 2,252 Ukrainians—, Kenmare (2,846), Killarney (2,575), Donegal Town (2,122), Tralee (2,544), Connemara North (1,178) and Westport (1,303).

In a press release issued by the Irish Tourism Industry Confederation (ITIC) in December 2022, the organisation estimated that 28%

of all tourism beds outside of Dublin had been contracted by the government to house Ukrainian and other refugees and estimated that the removal of those tourism beds would lead to lost income of one billion euros in 2023.[13] From 2022 to 2024, Co. Clare had the greatest number of tourism beds contracted by the government—consistently above 30%. Lisdoonvarna, world famous for its 165-year-old Matchmaking Festival, is located in the electoral district of Ennistymon, Co. Clare and its tourism industry has been decimated by the government's decision to place Ukrainian refugees in tourist beds. Local hotelier Marcus White, owner of the three-star Hydro Hotel (111 rooms), the three-star Imperial Hotel (100 rooms) and the three-star Burren Castle Hotel (81 rooms) contracted his hotels to the government. Similarly, The Burren Hostel (120 beds) and a variety of other independent hotels and guesthouses signed government contracts. By August 2023, an influx of 1,100 Ukrainians and another 100 refugees from other areas vastly outnumbered Lisdoonvarna's native population of 800.[14] Hotelier White, who has been a vocal supporter of government refugee policy, received (alongside co-director of Hydro Hotel Ltd, Somjai Kaewmahawong), €3.7 million from the Department of Integration for accommodating Ukrainians in 2022.[15] In 2023, he received €5.5 million and in the first quarter of 2024, he received €1.3 million.[16] The King Thomond Hotel in the town, registered to Marcus' father, James White & Co. UC, received €2.97 million in 2022 and just over €4 million in 2023[17] before changing the company business listing to Unlimited meaning they no longer need to publicly declare their finances. James White had first leased the hotel to the state as an IPAS centre in 2018 against the wishes of the people of the town and from 2018 to 2022, White received a total of €6.15 million from the state for the King Thomond Hotel alone.[18]

The extraordinary sums of money being given to private hoteliers were such that in May 2024, The Clare Echo reported that private individuals had started buying up properties in north Clare with the express intention to then lease them out to the government as IPAS centres to the detriment of the wider local economy.[19] What amounts to government bribery of tourist accommodation operators has led to a new boom for a select handful of opportunistic property owners, and it is radically shaping local communities. A 2017 study[20] by Fáilte Ireland found that tourists spend only 31% of their total spend on accommodation with the other 69% being spent in the local economy on food, drink, entertainment, sightseeing, transport, shopping and other things. When the government offered vast sums to tourism accommodation providers to give over their beds to asylum seekers, not only did they make those providers unimaginably wealthy overnight, they deprived non-accommodation tourism providers of paying customers, thus killing the wider industry, putting unimaginable financial strain on people in towns like Lisdoonvarna whose economy is largely based around summer tourism. It created an entirely new class system and pockets of extreme wealth and extreme subsistence overnight. The dual shock of losing one's livelihood and seeing accommodation providers made arbitrarily wealthy is a recipe for conflict in close-knit communities as well as a recipe for financial ruin. It is a pattern that happened across the country as a new class of hoteliers, reminiscent of the Anglo-Irish landed gentry in their Big Houses, became a powerful new economic class at the expense of the Irish taxpayer. In total, €2.1 billion was paid out to IPAS accommodation providers in 2023 alone.[21]

Simultaneously, in May 2023, The Irish Times reported[22] that the government policy of using tourism accommodation to house refugees had cost 10,000 tourism jobs nationwide to that point. Clare's biggest town, Ennis, had lost €15.4 million in tourism income and 415 jobs while Ennistymon had lost €5.10 million and 138 jobs. The figures were similarly bleak along the western seaboard where the government had disproportionally placed Ukrainian refugees. Killarney, home to 2,575 Ukrainians, lost €100.8 million and 2,722 jobs. In Westport, where there were 1,303 Ukrainians, losses stood at €33.3 million and 898 jobs. Nearly as many Irish jobs were displaced as there were Ukrainians coming into the West.

An abuse of goodwill

Despite the profound socio-economic changes and emerging class stratification brought by the government's migration policy, Irish people were largely welcoming of Ukrainians by mid-2023. But that would change. On the very same day, May 17th, that Varadkar announced from Reykjavik that there would be no cap on Ukrainian refugees coming to Ireland, he was forced to defend the government's handling of migrant placement into local communities.

The people of Clare had been overwhelmingly supportive of their Ukrainian guests throughout the first year of the conflict and by mid-2023, they made up 12.5% of the population of the Ennistymon electoral district—Co. Clare's tourism hub in the Burren[23]—and 7.28% of the population of the entire county. The people of Clare had been understanding as the government contracted over 30% of all tourist accommodation[24] in the county to house refugees despite being a county heavily dependent on tourism. They had even accepted the government's informal policy of non-consultation and non-consideration of the strain on local economy and services before moving large groups of refugees into areas, adopting a Merkel-esque "Wir schaffen das" or "We can do it" attitude. However, a year after the initial influx, Varadkar's government had grown emboldened by this kindness of spirit and his unquestioned and extraordinary powers of refugee dispersal. The balance of locals momentarily and consensually forgoing norms of government overreach in a time of crisis was becoming de facto policy. Whereas in early 2022 communities welcomed Ukrainian refugees out of a sense of solidarity, by mid-2023 it was increasingly apparent that it wasn't optional. This came to a head in the tiny village of Inch.

On Monday 13th of May, a bus carrying 30 asylum seekers arrived at Magowna House Hotel. The passengers were single men of Arab and African origin and not Ukrainian refugees. Locals had been kept in the dark about their hotel being turned into refugee accommodation until the last minute and they scrambled to protest the move. Barricades were set up at the entrance to the hotel. Local farmers cut access to the site by parking tractors on the roadway. A tense standoff ensued with several asylum seekers choosing to leave the site while others stayed. For one week, the locals held constant vigil outside the hotel. Speaking during Leaders Questions in the Dáil on May 17th, Holly Cairns, leader of the Social Democrats, laid bare just how chaotic the government's actions had been, stating, "The manager of Magowna House knew for three months that asylum seekers would be housed there, but nobody else was told. The local community was not told. Local politicians were not told. Not even the Clare Immigrant Support Centre, which has been providing outreach services for refugees for more than 30 years, [was] told."[25]

On that very same day in Reykjavik, Varadkar struck a defiant and authoritarian tone addressing events. He gave a cursory acknowledgement to the "genuine concerns" of locals before making two statements that would come to define the government's approach to refugee and asylum settlement going forward. He condemned the blockade outside of Magowna House stating, "Nobody should have their free access over public roads stopped in that way." He noted that Inch was just one of over 100 protests at asylum seeker accommodation in the weeks preceding, and rather than reflect on why such an extraordinary number of protests were occurring, he claimed that "There are people who hold extreme views, who hold racist views, essentially, and we have to stand up to that." Shaming protestors as being racist to delegitimise their grievances would become a feature of government responses to protests. And Varadkar further compounded the sense of anger that protestors felt at being labelled racist. While stating that the government could have been more transparent in providing information and consultation to communities in advance of asylum centres opening, he declared that "Information and consultation, as I've always said, is exactly that; it's not a veto...Nobody gets to say who can and cannot live in their area and we can't have that kind of situation." Importantly, the real issue at play in Inch was that the people of Clare had opened their doors to Ukrainian refugees as a temporary measure in a time of crisis, not to men of unknown origin. The government was slyly turning a proud moment of solidarity with Ukrainians into a forced long-term asylum industry. The kindling that would lead to the burning of Killaguile House was set. As of May 2023, government strategy was clear; there would be no negotiation with locals. Locals would not even know if asylum seekers placed in their communities would be Ukrainian or otherwise, dissenters would be labelled racist and no community would have a veto on who was being placed in their community. And so it played out from 2023 through 2024.

The very same week that the people of Inch protested the placement of unannounced non-Ukrainians in Magowna House, another community held a vigil outside of a building at the Airways Industrial Park in Santry, Co. Dublin. Local TDs, on short notice, had been informed that 303 asylum seekers would be placed in an industrial unit over a phased basis.[26] The building was owned by Goldstein Property ICAV, an offshore property investment company that also leased a building in Dublin's East Wall to the state.[27] Already before the war in Ukraine, Tifco Hotel Group (who own the Crowne Plaza in Santry), also an offshore company owned by the Apollo hedge fund, had been providing accommodation services to the state for IPAS individuals. In 2022, the group was paid €80 million in accommodation services. They were involved in a financial scandal in December 2021 when it emerged that they had leased all 209 rooms to the state for IPAS accommodation but hotel staff had been put up in up to seven rooms.[28] The Irish taxpayer was paying for the group's hotel staff accommodation. Scandal aside, this means that the people of Santry were already carrying more than their fair share of the asylum burden before the announcement that 303 new arrivals would be placed in their community.

The lease of the industrial building in Santry was simply a hard-nosed cash transaction between an offshore property investment firm and the state but for locals, it represented a direct threat to community cohesion and personal safety. Several members of the community who protested the site articulated a range of fears locals had, including a fear that women would feel vulnerable walking freely in the area with "303 undocumented males"[29] and that local services, especially medical services, would collapse under the weight of new arrivals.[30] When locals asked for a face-to-face meeting for more information on the centre, local politicians offered them a Zoom call.[31] On May 19th, as buses arrived to bring migrants to the site, several people, later identified as members of the National Party, blocked the road and waved Irish flags. Deputising Minister for Justice, Simon Harris, pounced on the presence of the hard right nationalist party, calling their actions "abhorrent" and denounced their use of the tricolour stating they "did not own" it. Despite protestors denouncing the National Party and their presence at the site, the damage was done. Santry protestors, like Inch protestors were all tarred with the same brush and labelled racist. Asylum seekers were eventually moved in, escorted by gardaí. No consultation, no veto.

In Donegal, where 6000 Ukrainians and 1,239 additional asylum seekers had been placed by October 2023, the town of Buncranna rebelled against the government's lack of communication and bait-and-switch policy of conflating non-Ukrainian asylum seekers with Ukrainian refugees. As in Inch, locals in Buncranna blockaded the entrance to a proposed migrant centre for 66 single non-Ukrainian males in the town, creating a human chain in the street to prevent the two buses carrying the migrants to the centre. Their stated reason for the blockade was that in the absence of a consultation process, the community feared the potential risks that "busloads of unvetted men"[32] posed to the community. It was a term that popped up with increasing frequency throughout 2023—unvetted males. On July 17th, locals in Ballybrack, Co. Dublin blocked the main street of the village as part of a protest against the placement of 60 male asylum seekers in a former Doctor's office with apartments overhead. Confirming the pattern well established by now, one protestor told The Irish Times[33] "We come out and stand here and protest to keep our children and grandchildren safe and we are called 'racist'. People are afraid. There is no one coming to speak to us. All the political parties do is use Facebook to call frightened women 'racists' and 'bullies'." The Times further reported that "Women in their 50s and 60s...said they had heard '60 unvetted males' were due to arrive by bus on Wednesday night and described communications to the contrary as 'lies'."

Inefficiency and dishonesty

By December, under intense pressure from social media, Varadkar was forced to confront claims that the government was pushing "unvetted males" into close-knit communities. Speaking two days after the burning of Killaguile House in Roscahill, he said, "I think we should have an open and honest debate about migration in this country but it has to be based on facts...It has to avoid anything that is othering or racist...I am concerned about a huge degree of misinformation."[34] Adopting a now familiar posture, the Taoiseach refused to acknowledge that the state's non-consultation and bait-and-switch asylum centre policy had played any role in the spread of "misinformation". Dismissing claims that single males being placed in communities were "unvetted", he continued "Everybody who comes into the country who claims international protection is photographed, is fingerprinted, is checked against a watchlist." Integration Minister Roderic O'Gorman later clarified "Their fingerprints are checked according to two EU bases in terms of had a claim been made in another EU member state and had they been involved in any element of criminality across an EU member state."

During a Dáil debate on International Protection on January 17th, 2024, Independent TD Carol Nolan asked Justice Minister Helen McEntee to make a statement on the verification process of asylum applicants. McEntee stated that as a first step, all applicants are photographed and fingerprinted. She went on, "These fingerprints are then checked against the EURODAC database, an EU-wide immigration database which stores the fingerprints of asylum applicants and those who have crossed borders illegally. EURODAC is not a criminal records database, however, the underpinning regulations permit law enforcement agencies to compare fingerprints linked to criminal investigations with those contained on EURODAC in certain circumstances involving serious criminal offences."[35] Journalist

Niamh Uí Bhriain followed up on McEntee's claims and found that while EURODAC *can* be used to investigate serious criminal offences, from 2015 to 2023, no Irish authority had ever accessed EURODAC for the purposes of investigating any serious criminal wrongdoing.[36]

Independent TD Michael McNamara asked McEntee how many asylum applicants' fingerprints were checked against the Europol Information System (EIS) in 2023. Europol is designed to cover all major areas of criminality including human and drug trafficking, organised crime and terrorism. Responding to McNamara, McEntee stated, "I am informed that An Garda Síochána does not input fingerprints on the Europol Information System (EIS)."[37] Not only did the Irish government not utilise EURODAC to vet for serious criminality as part of the asylum application process, but they also eschewed the EU's most useful tool in performing serious crime background checks on those entering the country. And while in both cases, using the systems for serious criminal background checks on asylum seekers is not their primary function, the fact remains that in no case were either one ever used as part of the vetting process of asylum seekers entering Ireland.

Again addressing Nolan, McEntee went on to explain that all asylum applicants entering Ireland are subjected to a Schengen Information System (SIS) check. This system assists in the execution of a European arrest warrant, tracking missing persons and helping to track terror-related individuals. It is primarily used to register alerts on individuals who have been denied access or stay in any EU country. She further pointed to iFADO, an image-based database which is used as needed by Irish Immigration Officers to share images of false or forged documents among EU member states. Like EURODAC, neither of these two systems are criminal records databases and are not suitable for vetting potential applicants for serious criminal activity.

EURODAC, SIS and iFADO *are* useful in determining if asylum seekers have registered elsewhere in the EU so that they can be returned to that nation under the Dublin Regulation. In an Immigration Policy Debate in the Dáil on January 24th, Michael McNamara

asked McEntee how many take-back requests were made by her
Justice Department in 2023, to which McEntee responded that she
didn't have the data to hand.[38] McNamara again confronted her at an
Oireachtas Joint Committee on Justice on April 23rd with figures in
hand. McNamara queried, "In 2023, the Department issued 188
transfer decisions. This means there were 188 cases where another
country said it was responsible for processing a person and that it
would take these persons back. Of these 188, three were transferred.
Will the Minister explain that?"[39] Flustered, McEntee attempted to
place the blame on the Dublin III system. Refusing to let her off the
hook, McNamara stated, in a line that all but won him his seat in the
upcoming EU parliamentary elections, "It shows the inefficiency of
the Department." McNamara's pithy punchline came after a three-
month delay, but it was devastating. In January, Carol Nolan had
already forced McEntee to make liars of Varadkar and O'Gorman
who had claimed that the state performed two fingerprint cross-
checks that could identify if an asylum seeker had been "involved in
any element of criminality across the EU". Now McNamara had
proven that even when the state did implement superficial vetting
using EURODAC and SIS and found 188 illegals through those
systems, all but three of those individuals were allowed to remain in
the state.

The vetting system was even more concerning for those entering
from outside of the EU. During Leaders' Questions in the Dáil on
January 18th, Michael McNamara, citing government figures, stated
that in 2022, 4,968 individuals presented at Dublin Airport without
proper documentation and 3,285 in 2023. Under Section 11 of the
Immigration Act 2004, it is a criminal offence to present in Ireland
without valid travel documents. Yet, as McNamara went on to point
out, only one prosecution was made, that happening in 2022.[40] In a
follow up on McNamara's claims, Newstalk made a Freedom of Information (FOI) request for the number of individuals seeking asylum
protection presenting at Dublin Airport without documentation or
with falsified documents and found that the figure was even higher
than that McNamara had been given. According to the FOI informa-

tion, in 2023, 4,712 people arrived at the airport seeking asylum. Of that number, 85% (4,007) presented with no or falsified documentation. The vast majority had no documents. Of the 4007, 80.5% (3,227) presented with no documents while 19.5% (780) had falsified documents.[41]

This means that in 2022 and 2023 alone, 8,975 non-Ukrainian individuals presented at Dublin airport seeking asylum with no or falsified documentation with only one case being prosecuted. Not only did these figures show that the government had presided over a catastrophic failure in migration policy in one of the easiest to manage points of illegal entry to the nation but they facilitated it by a lack of enforcement of existing immigration law. Again, it made a mockery of claims that asylum claimants were "vetted". And while those who presented without documents but had already registered in another EU country *could* be sent back to that country, McNamara proved on April 23rd that this only happened in three out of 188 cases.

Worse, all of the vetting measures spoken about to this point can only vet those asylum claimants who arrived in Ireland via another EU nation. However, in 2022 and 2023, the majority of asylum seekers came from outside the EU. In 2023, there were 13,277 total asylum applications in Ireland. In 2022 there were 13,649. In 2023, 15% of applications came from Nigeria, 11% from Algeria, 8.3% from Afghanistan and 8.3% from Somalia. In 2023, 19.9% came from Georgia, 12.9% from Algeria, 8.1% from Nigeria and 7.1% from Zimbabwe.[42] When asked by Carol Nolan to clarify how the government vets non-EU migrants in the January 17th Debate on International Protection, McEntee responded, "In relation to countries of origin which will not be a party to the EURODAC database, it would be in breach of our responsibilities in respect of refugee protection to contact the consular or gardaí authorities in relation to persons who have sought the protection of the Irish State as doing so may have the consequence of making such authorities aware of an applicant's presence in the State, and their claim for international protection."[43] The Justice Minister, presenting the fact as an abundance of empathy for the applicant, acknowledged that non-EU asylum applicants are not vetted at all upon claiming asylum in Ireland.

By early 2024, the facts were clear. A burgeoning number of non-Ukrainian asylum applicants entering the state and being pushed out into close-knit communities were not only unvetted, they were often found to have broken the law by entering the state without documentation, some had been served a return order to another EU nation and yet all had been allowed to remain in Ireland. The vast majority of those claiming asylum in 2022 and 2023 were from outside of the EU and no criminal vetting had taken place. The demonised protestors at Inch, Santry, Buncranna and dozens more communities were proven correct. The busloads of single men being forced into small villages and towns without consultation and without veto were unvetted. Ireland's asylum system was broken and it would get worse.

A broken system

In 2021 the Minister for Integration, Roderic O'Gorman, drafted a white paper to abolish Direct Provision and replace it with an "International Protection Support Service" by December 2024. A press release accompanying the white paper stated that "This new model will be focused on encouraging integration from day one and supporting applicants to live independently." [44]Under the new model, there would be two phases. In phase 1, asylum applicants would receive intensive English language and orientation programmes while in "reception centres" for the first four months after arrival. In phase 2, after four months, applicants would receive their own accommodation through approved local housing bodies, NGOs, through a wave of urban renewal schemes, through local community initiatives and through the private market. It marked a radical and generous shift in Ireland's asylum system. The white paper was published on the Department of Integration's website in eight different languages including Albanian, Arabic, French, Georgian, Somali and Urdu and these were also shared by the Department on social media.[45]

Prior to COVID, there had been a year-on-year rise in the number of people applying for asylum in Ireland. From 2016 to 2017 there was a 30% increase from 2,244 to 2,926. From 2017 to 2018 there was a 25.5% increase from 2,926 to 3,673. From 2018 to 2019 there was a 30.2% increase from 3,673 to 4,781. From 2019 to 2020, when COVID hit, there was a 67.3% decrease from 4,781 to 1,566. From 2020 to 2021 there was a 69.2% increase from 1,566 to 2,469. In 2022, after O'Gorman's white paper, numbers exploded. From 2021 to 2022 there was a 427.7% increase from 2,469 to 13,651.[46]

There is a strong stability in the nationalities of applications each year from before COVID (2016) to 2022. Clearly Ireland had developed a reputation among certain nationalities—Nigerians, Albanians, Somalians, Afghans—as a good bet to gain asylum. It seems likely that word had also gone around that Ukrainian refugees were being put up in holiday accommodation in world-famous beauty spots and that Ireland was, increasingly, a land of milk and honey for those seeking asylum. The languages of O'Gorman's multilingual white paper, however, correspond directly with applications from people speaking those languages during the 2022 boom. In 2022, the top nationalities of applicants were: Georgian (19.9%), Algerian (12.9%), Somalian (11.5%), Nigerian (8.1%) and Zimbabwean (7.1%). In a Dáil Debate on Asylum Seekers on 21st of February, 2023, O'Gorman rejected claims that advertising his white paper in eight languages contributed to the rise in asylum claims. He stated that "these are the most common languages spoken by those who were residing in Direct Provision accommodation at that time."[47] While his intent may have been to make sure that everyone in the asylum system in Ireland was able to read and understand the proposed new system, it obviously had the effect that those same people within the system sent word through various networks to others from their homelands that Ireland was a soft touch. The pattern was confirmed when in 2023, 13,277 asylum claims were made, again with the largest groups being those targeted by the languages in O'Gorman's white paper translations. Of the applications, Nigerians accounted for 15%, Algerians 11%, Afghans 8.3%, Somalians 8.3% and Georgians 8%.

By the beginning of 2024, not only was it clear that the government's vetting of non-Ukrainian asylum seekers was virtually non-existent, but the numbers coming in were spiralling out of control. Faced with a growing rejection of the placement of single unvetted males into close-knit communities by local protest groups, they were also scrambling to house ever more of them in IPAS centres around the country. Conflict seemed inevitable.

By December 2023, in a walk back of Helen McEntee's February 2022 open-door invite to "all Ukrainians" and Varadkar's May 2023 claim that there would be "no cap" on the number of Ukrainians Ireland would accept, reality had begun to sink in that Ireland's overly generous open-door policy was unsustainable. Ireland was, after all, attracting Ukrainians at a rate ten times the EU average with no sign of slowing down.

On December 11th, 2023, O'Gorman put forth tough new recommendations that would bring Ireland's Ukrainian refugee policy more in line with the rest of the EU. Under proposed legislation, new Ukrainian arrivals would no longer be entitled to the €232 jobseekers' rate of social welfare rather a reduced rate of €38.80—the same as any other asylum seeker—while living in state accommodation. Additionally, state-provided accommodation would only be given for 90 days. These measures came into effect in March 2024 and were extended to all Ukrainians in Ireland in September 2024[48] regardless of when they arrived. The effects of the policy were striking. In the month of December, 2023 when the policy changes were announced, the weekly average of Ukrainians arriving was 530. By the time they came into effect, the weekly average for March had dropped to 239. In 2023 alone, McEntee, Varadkar and O'Gorman's open-door policy to Ukraine had cost €2.1 billion in accommodation acquisition and a loss of €1 billion and 10,000 jobs in tourism. From the beginning of the crisis to the end of 2023, €650 million was paid out in social welfare payments.[49]

The government's decision to wind down Ukrainian asylum had little to do with economic and political responsibility. The numbers entering Ireland thanks to O'Gorman's eight-language open invite, cumulatively 27,000 for 2022 and 2023 showed no signs of slowing down and these new arrivals were badly clogging up the asylum system. It was increasingly obvious that Ukrainians were being pushed out to make way for O'Gorman's migrants. Despite the new arrivals being pushed—contentiously—out into IPAS centres around the nation, the backlog meant that by December 2023 there were not enough beds for those coming in. In response, the government offered single male asylum claimants coming into the country a tent and an increased social welfare payment of €113.50 and sent them on their way. By December there were 207 homeless asylum seekers camped out on Dublin's streets[50] and the figures exploded in the first months of 2024.

On December 6th 2023, in an attempt to slow down illegal migration across the English Channel from France, the UK signed a deal to send migrants to Rwanda for processing. Under the terms of the plan, up to 54,000 asylum claimants who had entered the UK illegally from a safe country would be sent to Rwanda.[51] As word of the scheme spread, there was a surge of asylum seekers arriving from the UK to Ireland via Northern Ireland in the first months of 2024 adding to O'Gorman's claimants. In the first seven months of 2024, there was a 90% spike in the number of non-Ukrainian asylum applications in Ireland. By July, there were 12,334 applications, almost the same number as the entire of 2022—the highest number ever recorded in the state. In the same April 23rd Oireachtas Joint Committee on Justice where Michael McNamara had forced Helen McEntee to admit that the Irish take-back system was virtually non-existent, she claimed that in the first months of 2024, 80% of asylum claimants entering the state had done so from the UK.[52]

The chaos made international headlines in March. As the city began preparations to welcome global dignitaries for annual St. Patrick's Day celebrations, there were 1,758 homeless asylum seekers in Ireland. 200 males had been living in filth and excrement on Mount Street, outside of the International Protection Office and their tents were cleared to make way for the celebrations with the occupants being bussed to IPAS centres in the vicinity.[53] On the morning before St. Patrick's Day, six coaches showed up near Mount Street and the homeless men were put on board. They were shuttled to a makeshift IPAS site in Crooksling, 20km from the city centre and their encampment on Mount Street was cleared and the street sanitised. O'Gorman stated that "International protection applicants at Crooksling have access to clean toilets and showers, health services, indoor areas where food is provided, facilities to charge phones and personal devices, access to public transport to and from Dublin City Centre and 24-hour onsite security."[54] Despite the services on offer, dozens of the men who had been bussed out to Crooksling turned heel immediately and returned to the city centre. Videos of the masses of men walking along the margins of the main road to the city went viral online adding to the sense that the government was out of its depth.

At the end of March Leo Varadkar stepped down unexpectedly as Taoiseach giving his successor, Simon Harris, the chance to replace the hapless McEntee and O'Gorman, return a semblance of law and order to the migration system and placate an increasingly enraged public evermore determined to protect their communities from unvetted males. In his acceptance as party leader at the Fine Gael Ard Fheis in Galway on April 4th, Harris struck a hard man tone declaring, "Under my leadership, Fine Gael will always stand for law and order. We stand for more Gardaí, with more powers and more resources to make our streets safe. We stand for tougher sentences for those who commit horrific crimes."[55]

On May 1st, attempting to deliver on his promise to be tough on law and order, Harris ordered that the tent city, which had popped up in the place of the one cleared in March on Mount Street, be cleared. 200 tents had once more popped up outside the IPO office with human and rotting food waste threatening a health crisis. Again the men were shipped off to Crooksling with a minority being sent to the 764-bed Citywest Hotel in the city whose operators had received €53.6 million in 2023 to house Ukrainians and other IPAS applicants.[56] Addressing the removals, the freshly minted Taoiseach said, "The situation had become completely unacceptable. The laws of our land must always be upheld and we cannot have unsafe and illegal encampments in our cities or towns."[57]

It provided positive headlines for the law and order Taoiseach but it meant nothing in practical terms. Within days, a new encampment had popped up on the banks of the Royal Canal, one of the city's most beautiful and well-loved walks. In an embarrassing game of whack-a-mole that dragged on throughout May, encampments housing hundreds of men were cleared on three separate occasions. On May 9th, 163[58] men were removed to tented accommodation on the grounds of the old Central Mental Hospital in Dundrum and to Crooksling. On the 21st, 89[59] men were again cleared to Dundrum. On the 30th, 109[60] men were cleared to the Citywest Hotel. Despite his soundbites, Harris had no control over the situation. Worse, he kept the ineffective McEntee and O'Gorman in their positions. As of the 20th August, there were again 30 tents along the Grand Canal and the total number of homeless male asylum applicants had risen to 2,509.[61] In an embarrassing low for Harris, on August 1st, High Court Judge Mr. Justice O'Donnell ruled that the state was in breach of the human rights of the homeless male asylum seekers, declaring, "A declaration that the respondents' failure to provide for the basic needs of newly arrived international protection applicants between 4 December 2023 and 10 May 2024, whether by way of the provision of accommodation, shelter, food and basic hygiene facilities or other-wise, is in breach of that class of persons rights pursuant to Article 1 of the Charter of Fundamental Rights of the European Union."[62]

Harris was able to somewhat distract from the tent city farce on the streets of Dublin by blaming UK Prime Minister Rishi Sunak for the chaos. Sunak, in turn, was happy to take the blame as it offered proof to the electorate in a General Election year that his Rwanda scheme was acting as a deterrent for illegal immigrants to the UK.[63] While the diplomatic spat offered some cover in Dublin, Harris was still tasked with moving those who were rounded up in each wave of tent clearances to accommodation elsewhere. He would be faced with the same hostility as Varadkar was and he would proceed in like; no consultation, no veto. Under greater pressure than Varadkar in terms of homeless asylum seekers and increased weekly arrivals from the UK, Harris was a man in a hurry and again, trying to prove his already dented law and order credentials, a man who would not be negotiated with.

"A loaded term—stop using it"

Harris had made his intentions about placing single migrant men in small communities clear on January 30th, 2024 when he said in a Dáil Debate on services for asylum seekers, "We cannot allow that excuse about lack of communication to in any way mainstream far-right language. Ireland is not full. Ireland is not only for the Irish. What is this 'unvetted male' situation?... It is a loaded term. Stop using it." Just as he had blamed the UK for the tents in Dublin City he would attempt to offload the blame for mounting criticism on social media and increasingly fraught protests at IPAS centres where single male asylum seekers were being placed as being "far right." He went on, "We need to stand united in the face of a small number of people who try to hijack the tricolour and undermine democracy."[64] Harris was attempting to poison the well of public opinion against legitimate local protestors at IPAS centres like Inch, Santry and Buncrana by linking them to "far right" protestors.

Harris further dismissed concerns coming from communities on the ground by casually dismissing the term "unvetted males" entirely, telling people to "Stop using it." Despite the evidence presented at that time by Michael McNamara, Carol Nolan and others that proved that asylum seekers coming to Ireland were not in any meaningful way vetted, his position was firm; stop saying "unvetted males" or you're "far right". Not only was his approach a preposterously cynical attempt to shut down legitimate concerns about catastrophic failures in government screening and placement of asylum seekers in small communities but he went on to further obfuscate the matter by intentionally conflating asylum seekers coming to Ireland with the contributions of legal migrants. Immediately after telling people to stop using the term "unvetted males" he stated, "Ireland is a country that relies on migrant workers to staff our health service. It requires them to build our homes and use them to work in our cafes, pubs and restaurants." If Harris thought he could shut down protestors at IPAS centres around the nation with linguistic gymnastics, he was in for a rude awakening.

Harris' May 1st clearance of 200 men from Mount Street to Crooksling and Citywest had a knock-on effect. To make room for those men coming out of the city centre, 60 more already settled in Crooksling needed to be moved on to make space. In the small town of Newtownmountkennedy in Wicklow, rumours had spread that the overflow from Crooksling would be heading their way. On March 14th the people of the village had set up a 24-hour vigil outside of Trudder House, a former care home for Traveller children in state care, when news broke that the site would be used to house 160 asylum seekers in tents to deal with the Dublin overflow. [65]The building had been in the care of the Health Service Executive (HSE) and was leased to the state for IPAS accommodation. Speaking to protestors on site shortly after the news broke, local councillor Shay Cullen said, "The lack of communication from the Department [of Integration] is so frustrating...Everything seems to be done in secrecy. When I spoke to one of the security team on site he said he didn't know what's going on."[66] No answers would be forthcoming. The community's 24-hour vigil managed to stall works on site as construction crews couldn't get through and on April 12th, someone attempted to set fire to the building.[67] The actions of outsiders provided tough-on-crime Harris to proceed with a very heavy hand.

On April 15th large numbers of the Garda public order unit were drafted in to clear protestors away from the site to make way for balaclava-clad construction crews to set up tented accommodation. Videos of the gardaí manhandling women went viral on social media and tensions mounted throughout the week. On April 25th tensions finally boiled over as protestors set a large bonfire outside the walls of the site and pulled down barriers surrounding it. A heavily armed Garda public order unit in full riot gear liberally pepper-sprayed and beat protestors. When riot police performed a shield wall charge on the crowd, they knocked a protester to the ground and continued to kick and beat him. When Gript journalist Fatima Gunning—who was covering the protests—approached in an attempt to get the gardaí to stop beating the man, she was pepper-sprayed.[68] The heavy-handed Garda response marked a new phase in the migrant crisis, injecting a level of state force not previously seen. It was a stark warning that pastoral Ireland was dead and gone.

Independent TD Mattie McGrath raised the matter in the Dáil on April 30th stating, "The abject failure of the Government's policy on migration is causing huge division. What happened in Newtown-mountkennedy last week is causing huge questioning of An Garda Síochána...The heavy actions there, which were reminiscent of Northern Ireland and the RUC [Royal Ulster Constabulary] and B Specials [Protestant Volunteer Corps], were shocking."

Harris responded curtly, "Shame on you."[69]

On May 1st, 60 single unvetted male asylum seekers were bussed into Trudder House with the number rising to 112 over the course of the next two weeks. The locals, who had, since March, expressed fears for their safety with the arrival of so many unvetted males, didn't have to wait long for problems to arise. On May 17th, one asylum seeker was hospitalised after he reportedly threw a rock at a security guard on site. Tensions boiled over when a group of 35 migrants attempted to overwhelm the security guards and leave the site. Gardaí were called to calm the situation.[70]

Harris' updated twist on the Varadkar policy would now become the norm. No consultation, no veto—riot squad.

This escalation would come to a head in July in Coolock, Co. Dublin. In mid-March an email purportedly from the Department of Integration began circulating which claimed that there were plans to place 500 asylum seekers in modular buildings on the site of the abandoned Crown Paints warehouse in Coolock. Locals immediately set up a 24-hour manned encampment outside the gates of the ware-house to prevent any site works. Under pressure, the Department of Integration was forced to acknowledge their plans to develop the site on Friday March 22nd and signalled their intention to proceed.

Outraged, more than a thousand locals took to the streets of Coolock to protest the following Sunday with further large protest marches on selected weekends thereafter.[71] Despite the protests—and the locals had particularly compelling concerns, as Coolock consistently ranks as among the most socially and economically deprived areas in Dublin and in the entire country[72]—they found that the no veto, no consultation rule applied to them just as it did every other community under Varadkar and Harris.

At 3am on Monday the 15th of July a large garda presence ferried construction workers onto the site. Gardaí removed protestors from their encampment at the gates before destroying it using a digger brought onsite by the workers. A metal fence was erected around the site and gardaí formed a line inside the barriers. Word quickly spread on social media of what was happening and locals asked for others to join them. By 10am a large number of locals had arrived and tensions with gardaí mounted. Barriers were torn down and mattresses that were placed at the entrance to the site as well as the digger that had been used to destroy the protestors' camp were set alight. Up to 50 gardaí were ferried in to handle the situation before the Public Order Unit arrived in heavy riot gear shortly after 1pm. The riot squad engaged in shield and baton charges on the protestors and deployed pepper spray liberally. Petrol bombs and debris were thrown at the gardaí and Garda vehicles were damaged as violence spiralled out of control throughout the evening. In all, 21 people were arrested[73] and many protestors were injured. The gardaí, under orders from Drew Harris, made two fatal errors on the 15th. The camp at the gates of the warehouse had housed protestors for four months as they performed their 24-hour vigil. Its brutal erasure in the middle of the night with heavy plant machinery was both a provocative and a symbolic act. It showed the protestors that all of their cold nights of peaceful protest meant nothing and could simply be swatted away like a fly by the overwhelming force of the state. Tearing it down enraged protestors. The second crucial error was the heavy-handed response of the public order unit. By shield and baton charging the irate demonstrators, pepper-spraying and injuring several in the process, the gardaí undoubtedly drew in the wider community. Some were no doubt outraged by the over-zealousness of the gardaí and others would simply have seen an opportunity to vent their unrelated grievances in the air of anarchy rapidly spreading throughout the area. Importantly, Justice Minister Helen McEntee had been informed about and robustly defended the actions of the gardaí throughout the day. In a tweet later in the evening, she stated, "I am appalled at the violent scenes in Coolock today. This is thuggish criminal behaviour and has no place in our society. The Garda Commissioner has kept me updated throughout the day and he has assured me that everything will be done to bring those responsible to justice."[74] Simon Harris was, predictably, steadfast in his support of the gardaí stating that they had shown "extraordinary professionalism". [75]Over the course of the next week, the warehouse was set ablaze on five separate occasions.[76]

Undeterred, two days after the violence, O'Gorman announced that the migrant centre at Coolock would proceed as planned and he additionally announced that the state was in the process of sourcing 30 large buildings to accommodate up to 1,000 asylum seekers each to be operational by 2028.[77]

The machine ground grimly on.

On social media, there was a growing consensus that this was a government increasingly at war with its own people in a manner not seen since colonial times. Echoes of the past grew louder. In Dundrum, Co. Tipperary, a small village of 165 people which had willingly hosted 270 Ukrainians in 2022 and 2023, locals were told in June 2024 that those Ukrainians would be replaced by asylum seekers. Those asylum seekers would come to outnumber locals. At a June 4th town meeting which saw 400 people—more than double the village of Dundrum—show up to support the villagers, local man Raymond Heaney gave an impassioned speech calling the planned arrivals a "plantation". He stated, "We are currently in the midst of a plantation. Our whole culture, our whole way of life is going to be diluted and ultimately decimated."[78] His choice of words was deliberate. The last time that such numbers of foreign men were forced into

Irish communities, no consultation, no veto, was during the Cromwellian plantations of the 1650s. It was a term growing increasingly common on social media. Further, it was Cromwell who imported the landed estate system which would make English and Anglo-Irish occupants of the Big Houses very wealthy. When an investigation by the Irish Mail on Sunday found that almost half of the top-earning asylum accommodation providers in the nation, including Tifco and Goldstein in Santry, were based overseas, it raised comparisons to absentee landlords who once grew fat in London off their Irish estates regardless of the impact on and protestations of the natives.[79]

Crucially, just as Ireland was a democracy in name only in the late colonial period, so too today, is Ireland in the midst of a democratic crisis. On May 17th, 2024, The Irish Times published a poll that found that 63% of Irish people wanted "a more closed migration policy." The same poll found that 79% wanted the government "to do more to manage the issue of migration."[80] On May 28th, a Red C poll found that 72% of Irish people wanted "very strict limits on the number of immigrants coming to live in Ireland."[81] Yet, since the previous General Election in 2020, Sinn Féin, the largest opposition party, had supported government migration policy in all crucial matters. It wasn't until the party suffered an unexpected backlash from its base in Local and European Elections on June 7th, 2024 that it attempted to pivot from the government line. A new party policy document was published on July 23rd shortly after the Coolock violence but rather than promise any meaningful rollback of the government's no veto, no consultation policy, it simply promised not to locate IPAS centres in economically disadvantaged areas. The plantation of unvetted males would continue against the will of the people—all political options were closed to them.

To understand how Ireland got to the point where a government, with the consent of their main opposition rivals, could run roughshod over the electorate, one must understand that Ireland is not a democracy quite like any other Western European nation.

Ireland is a crippled democracy.

2

A CRIPPLED DEMOCRACY

On January 7th, 1922, the Dáil voted 64 to 57 in favour of the Anglo-Irish Treaty which led to the birth of the Irish Free State (Saorstát Éireann) on December 6th of that same year. Two days after the vote, Dáil President Éamon de Valera resigned his position stating, "Unfortunately, on the Treaty we cannot co-operate...We will be there with you against any outside enemy at any time. Meantime you must simply regard us as an auxiliary army with a certain objective, which is the complete independence of Ireland...I am against you on principle...We will not interfere with you except when we find that you are going to do something that will definitely injure the Irish nation."[1]

De Valera led his anti-treaty Sinn Féin followers out of government and wouldn't return until October 1926, almost three and a half years after the end of the Civil War as leader of the newly founded Fianna Fáil. De Valera understood that a continued policy of Dáil abstentionism and a sustained period in the political wilderness would hand the shaping of the Irish nation to pro-treaty Cumann na nGaedheal during its crucial foundational phase. His return, after the spilling of so much fraternal blood and the loss of six sitting Dáil members on both the pro- and anti-treaty sides, led to two bitterly opposed factions—but opposed mainly on the matter of nationalism. Nationalism aside, Fianna Fáil and Cumann na nGaedheal—Fine Gael from September 1933—had to deal with running the pre-industrial, pre-capitalist nation that they had inherited from the British Empire. In doing so, they would show such an extraordinary lack of ideological difference over the coming decades that it was as though they were, once more, a family united.

The immediate heat was taken out of the old civil war divisions after Fianna Fáil came to power and held onto it for sixteen years until 1948. In this period, Fianna Fáil, adopting a nationalist agenda, picked apart the Anglo-Irish Treaty. On May 3rd, 1933, de Valera won a Dáil majority (76 to 56) in support of the Constitution (Removal of Oath) Bill[2] to remove the oath of allegiance to the British crown which had to be recited in order to take one's Dáil seat. On December 12th, 1936, Fianna Fáil pushed through the Executive Authority (External Relations) Act[3] which gave the Irish government expanded treaty-making powers and greater rights in appointing consular representatives and diplomats. The Act resulted in the removal of the post of Governor General whose role had previously been to oversee the Oath of Allegiance in the Dáil. On April 27th, 1938, Fianna Fáil passed the "Agreements Between the Government of Ireland and the Government of the United Kingdom" (Anglo-Irish Agreement) which saw the return of the three deep-water ports at Berehaven, Spike Island and Lough Swilly, which had been retained by Britain in the 1922 Anglo-Irish Treaty. It was the crowning moment of de Valera's nationalist agenda.

Speaking to the Dáil as he motioned for approval, de Valera stated, "I do not think it is necessary for me to stress to anybody who has desired the independence of this country the importance of that agreement from the point of view of Irish sovereignty. The ports are handed over unconditionally...Among the Articles of the Treaty of 1921 that gave most offence to national sentiment were these, because they meant that part of our territory was still in British occupation." He went on to state that only one more step remained in the nationalist agenda, that of unification. "These Agreements, as a whole, will remove from the field of dispute between Great Britain and ourselves all the major items now, except that one. The whole Irish race can now concentrate upon that one, and, with a united effort, I believe, as I have said already, that a completely independent, sovereign Ireland will be achieved."[4]

On the 21st December, 1948 the Republic of Ireland Act was signed.[5] At a Dáil debate and second reading of the Bill on November 24th, then Taoiseach, Fine Gael's John A. Costello asked, "Why are we doing this?" Before answering, "Because of our instincts and our tradition and our history, the institution of the Crown has been regarded as a badge of servitude and those instincts can never be eradicated from the tradition and the blood of any Irishman."[6] Not only did the signature of the Act put to an end 800 years of British rule in what was now the Republic of Ireland, but it also, in real terms, resolved Fianna Fáil and Fine Gael's primary ideological point of division—the nationalist question. While de Valera quietly supported the passage of the Republic of Ireland Act, future Fianna Fáil leader and economic nation shaper Seán Lemass put up a good show of trying to maintain the distinction between the two parties based on Civil War grievances when he took umbrage at Costello's praise for Michael Collins, recalling Collins' powerful speech during the Dáil debate on the Treaty on 19th December 1921.[7] Collins said, "I do not recommend it for more than it is. Equally I do not recommend it for less than it is. In my opinion it gives us freedom, not the ultimate freedom that all nations desire and develop to, but the freedom to achieve it." Lemass snapped back, "I am told that the Treaty was a stepping stone to freedom. It was nothing of the kind. On behalf of those who fought with me, those friends of mine who died or who were broken or exiled in opposition to the Treaty, I am going to deny that assertion with all the vehemence I can. It is not true."

Despite Lemass' protestations, the nationalist heat was gone from Irish politics after 1948, and so Fianna Fáil and Fine Gael were confronted with the reality that they had little else to differentiate one from the other policy-wise. Socially, morally and in matters of education, both parties had abdicated responsibility to the Church.

On the 29th December 1937, the new Constitution of Ireland came into effect. Article 44.1.2 stated, "The State recognises the special position of the Holy Catholic Apostolic and Roman Church as the guardian of the Faith professed by the great majority of the citizens."[8] The new constitution gave protected status to all faiths but gave special recognition to the Catholic Church. As the Dáil debate on the matter on Friday 4th June, 1937 indicates, there was little pushback from the chamber on the idea that the Catholic Church should be especially privileged. Defending the subsection, de Valera stated "The recognition of an obvious fact is there, and that fact must have considerable influence in the life of the State. It is bound to have. There are 93% of the people in this part of Ireland and 75% of the people of Ireland as a whole who belong to the Catholic Church, who believe in its teachings, and whose whole philosophy of life is the philosophy that comes from its teachings. Consequently it is very important that in our Constitution that fact should be recognised." Assigning the Catholic Church a special position in the Constitution would have made perfect sense to a majority of Irish politicians and the public. In 1937, the power of the church was at its zenith. Also, internationally, Ireland was not entirely out of step in affording the Church a privileged position. Article 7 of the Italian Constitution (1947), for example, reaffirmed the Lateran Treaty of 1929 giving the Vatican and church special status in the then newly unified Italy.[9]

Where Ireland was very out of step with the rest of Western Europe in the 1930s however was in its cultural homogeneity. Ireland was a pre-industrial, overwhelmingly farming and Catholic nation. Catholicism was a deeply embedded pillar of Irish daily life and as such, both political parties needed to be on good terms with the church. In fact going against it would be an act of political suicide. As recounted by Fahy,[10] when the American Jesuit, Bruce Biever came to Ireland as late as the early 1960s to conduct sociological research, he found that the stereotypes of a deeply devout nation were indeed true. When members of a large-scale attitudinal study group were asked if they would side with the church or state in the event of a disagreement, 87% said they would side with the church. When confronted with the statement that the church can and does more for the welfare of society than any other institution, 88% agreed. And when presented with the statement "whatever the church tells me to do I will do whether it makes sense or not", 61% of people agreed.

Quite the opposite of coming into conflict with the Catholic Church, the men who drafted the Constitution were men of devout faith on the whole and so both Fianna Fáil and Fine Gael were happy to offload social, moral and educational matters to the church. It was logical. This was out of step with the European post-War order where the Christian democratic model, typified by the CDU in Germany, the Christian Democracy Party in Italy and the Christian Social Party in Belgium, among others, was necessary in nations where there were diverse religious groups and significant ideological differences among parties. In Italy, for example, in the 1948 General Election, one year after enshrining the primacy of the Catholic Church in their constitution, the Christian Democrat party won 49% of the vote but the Popular Democratic Front, an alliance of communists and socialists, won 31%. Aside from these two, there was a plethora of smaller leftist, right-wing, monarchist and peasant parties. In this broad left/right political axis, it was deemed essential for the Church to have a pressure group in parliament to look after their interests. That was not necessary in Ireland.

From 1922 to 1962, primary and secondary schools were managed by the Catholic Church with bishops opposing any managerial interference by laity. In primary schools, the local parish priest was responsible for management and secondary schools fell under the direct jurisdiction of the bishop. Some religious orders had the freedom to set up independent schools but would never do so without the approval of the bishop. Schools were overwhelmingly staffed by priests and religious brothers and sisters, with the Christian Brothers and Sisters of Mercy dominant. In 1922, there were 963 religious teachers in secondary schools in the Free State compared to 498 lay teachers and this ratio remained largely the same by 1962 when Bruce Biever arrived in Ireland.[11]

An emerging industrial nation

As Ireland was a rural society—the 1936 census showed that 57.3% of all people lived outside of urban areas, towns and villages[12]—there were no radical urban or industrialist workers parties. Communism never took root in Ireland and Eoin O'Duffy's anti-Communist Army Comrades Association (also known as the Blueshirts) merged with Cumann na nGaedheal, the pro-treaty National League Party and the splinters of the former Farmer's Party to form Fine Gael in September 1933. The Labour Party, which had served as Cumann na nGaedheal's primary opposition prior to Fianna Fáil's Dáil entry, were sidelined by the centrality of the nationalist question and Fianna Fáil's similar economic platform in the 1930s. They never again came close to their 17-seat success in the 1922 Dáil and, as the third wheel of Irish politics in the 20th century, they largely existed simply to prop up Fine Gael as a coalition partner. What this effectively meant is that unlike in contemporary European nations, Irish democracy, almost from its inception, was dominated by two parties—Fianna Fáil and Fine Gael —each of whom didn't see themselves as parties beholden to a certain percentage of the electorate or any hard and fast political ideology outside of the nationalist question. They both believed that they could appeal to and govern all of the electorate.

As the nationalist question faded, and social and educational matters were offloaded to the church, the narrowest of political spectrums in Western European politics grew ever narrower with differences between the two parties largely confined to their economic platforms.

The Free State that Cumann na nGaedheal inherited from the British Empire was a pre-industrial and pre-capitalist colonial outpost overwhelmingly dependent on agricultural exports to Britain. In order to survive as an economically viable independent state, rapid industrialisation, developing a robust private enterprise sector and diversifying exports were essential—no easy feat in the midst of the Great Depression and amid the ruins of the Civil War. Added to this, unemployment figures in Ireland were significant. The

1926 census listed 78,071 being unemployed. While this figure amounted to a 6% unemployment rate nationally, there was great variance with rural areas reporting significantly lower unemployment rates than urban areas. Dublin and Waterford, for example, had a rate of 12.5%, Cork 14.5%. While Connaught had an unemployment rate of only 1.2%, many in the agricultural sector were underemployed. [13]From 1922 to 1932, Cumann na nGaedheal favoured a laissez-faire economic model with minimal state interference in economic matters, with a strong focus on balancing the books and raising capital through public sector cuts rather than increased taxation. In doing so, W. T. Cosgrave hoped to create the conditions under which private enterprise could flourish. In practice, as Barry has argued,[14] Cumann na nGaedheal's economic policy was more interventionist and developmentalist than laissez-faire. In Industry, Agriculture, and Housing, Cosgrave implemented a number of interventionist policies in a bid to stimulate the fledgling Free State economy.

In order to boost native industrial production and to lure British manufacturers to the Irish Free State, Finance Minister Earnest Blythe, despite protestations from some within his own party, announced in the Dáil on April 25th, 1924 his intention to impose a series of tariffs on certain imports. Boots and shoes were the primary focus of tariffs with Blythe explaining that such an industry should be homegrown and would provide a secondary boost to tanneries and livestock breeders. At that point, the Free State was importing £2 million worth of boots and shoes from Britain—almost 95% of all shoes. He proposed a 15% customs duty. Similarly, tariffs were placed on confectionery, soap, candles, brown and green glass bottles, motor bodies and tobacco.[15] The immediate results of the tariffs were positive, with several British companies—including tobacco manufacturers Players, confectionery company Rowntree and several others—opening factories in Ireland. By 1926, nine to ten thousand jobs had been created in those areas affected by tariffs.[16]

To further boost industrialisation efforts, Cosgrave understood the need for a reliable electricity grid for factories to avail of. On the

4th July 1925, the Shannon Electricity Act provided state funds for the construction of the Ardnacrusha hydro-electric power plant on the mouth of the River Shannon. The state entered into a £5.2 million contract with German firm Siemens to build the power station and the 1927 Electricity Supply Act[17] established the Electrical Supply Board (ESB), thus nationalising electricity supply in Ireland. The move was met with withering criticism by Independent (later Cumann na nGaedheal) deputy Major Bryan Cooper who called the project "a most admirable model for a future measure of State Socialism."[18] Cooper aside, most criticisms were directed at the contract for the project going to a German company but overall the project was seen less as the beginning of state socialism and more as a statement of intent by an ambitious emerging industrial nation. Indeed, the project captured the public imagination such that the Great Southern Railway had to put on extra trains to deal with the number of tourists coming to see the engineering marvel. From June 1928 to March 1932, 185,000 or 6% of the entire population of the Irish Free State visited Ardnacrusha.[19]

In 1926, 53.4% of workers in the Free State were employed in agriculture, fishing and forestry, compared to 13% of people who were employed in industry. Throughout the 1920s, agricultural exports to Britain accounted for more than 90% of all Irish exports. Again, through limited state interventions, the Minister for Agriculture, Patrick Hogan understood that the financial success or ruin of the state would depend on agricultural exports. He rejected the idea of placing tariffs on agricultural-related items from Britain for fear that it would result in retaliatory tariffs and instead encouraged Irish farmers to focus on dairy, bacon and cattle production, areas which could secure favourable prices in the UK export market. As Minister for Agriculture, then the most valuable portfolio to the Irish economy, Hogan best embodied the government's laissez-faire credentials but he did make notable interventions in areas of livestock breeding and the establishment of the Irish sugar industry. Generous subsidies were offered for the production of sugar via the 1925 Beet Sugar Act.[20] In a flagship economic project by Cumann na nGaedheal, sugar industry experts from Belgium and Czechoslovakia were advised on how best to cultivate the sector. In 1926 the Irish Sugar Manufacture Company in Co. Carlow was established and both the factory and local farmers growing sugar beet were protected by generous state subsidies.

Similarly, in a bid to boost the quality and reputation of Irish beef exports, Hogan oversaw the Livestock Breeding Act of 1925[21] which gave the government considerable regulatory powers. The act stipulated that all bull owners must apply for a licence and that those with bulls deemed inferior to breeding standards would be required to have the animal destroyed. The 1927 Agricultural Credit Act[22] provided government funding for the Agricultural Credit Corporation to provide low-interest loans to farmers. Also in 1927, the state intervened to purchase the distressed former Condensed Milk Company, the largest private dairy in the state with the intention of integrating it into wider dairy co-operative societies over time. The move had a major stabilising and regulatory effect on the Irish dairy sector into the 1970s and provided essential relief to dairy farmers in Cork, Kerry and Clare.[23]

Considering the immense internal and external pressures the Irish Free State faced in its first decade and the general success of Cumann na nGaedheal's interventions in economic affairs, the government faced little criticism that actually landed. What would lose Cumann na nGaedheal the 1932 election and hand power to Fianna Fáil for the next sixteen years was their cuts to pensions and civil service pay. Government spending was reduced from £42 million in 1923/24 to £24 million in 1926/27 with cuts made to old age and blind persons' pension via the 1924 Old Age Pensions Act[24] as well as pay cuts for teachers and gardaí in 1923. Blythe's unwillingness to increase the pension payments until 1928[25] gave his political opponents an easy stick with which to beat him. For Blythe, the revenue was simply not there from tax receipts to give to pensions. Because a low tax rate was the cornerstone of the government's industrialisation plan, it meant less public expenditure. Blythe was loathe to raise taxes to afford a raise in pension because, as he explained in a Dáil debate on the matter on the 29th February 1928, "Taxation has a very definite reaction on the cost of living, and the value of any pension that may be given to old age pensioners depends on the cost of living."[26] Increased taxation would lead to an increased cost of living which in turn would gobble up any increase in pension payment. Blythe's commitment to balancing the books and fiscal responsibility in a perilous time for Ireland was entirely noble. However, it was easily exploited politically.

Cumann na nGaedheal's economic legacy is one of financial responsibility, a realism that advanced established strengths (agricultural exports), limited intervention, industrial development and pragmatism over ideology. That would change radically in the following 16 years.

Fostering state dependency

De Valera's Fianna Fáil won the 1932 election with a protectionist economic platform that promised 100,000 jobs in industry, agriculture and tourism, an increase in wages for agricultural workers and promises to break economic trading dependency on Britain. Fianna Fáil also promised greater state interventions to build more badly needed houses for the poor as well as guarantees that public sector pay cuts would not be applied to low-income earners. It was a giveaway bonanza that financially prudent Cumann na nGaedheal wouldn't offer. As part of its nationalist platform, alongside promises to remove the oath of allegiance and dispense with the office of Governor General, Fianna Fáil also promised to withhold land annuities—payments due to the British government as part of the Treaty, later formalised in the 1923 Land Act.[27] The land annuities were debts paid by Irish farmers to the British Treasury in repayment for loans given to them to purchase land from the end of the Famine until the start of the Irish Free State. The annuities, more than £120 million in total, resulted in a £5 million per year repayment[28] which amounted to approximately 10% of the government's total revenue. It was a major contributing factor to Cumann na nGaedheal's fiscal tightfistedness and to put it in context, the Ardnacrusha power plant cost £5 million while the Carlow sugar factory cost £3 million.[29] De Valera's promise to withhold the annuities was, obviously, extremely popular with small farmers and would free up large amounts of money to fund his other economic policies. When he won the 1932 election, he did just that.

De Valera withheld annuities due to the British Treasury on July 1st and in doing so triggered a retaliation from Britain which placed a 20% tax on all Irish imports. De Valera met with British Prime Minister Ramsay McDonald on the 16th July at Downing Street but could find no solution to the issue. While de Valera was in London, Cosgrave gave a withering verdict of de Valera's actions stating, "Those who are trustees in respect of defenceless people ought not to allow those defenceless people to be made the sport of politics, and the most defenceless people in this country are going to suffer most in respect of this thing. 200,000 farmers in this country have uneconomic holdings."[30] To test if he had a mandate to engage in a potentially devastating trade war with Britain, de Valera held a snap election in 1933 which Fianna Fáil again won. In response to Britain's 20% tax on agricultural imports, Fianna Fáil responded with similar tariffs on coal, grain, steel, electrics, machinery and cement.

At the beginning of the trade war, Ireland exported approximately 800,000 cattle, 600,000 sheep and massive numbers of pigs to Britain annually.[31] While the trade war was financially devastating for larger farmers, who were on the whole Cumann na nGaedheal voters, Fianna Fáil, who had aggressively courted small farmers during their 1932 and 1933 election campaigns, supplemented their lost income with subsidies and farmers' benefits. In his first year in power, De Valera increased public spending by almost 20% (£24 million to £29 million) on increased pensions, housing, infrastructure and social welfare.[32] The 1933 Unemployment Assistance Act[33] expanded the social welfare state considerably and the 1934 Public Assistance Bill[34] granted local authorities powers of compulsory purchase of private land in order to assist with social housing. Whereas Cumann na nGaedheal engaged in limited intervention and exercised extreme discipline in balancing the books throughout the turbulent 1920s, de Valera placed the state at the heart of the economy and became its principal driving force.

To boost industrial development, Fianna Fáil passed The Industrial Credit Act, 1933[35] and formed the Industrial Credit Company to finance industrial projects. The Control of Manufactures Acts of 1932[36] and 1934 established the grounds for de Valera's vision of a protectionist, Irish-owned industrial sector. The act required non-Irish businesses to be licensed and required a majority of shareholders and board members of businesses to be Irish. The act gave the government significant control over industrial development through licensing. Building on Cumann na nGaedheal's 1924 tariffs on footwear, in 1934, Fianna Fáil introduced an increased 30% tariff on footwear imports. By 1935 there were 23 footwear manufacturers in the Free State. Ironically, the move to impose prohibitively large tariffs as part of a nationalist economic model simply encouraged several British manufacturers to move to Ireland. John Rawson & Son Ltd set up a ladies' footwear factory in Dundalk which employed 500 people and produced 13,000 pairs of shoes a week. By the end of 1935, a third of Irish shoe companies were British-owned and half of the industry's employees belonged to British companies. Fianna Fáil, who had aimed to promote native industrial growth to break economic ties to Britain, realised that in order to industrialise rapidly, they would have to grant operational licences to British companies. In 1932 there were 1,936 people employed in the footwear industry and by 1936 this number stood at 5,974. Because shoe sales were limited to the domestic market due to protection measures, the sector had reached saturation by 1938 and began to collapse.[37]

The limitations of Fianna Fáil's protectionism and ongoing trade war meant that most other industries that developed during this time period found themselves faced with the same issues as the footwear industry. With limited or no access to the international market, Irish industry led to simple commodity production of small enterprises propped up by subsidies. This had a knock-on effect that industrial wages were poor, and so housing for the increasing numbers of workers moving from rural to urban areas had to be further subsidised by the state. Between 1932 and 1939, Fianna Fáil embarked on a massive campaign of local authority apartment and house building schemes for rent to urban working-class industrial workers. In that time Dublin Corporation built 6,019 rental cottages. Compared to the previous 8-year period under Cumann na nGaedheal, the corporation had only built 229.[38] This state-sponsored house boom put Fianna Fáil's interventionist economic model in sharp contrast to Cumann na nGaedheal's. Realising that the backlog in housing had reached a crisis point after building had all but stopped during the War of Independence and the Civil War, Cumann na nGaedhael wished to subsidise private enterprise over corporation-built homes. The 1924 Housing Act[39] prioritised private enterprise by supplying grants to individuals to build their own homes. When Dublin Corporation created a large suburb of homes for purchase at Drumcondra, the government subsidised the down payment. Aside from producing far fewer housing units because of their non-interventionist principles, Cumann na nGaedheal's housing subsidies tended to favour middle-class workers. Fianna Fáil's expansion of local authority housing and rentals endeared them to the working class.

When de Valera signed the 1938 Anglo-Irish agreement that brought the trade war to an end along with returning the treaty ports, he was hailed for having land annuities written off with a one-time payment of £10 million. For diehard nationalist supporters, the temporary financial hardships they had endured were worth it though the trade war had been devastating. Unemployment soared from 28,934 in 1931 to 138,000 in 1935. Emigration had increased and many big farmers had been ruined. While industrial output had increased, it was inward-looking and underdeveloped. Much of Fianna Fáil's industrial policy was a continuation of Cumann na nGaedheal's early policy—to spur domestic industry under protection. This resulted in an expansion of footwear, textile and sugar industries already developed by Cumann na nGaedheal and saw the growth of new sectors such as peat harvesting and cement production with Cement Ltd—later Irish Cement Ltd—opening two major factories at Drogheda and Limerick. However, when all was said and done, in 1938, agricultural exports to Britain remained Ireland's economic lifeblood and Britain still accounted for over 90% of all Ireland's exports.

But the lasting legacy of this period, aside from a shift from quasi-laissez-faire or developmentalist economics under Cumann na nGaedheal to a protectionist model under Fianna Fáil, was the fostering of a culture of dependence on state subsidies and handouts. In a culture of subsidies and a lack of competition, native industrialists often produced sub-standard goods unfit for export. Expanded social welfare payments, particularly to small farmers, fostered a culture of dependency on the state.[40] Similar grants to impoverished Gaeltacht areas, such as the £2 grant per child to Irish-speaking households could easily be seen as a cynical means of buying off the electorate. De Valera didn't just dismantle the Treaty when he came to power, he dismantled Cumann na nGaedheal's small government model, replacing it instead with a paternalistic, if not socialist economic model. The issue, of course, is that once Fianna Fáil fostered a culture of state dependency, there was no going back. In order to ever lead the country again, Fine Gael would have to abandon any aspirations to a laissez-faire economic model and join the handout state.

Ireland's steadfast neutrality during WWII and continued protectionism after the war led to the nation being increasingly isolated from Europe's post-war Marshall Plan-financed economic recovery and boom, leading to economic stagnation and decline in the 1950s.

In February 1948, Fine Gael cobbled together a coalition—known as the 'first inter-party' government—with Labour and three other minor parties and independent support.[41] The government's first move was to kill the nationalist question once and for all by signing the Republic of Ireland Act in December of that year. It was the highlight of their time in office. In power from 1948-1951 and again with a reshuffled coalition from 1954-1957 with a Fianna Fáil government sandwiched in between, they stuck to Fianna Fáil's economic model of protectionism. Chastened by sixteen years out of power, they understood that de Valera's populist model of state dependency meant there could be no returning to the economically conservative days of Cumann na nGaedheal. Instead they leaned in all the more to show that Fine Gael could throw open the public purse just as well as Fianna Fáil. They were happily assisted in this with the socialist elements of their Labour and Clann na Poblachta coalition partners. William Norton, Labour leader and Tánaiste, was Minister for Social Welfare. He increased the old age pension by 50% in his first year as well as adding significant increases for widows, orphans and the blind. Fellow Labour Party member and Minister for Local Government, Michael Keyes showed de Valera that they were good students. While Fianna Fáil managed to build 1,460 houses under social housing schemes in 1947, Keyes built significantly more year-on-year, peaking at 12,046 in 1950. Clann na Poblachta's Minister for Health, Dr Noel Browne, in a period of badly needed modernisation, boosted spending in his department from £617,905 in 1947 to a massive £5 million in 1951.[42]

During this decade of political chop and change there was very little to distinguish Fianna Fáil and Fine Gael. The two inter-party governments of the 1950s continued Fianna Fáil's protectionist model, refusing to move away from the Control of Manufactures Act, ensuring Ireland's industrial sector's continued economic stagnation and decline behind tariffs with a focus on producing lower quality simple commodities for local supply. During this time, Fine Gael understood that protectionism and an expanded social welfare state would lead to economic ruin but they also understood that any attempt to radically change course would lead to another period in the political wilderness. Emigration rose throughout the 1950s, leading to a net loss of half a million people throughout the decade. The year 1961 marked the lowest population in the history of the state with 2,818,341 people.[43]

Pivoting to an open economy

The demographic bleeding was unsustainable and Costello finally, in 1956, realised that he needed to be decisive. During a Dáil debate on October 24th, 1956, while being confronted about record migration in Co. Mayo specifically, but across the rural west generally, he announced details of his Policy for Production, a speech he had delivered to cabinet members on October 5th. In it he laid out an ambitious and liberal economic vision which included providing a 50% tax break on surplus exports. This was a crucial reversal of decades of protectionism and an inward-looking industrial model. Ireland would open up to the world once more. In reality of course, and despite the nationalistic Dáil speeches of breaking economic dependency on Britain and building up domestic industry, even with the introduction of heavy tariffs and the Fianna Fáil Control of Manufactures Act, foreign—mainly British—firms had continued to prop up Irish industry. And despite the bluster, both parties had pursued very similar economic policies since the 1930s. That would continue.

Costello's epiphany came too late. Less than six months after his announcement, Fianna Fáil were back in power and would stay in power until 1973—another unbroken sixteen-year stretch that consigned Fine Gael once more to the political wilderness. Fianna Fáil's Sean Lemass took over from de Valera in 1959 and along with his Secretary at the Department of Finance, T.K. Whitaker, he is recognised as shaping the Ireland we know today. In actuality, however, much of Lemass' innovation was built on the back of Costello's lesser-known revolution. Costello's tax breaks on exports along with grants for new factories attracted international companies to set up in Ireland. Indeed, in the 1920s Lemass had been a critic of economic protectionism and would have fitted in quite neatly with Cumann na nGaedheal. It was logical for him to simply build on Costello's foundation.

In 1958, T.K. Whitaker, the Secretary of the Department of Finance who had been put in place by Fine Gael Minister for Finance Gerard Sweetman, produced a report called *Economic Development*.

The document formed the basis of the Lemass economy. In November 1958, ideas expressed in Economic Development formed the basis of a white paper called *Programme for Economic Expansion* which marked a radical shift in economic direction. Key points outlined in the white paper included a growing realisation that there would inevitably be a European Free Trade Area that Ireland could not compete with and with that in mind, Ireland would need to be able to adequately compete with international industrial competition in the export market and that there would have to be a complementary upgrade in industrial production for the home market to compete with industrial imports. Protectionism was officially over.

To meet this new direction, the white paper prioritised foreign investment. The Industrial Credit Company would underwrite long-term and low-interest loans for companies setting up in Ireland. It would provide capital for hire-purchase schemes for plant and machinery, and it would offer advice on how to raise capital. While giving a nod to Costello's tax breaks, the white paper made clear that further tax breaks would be given where deemed necessary. Funds were to be made available for research, training and technical assistance. A lump sum of £4 million was made immediately available in grants for industrial development in underdeveloped areas and, importantly, the Industrial Development Authority (IDA),[44] set up by Costello in 1949 as an independent body under the guidance of the Department of Finance, was given expanded responsibilities to attract foreign development into Ireland. The white paper estimated that the total cost of effecting this new economic policy over the five-year period from 1959-1964 would be £273 million and where necessary, external debt would be accrued to fund it.[45] Ireland had joined the IMF and World Bank the year before in anticipation.

The Industrial Development Bill,[46] enacted in July 1958, dismantled the protectionist restrictions of the Control of Manufactures Acts of 1932, paving the way for foreign investment. The 1963 Imposition of Duties Bill[47] reduced tariffs on swathes of goods while the 1965 Free Trade Agreement[48] began the process of removing all trade restrictions between the United Kingdom and Ireland.

A second goal for Lemass' liberalisation of the Irish economy, subtly hinted at in reference to a potential European free trade area in his white paper, was his desire to join the European Economic Community (EEC). His predecessor de Valera had been passionately against the notion, preferring isolation or self-determination as a matter of economic as well as nationalist policy. Lemass, seeing Ireland's best chance at economic divestment from Britain being access to the European market, applied to join the EEC on July 31st, 1961. Lemass understood that Ireland's economy, being overwhelmingly reliant on British exports could only join if Britain did. Britain's application was vetoed by Charles de Gaulle's France in January 1963 and again in May 1967, leaving Ireland ever dependent on Britain, though the 1965 Free Trade Agreement between Ireland and Britain yielded mutual economic benefit. Ireland was finally granted access to the EEC along with Britain in January 1973 and the intervening years had allowed the country to build up a robust native industry to deal with massive new export markets.

In the first five years of the Lemass plan, GNP rose by over 4% per annum. In 1963 production of transportable goods—turf, mining, manufacture, quarrying—was 45% greater than in 1958. Metal, engineering, textile, chemical manufacture expanded rapidly and exports of manufactured goods rose by 90% from 1958-1963. Agriculture also saw impressive gains with cattle exports for slaughter, which accounted for approximately 80% of total agricultural exports, growing rapidly, leading to a 7% increase in productivity in 1963 compared to 1958. However, despite this increase in production, there was a huge decline in agricultural employment as the government's push for industrialisation led to massive rural-to-urban migration and the loss of 47,000 jobs in fishing, farming and forestry between 1958 and 1963.[49] Indeed, this period saw the birth of an industrialised nation. While in 1926, 53% of people were employed in fishing, farming and forestry in Ireland, by 1981, that figure had dropped to 18.9%.[50] In the 1960s, 350 foreign firms opened in Ireland thanks to the generous tax breaks and state capital investments. Major firms included General Electric and Pfizer and these foreign firms accounted for 70% of new employment and 90% of increased exports in transportable goods.[51]

As foreign direct investment (FDI) in industrial development became the new focus of the Irish economy, Irish agriculture was the chief beneficiary of EEC accession. Despite losing its cherished place as the main driving force of the Irish economy, it remained an essential vote-winner for both Fine Gael and Fianna Fáil. After all, it had been the protection of farmers and the refusal to pay land annuities that had sparked Ireland's drive to protectionism. The farm, complete with the pastoral images of a fast-disappearing way of life it conjured up, was the bedrock of nationalist idealism and though the national question had largely been resolved, that imagery remained a crucial ideological differentiator between the two parties. Fianna Fáil saw itself as the protector of the small farmer and Fine Gael had come to be associated with the prosperous farmers through their commitment to free trade in their Cumann na nGaedheal days. Farmers couldn't, then, be abandoned but also, new economic realities dictated that government funds must also be directed into new urban and industrial developments. Successive governments looked to the EEC to subsidise Irish farming. Thanks to their longstanding position as Ireland's leading economic sector, Irish farmers had two powerful lobby groups in the form of the Irish Farmer's Association (IFA) and Irish Creamery Milk Suppliers Association (ICMSA) and through the pressure applied by them, throughout the 1970s, Irish EEC policy effectively became agricultural policy. In Ireland's first decade as a member of the EEC, over 70% of direct grants and subsidies were given to the agricultural sector—a total of £707.1 million.[52]

The blueprint for Irish economic growth into the present day was set. What is remarkable with the economic developments of the 1950s and 1960s is the degree of consensus among both Fianna Fáil and Fine Gael. Throughout the 1950s, Fine Gael went with Fianna Fáil's disastrous pursuit of protectionist policies. When Fine Gael finally came to its senses in the late 1950s and plucked up the courage to move closer to their Cumann na nGaedheal roots of free trade and low taxation, Fianna Fáil were happy to run with that model and make it their own. From 1956 onwards, there has been remarkably little difference between the two parties in economic policy with a low tax, FDI, and pro-EU sentiment at the heart of both offerings. Importantly, underlying both parties' shared vision has been an ongoing commitment to de Valera's dependency culture which has led to a continued crippling of native industry and innovation and interventions in social spending. The 1960s established an Ireland that was outwardly economically liberal and dependent on foreign investment to prop up its industrial growth and on the EU to prop up its independently unsustainable farming sector. Inwardly, however, it fostered state dependency and stifled native innovation through grants and subsidies. Throughout, both parties believed they had a claim to every vote of the electorate and increasingly, elections would be decided based on old loyalties, external economic disruptions, the rise of magnetic personalities such as Garret Fitzgerald (Fine Gael) and Charles Haughey (Fianna Fáil) and, above all, state dependency —who is offering the best handouts package come election time. By the late 1950s, a vote for one party over the other had little to do with a hope for radical change in political direction or the hope of improving one's own standard of living.

Despite the ups and downs of international pressures such as the 1973 oil crisis and the inflation crisis of the early 1980s that marked a decade of economic stagnation for Ireland, the economic model established by Lemass endured. In 1993, on the eve of the Celtic Tiger, 80% of Irish non-agricultural exports were produced in foreign-owned businesses. Said foreign direct investment was underwritten by government expenditure funded by taxation and debt. Agriculture remained the single most important industry accounting for 10% of GNP and one-fifth of all exports, and it remained unable to sustain itself economically outside of EU grants. 75% of agricultural production was accounted for by meat and dairy exports.[53] However, favourable prices spurring production and the accession of Greece, Spain and Portugal throughout the 1980s led to a massive surplus of food piling up in Brussels. Initially, the EEC had purchased agricultural surplus, storing what could be saved to keep prices stable. It was a massively unsustainable protectionist endeavour. By 1985, approximately 75% of the EEC's budget was being spent on the Common Agricultural Policy (CAP). Equally, the Irish economy, dependent as it was on agricultural exports, could not afford to widen its non-EEC export market and have Irish beef and dairy compete in the global market where prices, without EU subsidy supports, would be slashed dramatically. After a series of reforms in the 1990s which included a switch to direct subsidy payments to farmers from the EU, Irish agriculture has grown almost entirely dependent on the EU.

As of 2023, agricultural exports accounted for approximately 6% of GNI and 9.3% (€18.3 billion) of all Irish exports. Dairy and beef exports accounted for 51% of all agricultural exports and Britain remained the primary export destination, accounting for 38%. Exports to the EU accounted for 34% while exports to the rest of the world accounted for 29%.[54] Ireland's century-long bid to divest from the UK had initially led to significant subsidisation by successive protectionist governments up to EEC accession in 1973. After accession, the government was able to hand off subsidisation to Europe and that has remained a constant. A March 2020 press release by Teagasc, the national agriculture and food development authority, reported that the EU's Basic Payment Scheme—direct subsidies— paid out €1.2 billion annually to Irish farmers. These payments made up, on average, 74% of Irish farmers' income.[55] The cost of breaking agricultural economic dependency on Britain over a century has been to foster absolute dependency on the EU. This dependency has made Ireland one of the most pro-EU nations in Europe as successive politicians from both Fianna Fáil and Fine Gael chose to see the EU as a handout cash cow rather than an external policy enforcement gun to their head.

Offshoring industrial growth

While Irish agriculture is entirely in the hands of the EU, it is a similar story for Ireland's industrial base which is overwhelmingly foreign-owned. A lasting legacy of de Valera's protectionist model was that Irish industrialists didn't have to compete in the external market and as such gained a reputation for being limited in ambition and disincentivised to produce world-class goods and services. Good enough was good enough. Writing in 1973, Fogarty[56] recounted the experience of an Irish businessman who had gone to Britain to learn his trade and returned to Ireland to set up a business. The engineer remarked, "I have been rather horrified in fact, since I came back to Ireland, at the low moral values here...People make appointments which they do not keep, which, in fact, they make glibly with no intention of keeping. Business people will make promises which they can't keep, and they seem to think they are doing you a favour by making the promises, that this is as far as they are expected to go." Another engineering businessman spoke of the poor work ethic of employees, wishing that they would "be here in the morning before a quarter past ten" and complained, "O.K. they want to work a five-hour day: don't spread it over eight or nine hours and hold everybody up as well." Another businessman mused that the casual way of rural routines had bled into the industrial sector stating, "We are a casual people. My opinion is that we have come very far very quickly in Ireland, and that our roots and inheritance are such that we haven't developed a maturity to cope with this advance. We express it in not getting involved, in immature drinking, in immature attitudes to life generally." Writing in 1993, Keating and Desmond[57] found that little had changed concluding, "On the whole the picture that emerges from a review of their [Irish entrepreneurs'] practices and perfor-mance is one that leaves the impression of an easy-going, complacent entrepreneurial community, too many of whose members are content with a neat little profit made on the home market and too few of whom are interested in taking on the challenge of developing new products for new markets in the internationally-traded goods and services sectors."

The opening up of the Irish industrial sector to foreign direct investment (FDI) throughout the 1960s was a quick way to get around the native industrialists' learned helplessness. With expansion throughout the 1970s, 1980s and into the new millennium, the IDA focused on attracting multinational market leaders in computing and IT, pharmaceuticals and medical equipment production. In the 1980s, IT firms Microsoft, Intel and Motorola set up in Ireland. They were joined by Dell, IBM and HP in the 1990s as well as Google, eBay, PayPal, Yahoo, Amazon and Facebook in the early '00s. Medical behemoths Medtronic, Pfizer and Stryker among many others employ thousands in Ireland. Up until 1997, the FDI economy worked to the benefit of the Irish people. Industrial investment needs were met by native stock. Until 1994, Ireland had a negative net migration figure.[58] In 1994, Ireland was the last EU nation to enter into net positive migration figures and this was driven by worker demands of the FDI economy. In 1996, Ireland's GDP per capita was 129.3% the EU average. This, however, would be the last year in which FDI recruitment needs were largely supported by the native population. From this point on, further economic expansion would be reliant on immigration, both of returning nationals and non-nationals. Unemployment stood at a record low of 3.7% in October 2000[59] and at this point, it would have been prudent of newly elected Taoiseach Bertie Ahern to cool off FDI recruitment to keep pace with natural population growth. He chose a radically different option.

The 1997 Finance Act[60] announced the implementation of a 12.5% corporation tax rate—reduced from 32%—on trading profits to be implemented over a phased basis. It came into full effect in 2003 and remained the bedrock of the Irish FDI economy until 2021. The 'Two Pillar' OECD agreement, which Ireland signed up to that year, imposed a 15% corporate tax rate on multinationals earning over €750 million. This 12.5% tax break attracted a massive spike in foreign direct investment over the next two decades. By 2003, FDI contributed €171.9 billion to the Irish economy. By 2005, 80% of foreign exports were accounted for by foreign-owned companies and these companies employed 132,728 Irish people.[61] As international markets cooled ahead of the 2008 global financial crisis, FDI slowed to a contribution of €118.9 billion in 2006 and employment figures had stalled.

In a bid to boost productivity, Finance Minister Charlie

McCreevy, who had introduced the 12.5% corporation tax in 1997, leaned into the construction sector by heavily subsidising developers and wealthy investors to purchase property through a series of tax incentives. His 1997 Taxes Consolidation Act[62] and subsequent 1998 Finance Act[63] allowed developers and investors to avail of massive tax breaks for construction of commercial and rental developments. These developments were funded most prominently by Anglo-Irish Bank (AIB) under the stewardship of Sean Fitzpatrick who would become the face of Celtic Tiger excess and sleaze. He was forced to step down from the bank he had built after it emerged he had been hiding personal loans in excess of €100 million which he had taken out for property speculation.[64] By 2008, one-quarter of AIB's loans—€17.7 billion—was lent to developers. The majority of this sum was given out to just 15 clients each with at least €500 million in loans.[65] Under the 1998 Finance Act, the Counties of Cavan, Leitrim, Longford, Roscommon and Sligo were specifically identified to avail of tax relief for construction projects. This led to an absurd building boom that resulted in some of the most rural and underdeveloped counties in Ireland being flooded with new housing estates. By 2006, 6,452 houses had been built in Leitrim but almost 22% of all housing in the county remained empty. The rate of building was such that by 2006, 15% of all houses in Ireland were empty.[66] From 2002-2007, public spending increased by €23 billion, private household borrowing doubled, and for the first time, construction industry employment—heavily supported by immigration from the new eastern European EU accession states—surpassed employment in manufacture. By 2006, the percentage of population employed in construction was higher than in any other industrialised nation. By 2007, 25% of government revenue—expenditure on public services—came from the construction sector.[67] It marked the most radical and unsustainable divergence in economic planning in the history of the state. One that would cost the taxpayer dearly.

Fianna Fáil had managed to retain power for 14 years throughout the Celtic Tiger period, almost as long as de Valera's 16-year run in the 1930s and 1940s by resorting to much the same tactics as he had—

social welfare bonanzas. The social welfare budget doubled between 2001 and 2007 with significant public service spending in the run-up to the 2002 and 2007 elections. Spending increased by 21% in 2001, 14% in 2002 and 13% in 2007 without any restructuring of the wider budget. Increases were given to pensioners, unemployed, carers, single parents and more.[68] It was a naked cash-for-votes scheme, a Fianna Fáil tactic as old as the state.

However, as Cosgrave tried to warn in 1927, there is always a larger cost to profligate public spending and a failure to balance the books, and the Irish taxpayer was about to pick up the tab. The cost to the taxpayer in tax breaks for developers amounted to more than €1 billion over the Celtic Tiger years and when AIB, Bank of Ireland, Permanent TSB and other financial institutions collapsed in 2008 as international debtors refused to extend credit, the taxpayer was again left with a tab for €64 billion as the government took the decision to bail them out.

Mounting debt and deficits, left from the loss of 25% of public revenue that the building sector supplied, meant international markets were unwilling to lend money. The government was forced to take the humiliating step of seeking a bailout from the European Commission, European Central Bank and International Monetary Fund. In December 2010, €67.5 billion was lent to Ireland to be paid back over a three-year period. This was the most crucial moment in Irish economic and political history. Fianna Fáil, which had been in power throughout the Celtic Tiger years would now, one would think, finally be flung into the political abyss never to return, and the nation could reset its economic and political direction. No such luck.

On the 9th March 2011, Fine Gael took over, backed, as usual, by Labour. The Celtic Tiger property speculation fever-dream aside, it was business as usual. FDI industrial development under the 12.5% corporation tax deal continued to be the sacred calf of the Irish economy. While the 12.5% tax deal had been brought in under Charlie McCreevy in 1997, that number hadn't been near low enough for Fine Gael. Recently released state papers show that as early as 1984, Fine Gael leader John Bruton had discussed with Finance and the IDA on how to allow US multinationals to pay "little or no tax"[69] and both parties have been extremely accommodating in helping foreign multinationals to use Ireland as a tax haven to avoid paying billions of dollars in taxes elsewhere. The recent Apple scandal showed that the company signed two deals, one in 1991 and one in 2007—both Fianna Fáil governments—which allowed the company to pay less than 1% tax on profits over the period 2004-2014. All sales for Africa, India, Europe and the Middle East were counted as sales by Apple Ireland and these profits were then funnelled elsewhere. In 2016 the European Court of Justice (ECJ) ordered Apple to pay taxes worth €13 billion to Ireland, a ruling upheld on appeal in September 2024.[70] Though the sweetheart deal with Apple was brought in under a Fianna Fáil government, when the ruling was handed down in 2016, both Fianna Fáil and Fine Gael came out strongly against the decision with then Fine Gael Taoiseach, Enda Kenny telling the Dáil, "It is not true that Apple was provided with more favourable treatment than others. There was no preference shown. The law was applied fully and appropriately, and Apple paid its taxes due in Ireland." He added, "Today, this House has an opportunity to send a strong message that we stand together in challenging the presentation that the Commission has made."[71] Fine Gael and Fianna Fáil joined hands across the aisle to protect their decades-long joint economic plan.

Under Fine Gael, corporate tax receipts skyrocketed in the post-crash years. In 2011 there were 149,697 people employed in foreign-owned companies in Ireland.[72] This increased by 65% to 247,195 workers in 2020. Over that same period of time, corporation tax receipts went from €3.52 billion in 2011 to €11.83 billion.[73] Yet, as seemingly rosy as the economy was, after the 2020 General Election, both Fine Gael and Fianna Fáil received historic low returns. Fianna Fáil took 38 out of 160 Dáil seats—their lowest ever performance in a General Election besides their 20-seat haul in 2011 directly after the Celtic Tiger collapse. Fine Gael won 35 seats, their second-lowest return since 1948 when the party won 31 seats when there were only 147 available. The election had the second-lowest turnout in the history of the state at 62.9% beaten only by the 2002 election which had a turnout of 62.5%. To keep a surging Sinn Féin—who won 37 seats—out of government, Fianna Fáil and Fine Gael did what had been a long time coming. After the 2020 election, they admitted that they were simply long-surly siblings pursuing the same government agenda, and went into government together as coalition partners, with the Green Party making up the numbers to form the 33rd Dáil. The FDI economy didn't miss a beat. By 2022, 294,072 people were employed by foreign-owned companies[74] and corporation tax receipts contributed €22.6 billion—27.5% of net tax receipts for the year.[75]

Indeed, things were apparently going so well under joint Fine Gael and Fianna Fáil rule that on Saturday 2nd December, 2024, Taoiseach Leo Varadkar stood before the world at the COP24 UN Climate Change Conference in Dubai and stated, "Ireland is a wealthy country". He told the global dignitaries in attendance that cash-rich Ireland "will double our climate finances to at least €225 million a year by 2025" and that €150 million would be invested in 2024 alone.[76] As a show of good will, he donated €25 million on the spot to the UN's Loss and Damage Fund—an international pot of money for "assisting developing countries that are particularly vulnerable to the adverse effects of climate change."[77] Ireland was rich, and Varadkar basked in the applause of the world as he promised away millions on climate initiatives at home and abroad. And on paper he was correct. Ireland was rich. In May 2024, Global Finance magazine ranked Ireland the third wealthiest nation in the world with a GDP per capita income (PPP) of €105,000.[78] In a September 2024 article, the Financial Times salivated, "Officials preparing Ireland's upcoming budget face a situation most of their peers elsewhere would love to have: an €8.6 billion surplus and an economy that grew five times faster than expected last year."[79] And yet, if one were to ask the Irish, particularly younger Irish people, if they felt rich, the answer for most would be a resounding 'No'.

A wealthy nation on paper only

Little of this fabulous wealth that had been flowing into public coffers had made its way down to the general public. Indeed, back in 2012-2014, the respected "World Happiness Report"—a long-running survey that partners with the UN, Gallup and the Oxford Wellbeing Research Centre—had found that Ireland ranked 18th in the world's happiest nations, despite going through a crushing recession and a humiliating national economic bailout.[80] The self-reporting survey asked respondents to score their happiness based on a series of questions relative to six indicators: GDP per capita, social support, healthy life expectancy, freedom to make life choices, generosity and perceptions of corruption. One would have to say that the 18th place in the rankings was not bad considering the bleak future Ireland faced in 2012. Fast forward to 2024, where Leo Varadkar was confidently letting the world know that Ireland had money to burn, one would expect the nation to be soaring somewhere close to the top of the happiness rankings. Not so. In the 2024 rankings which cover the period from 2021-2023, Ireland had risen only one place, to 17th. Alarmingly, for the under 30s, Ireland ranked 21st, well behind nations like Romania, Lithuania, Costa Rica and El Salvador.[81]

It got worse. A May 2024 report by Eurofound, an EU agency for social and work-related study, found that 61% of all Irish young people between the ages of 15-29 were either 'planning to migrate' or 'wished to migrate' to another country within three years. This was the highest figure of all EU nations.[82] Irish young people, more than any other EU nation, wanted out of their home country. Also in May, a poll by The Journal and Ireland Thinks found that 41% of 18-34 year-olds were 'actively planning to emigrate' or 'would like to'. 90% of those 'actively planning to emigrate' were either living at home with their parents or renting privately as were 76% of those who 'would like to' emigrate. This link to home ownership and emigration was in line with an Irish Central Bank study released in March 2024 which found that the primary driving factor in wealth inequality in Ireland was property ownership.

The study found that 97% of the wealth in Ireland was held by property-owning individuals. The top richest 10% in Ireland owned almost 50%[83] of the net wealth of the nation but, importantly, private renters, of whom there were 330,000 in the state, or 21% of the private property market in 2022, held just 3% of the wealth.[84] This disparity was driven by a sharp increase in property value due to Ireland experiencing the worst housing crisis in the history of the state. Young people were simply not able to get onto the property market because of the astronomical prices of houses. Despite some 15% of houses in Ireland laying empty in 2006, being the products of wild property speculation and tax havens for developers, most of those houses were in undesirable locations far away from urban employment zones, were taken into receivership by the national bad assets management bureau (NAMA) or stood as unfinished 'ghost estates' until they were finally demolished in the wake of the Celtic Tiger collapse. By 2022, 2006 and the expectation to own a home was a world away for first-time buyers. 64.8% of 30-year-olds in the private property market were renters but a March 2024 report by leading property rental and property website Daft found that the average rent nationally was €1,922 and well over €2,000 in Dublin, Limerick, Cork and Galway. This represented a 7.1% national increase in rent in one year alone.[85] House prices similarly rose by 6.7% over that same one-year period with the national average price for a house in March 2024 being €340,398. Galway, Limerick and Cork saw on average a 10% increase in house prices. The most expensive regional average house price was in South Dublin at €694,602.[86] Importantly, over the same period—the 12 months to Q2 2024—average weekly earnings nationwide only rose 4.7%.[87]

All renters, but particularly young renters earning below the national average wage, could look at the widening gap between earnings and property prices (rented and bought) and understand that the chances of them ever being able to save a 10% deposit for a mortgage was an increasingly slim prospect. The May Eurofound report found that 40% of Irish people in employment between the ages of 25 and

34 were still living at home. This compared to 12% of Germans, 12% of French, 2% of Swedish and 2% of Finnish young people.

Adding to these pressures, the government, rather than assisting young people to get on the property ladder, was actively competing against them. Despite Simon Harris' promise to ensure 50,000 new houses per year under his stewardship, The Irish Times, on May 21st, published a leaked report from the Housing Commission that found that there was a housing deficit of 212,500 to 256,000 houses. This would require building 62,000 houses per year until 2050 to clear the backlog.[88] In 2022, there was a total of 29,726 builds and in 2023, there were 32,695—far short of demand.[89] Worse, when these buildings came on the market they were snapped up by private investment funds and the government itself, squeezing young private purchasers out of the market. An August 2024 report[90] by Ireland's leading prop-erty retailer, DNG found that out of 17,039 total house sales in Ireland in 2023, 42% (7,206 units) were sold as part of block sales. That left a total of 9,200 homes nationwide for purchase on the private market. The study identified private investment firms, charitable organisa-tions and state institutions such as housing authorities among the leading groups purchasing blocks of property. Absurdly then, the government, alongside investment firms, helped remove 42% of prop-erty from the private market, thus ramping up prices for private buyers for the remaining 58% of houses, while putting the cost of the government purchases back on the taxpayer. Private buyers were paying double, and those working young people at home with their parents with no hope of moving out were paying for state-purchased homes for others.

The logical solution for Ireland's propertyless educated and hard-working youth? Emigrate and hope for a fairer shake abroad.

And emigrate they did. In the twelve months to April 2024, 69,000 people—of whom 34,700 were Irish citizens—emigrated from Ireland —the highest figure since 2015. This milestone was far surpassed by the number of people immigrating to Ireland in 2023—149,200 who entered legally for employment with an additional 13,277 asylum applicants—a seventeen-year high. This was the third year in a row that immigration to Ireland had broken 100,000, placing ever more pressure on a rapidly collapsing housing system.[91] Indeed, by the start of 2023, 22% of the population of Ireland had been born overseas.[92] Irish fertility rates have been below replacement levels (2.1) every year since 1990. Yet, from 2003 to 2023, the population of Ireland ballooned from 3.99[93] to 5.28[94] million. That radical increase in population has been overwhelmingly driven by mass legal immigration to service the FDI economy and it has directly led to the current housing crisis.

For decades, tech has been the focus of the Irish FDI economy and since the early 2000s, it has taken an even more central role. The inflated GNP that Ireland currently enjoys is increasingly thanks to a handful of tech powerhouses such as Google, Facebook (Meta), Amazon and Apple. Aside from the 'Double Irish' tax loophole, tech companies like Apple are uniquely suited to take advantage of Ireland's 'Capital Allowances for Intangible Assets' (CAIA) tax loophole. By shifting the company's Intellectual Property (IP) to Ireland, Apple and other tech companies were able to continue to shield billions of euros in international profits from taxation even after the 2016 ECJ ruling against the company by paying corporation tax on Irish sales and no tax at all on other non-US sales which were held in Ireland. This shifting of IP as intangible assets to Ireland—€90 billion across several firms in 2015 alone—led to a massive 26.3% spike in GDP.[95] This non-tangible boost to the balance sheet would later become known and derided by the renowned economist Paul Krugman as 'leprechaun economics'.

The massive tax incentives for tech companies to set up in Ireland were extraordinary. And while Ireland was making a tidy profit off the tax they did gather from these companies, the arrangement came with significant risks. The shifting of big tech assets to Ireland led to an extraordinary reliance on tech for corporate tax receipts. In 2020, corporation taxes contributed €11.8 billion or 21% of total tax receipts to public coffers. Of this figure, Apple, Microsoft, Google and Facebook contributed €5.018 billion, or 42.5%.[96] Aside from economic over-reliance on a single industry, there were other issues.

Ireland is a nation which has never been interested in computing in large numbers. At the height of the Celtic Tiger, there was a 70% drop in applications for computing degrees between 2001 and 2003. Graduate numbers for computing degrees at DCU dropped from 224 in 2005 to 74 in 2008.[97] A comprehensive 2021 study by the Higher Education Authority (HEA) found that computing had the lowest rate of graduation of any degree course in Ireland, with only 55%-56% graduating. Despite being the best paid profession on average in Ireland in 2018, from 2014 to 2018, there was an 8% drop in students starting computing courses.[98] Google, which, using the 'Double Irish' loophole, only paid 1% tax on total profits funnelled to Bermuda through Ireland in 2017, overwhelmingly employs non-Irish workers. 70% of Google Ireland's staff are immigrants.[99] This figure appears to be similar for computer science positions in Apple[100] and Amazon[101] based on applications for work permits for non-EU workers. Aside from major tech firms setting up base in a profoundly unfit employment market and paying a fraction of their annual tax on profits, while adding to mass immigration, these foreign employees are earning at the very top end of the Irish employment scale. This means that immigrant workers in major tech companies are helping to price natives out of the housing market, adding to the frustrations of the 40% of working young people living at home with their parents.

Since the early 1930s Ireland had been on a path of political coalescence between Fianna Fáil and Fine Gael. The first blow was struck by de Valera whose handout state made it impossible for Fine Gael to compete as an economically open, low-tax, and minimally interventionist opponent in government. By the late 1950s, both parties had coalesced behind a foreign direct investment and EU subsidy economy, which remains the basis of the Irish economy today. This economy left farmers dependent on EU subsidies for survival and abandoned native industrialists for the easy fix of multinational investment. The increased focus on attracting big tech companies on minimally beneficial tax returns for Ireland has come with a new abandonment of the native worker by Fianna Fáil and

Fine Gael. They first devalued the Irish worker in 1994 when successive governments continued to inflate the FDI economy past native worker supply levels. In the post-Celtic Tiger era, successive governments have abandoned Irish workers entirely by pursuing a tech industry for which native workers do not exist. In the era of the Fianna Fáil and Fine Gael coalition, the FDI economy is increasingly a big tech economy—and that is an immigrant economy. A new, immigrant urban middle class is emerging in wealthy urban developments, adding pressure to an in-crisis private housing market squeezed by investment firms and government block buying to leave native young people out-skilled, stuck on the assembly line floor, out-priced and living at home.

So what are the political options available to Irish people who feel locked out of the housing market and see the Fianna Fáil and Fine Gael FDI and EU federalism model as being the root of their problems? The answer is, very little. Sinn Féin are the largest opposition party in the Dáil and on the crucial issues of government over the past decade, they have acted as silent partners to Fianna Fáil and Fine Gael. In 2022, the government proposed a highly controversial Criminal Justice (Incitement to Violence or Hatred and Hate Offences) Bill. It made international headlines when Elon Musk said he would challenge any such bill in Irish courts and called the proposed legislation "a massive attack against freedom of speech". Sinn Féin's main complaint was that the bill didn't go far enough to clamp down on hate speech against illegal immigrants.[102] In 2015, they vigorously supported the 2015 Gay Marriage Act[103] along with Fianna Fáil and Fine Gael. In 2018 they supported the Health (Regulation of Termination of Pregnancy) Act put forward by Fine Gael.[104] In 2022 and 2024 they supported Fianna Fáil and Fine Gael in passing one of the most liberal surrogacy laws in Europe.[105] When Fianna Fáil and Fine Gael introduced two referenda on March 2024 to amend two sections of the constitution to remove specific references to women's role in the home and to broaden the meaning of families to include 'durable relationships' outside of marriage, Sinn Féin supported it so much that leader Mary Lou McDonald promised to re-run the referenda if they failed to pass.[106] All of these issues, of course, are social issues. One could argue that Sinn Féin's support for each says less about Sinn Féin, which is a socialist party that sits in the most left-wing group of the EU Parliament—'The Left'. Rather it shows very adequately just how left-skewed Irish politics has become. Importantly, over decades, they have offered no alternative to Fianna Fáil and Fine Gael's FDI economic model. Sinn Féin have acted as silent partners, not opposition to Fianna Fáil and Fine Gael in shaping modern Ireland.

A government with no opposition

After chastening defeats in the March 2024 referenda, followed by a massively disappointing return of 12% of first preference votes in the June Local Elections, Sinn Féin attempted to strike a more hard-line tone on migration. A position, as it turned out, which was essentially the same as the government's. Having provided no meaningful opposition to Fine Gael and Fianna Fáil's no consultation, no veto migrant centre settlements prior to their beating in Local Elections, Sinn Féin produced a new twelve-page policy document entitled "International Protection: A Fair System that Works".[107] With this, the party attempted to win back urban working-class voters in places like Coolock and the East Wall as well as rural voters who were republican but socially conservative. However, the policy document made no promises to stop the massive flow of IPAS applicants entering the country, simply pledged to speed up the process by tripling the number of civil servants at the International Protection Office to 1200 at a cost of €50 million. The policy promised to not place IPAS centres in deprived areas—where their urban voter bases were located—rather, they would place them somewhere else in the country with better facilities. It promised to abolish private profiteering on IPAS accommodation but instead place the centres on publicly owned land, meaning the cost remained with the taxpayer. The document did state that Sinn Féin would "create a standard, transparent and consistent approach to community consultation, including opportunity for submissions", however, at a press conference launch of the document on July 23rd, McDonald stated that the consultation process would not include a 'veto' for any community. Sinn Féin's new 'conservative' migration policy was simply the government position with a fresh coat of paint—meaningless consultation, no veto.

Crucially, and where Sinn Féin disappoint most as an opposition party, is that their core economic policy is the same as Fine Gael and Fianna Fáil's. Ahead of the 2016 General Election, Sinn Féin unveiled a superficially socialist manifesto that promised wealth taxes for high-income individuals as well as promising to cut tax for lower income earners. When asked whether or not Sinn Féin would push for reform of the 12.5% corporation tax, Gerry Adams vowed that the party would, alongside Labour, Fine Gael and Fianna Fáil, fight any tax regulation attempts by the EU in the wake of the Apple scandal.[108] Again in 2024, the party, then under the leadership of Mary Lou McDonald, reaffirmed its commitment to the 12.5% corporation tax rate (15% for companies with turnover of more than €750 million as agreed by the current government as part of the Two Pillar OECD agreement signed in 2021). In the Party's 2024 EU Election Manifesto[109] they reaffirmed the traditional Fianna Fáil and Fine Gael line of calling for an increase of CAP subsidies for Irish farmers, increased voice for Irish farmers at policy decision level in the EU, a promise to fight for the family farm model, a commitment to seek funding for EU environmental initiatives for Irish farmers and a promise to retain Ireland's Nitrates Derogation. Nitrates Derogation allows Irish farmers to increase dairy livestock per hectare of grassland if the farmer submits to a series of ongoing environmental testing and restrictions on farming practice. Sinn Féin's EU agricultural policy was almost indistinguishable from both Fianna Fáil's EU manifesto[110] and Fine Gael's.[111] With the same driving economic policy—12.5% corporation tax FDI model combined with continued EU CAP over-reliance, Sinn Féin find themselves completely aligned with Fianna Fáil and Fine Gael in their core economic vision for Ireland. This leaves all three parties with no significant economic division, which leaves them reliant—like Fianna Fáil in the de Valera and Celtic Tiger years—on vote-buying through government give-aways, come election time, to give the electorate the illusion of choice. And even here, there was no great separation between parties.

Ahead of the 2019 General Election, all three parties promised pension increases. Fianna Fáil and Fine Gael promised the exact same—to increase the weekly State pension by €25 over the course of five years. Sinn Féin promised to increase it by €20.[112] Fine Gael and Sinn Féin[113] both promised to raise the weekly universal subsidy for childcare from €20 to €100 over the course of five years, Fianna Fáil promised to raise it by €80.[114] Fine Gael promised an extra 2,600 hospital beds and 5000 extra nurses, Fianna Fáil also promised 2,600 extra hospital beds but 4000 extra nurses.[115] Sinn Féin promised 1,500 extra beds and 2,500 more nurses.[116] Among a plethora of tax breaks and subsidies, Fine Gael promised to build 60,000 social houses over the course of five years while Fianna Fáil promised 100,000 social and affordable houses.[117] Sinn Féin promised 100,000 social houses.[118]

As the 2024 General Election loomed and each of the three major parties ramped up their latest round of social welfare handouts in health, pensions, housing and more, no establishment politician acknowledged the root cause of strain on those social services—a population explosion caused by mass immigration, needed because of each party's unwavering dependency on the tax-avoidance FDI economy. Ireland is a crippled democracy where voters have only the illusion of choice each time an election comes around. It is the reason that elections are met with lower and lower turnouts, with a historic low of 59.7% in 2024. It is the reason young employed people are living at home with their parents without hope of ever owning their own home. It is the reason Ireland leads the EU in the number of young people who want to leave their homeland. It is the reason that Irish people are told by their leaders that they are a rich nation yet they struggle to pay childcare costs. It is also the reason that Ireland is burning.

3

AN EMPTY VESSEL

C ulture and identity, the everyday habits and customs that bind a people together, lie unexamined in times of plenty. It is only in times of existential threat that we are forced to confront who we are and what makes us different from all the other peoples of the world. Viking, Norman, Cromwellian violence could not shake the Irish from their sense of self. And when the sword blunted on the back of the Gael, resort to legal persecution proved more effective. Legal documents also give us a sense of how outsiders defined Irish identity at various times throughout the colonial era. In 1366, The Hundred Years War was going poorly for the English, there was a succession crisis and the English stronghold inside the Pale had not recovered from the loss of approximately 14,000 people during the Black Death. Fearful that the Irish would usurp the weakened colony, Lionel, Duke of Clarence, son of Edward III and the Lord Lieutenant of Ireland, summoned Parliament in Kilkenny and signed into law a number of statutes to prevent the fraternisation of the English and the Irish. The statutes provide a fascinating insight into what the 14th-century English considered to be the defining traits of the Irish.

The statutes demarcated the two groups as different peoples with distinct laws and customs. The English were not allowed to marry or carry on a romantic affair with an Irish person, nor were they allowed to foster (adopt) an Irish child. The English were forbidden to speak Irish, wear Irish clothing, ride a horse in an Irish fashion—that is without a saddle—or enter into negotiations under Brehon Law. The Irish were forbidden to enter any English church for worship or clerical training and the English were forbidden from receiving Irish 'minstrels'—musicians, storytellers, poets and other performers.[1] The Statutes of Kilkenny identify the Irish as distinct from their nearest neighbours culturally through law, language, music, storytelling and clothing and racially by land and ethnicity. Importantly, the statutes were enacted in large because Irish culture and identity were attractive to the English colonisers who lived among the Irish. Many English had adopted the customs and appearance of the Irish, and setting clear boundaries between the two was deemed necessary to prevent the English from assimilating.

The wars of the mid-17th century which led to Cromwell's brutal conquest of Ireland left the native Irish nobility smashed, impoverished and banished to only one-fifth of the Island, confined to the province of Connaught and Co. Clare. The arrival of the native elite into Connaught was a humiliating ritual. The transplantation certificate of James Butler Lord of Dunboyne of Tipperary showed that the once noble Irishman was left in possession of only four cows, ten carthorses and two pigs upon expulsion. Viscount Maurice Roche of Fermoy, who had been a commander against Cromwell, arrived in Connaught penniless and with four daughters. He was given no new lands and he died a pauper.[2]

While at first it seemed that all native Catholics would be banished to Connaught under Charles Fleetwood, then Lord Deputy of Ireland, it was under Henry Cromwell, son of Oliver, who became Lord Deputy in 1655, that the threat of mass expulsion of all natives was averted. Under Henry, pragmatism prevailed—labourers and tradesmen would be needed to make freshly planted estates profitable and so the Irish peasantry avoided being uprooted from their ancient villages along with their customs. The humiliation of the native Irish nobility and their replacement by a new Anglo-Protestant elite marked the beginning of a sustained process of Anglicisation of the native Irish.

From 1695 through the first decade of the 18th century, as punishment for supporting the Catholic James II against the Protestant William of Orange in the 1689 Rebellion, the Irish Parliament, comprised of Anglo-Irish Protestants, enforced a series of Acts designed to break the back of Irish resistance once and for all. The aim of the Penal Laws as they would become known was to remove the Irish from ownership of their lands and to reduce them to a profound state of spiritual and academic ignorance that would render them eternal peasants. Whereas the Statutes of Kilkenny 300 years earlier were designed to prevent the Anglo-Irish from being seduced by the vitality of native Irish culture and custom, to prevent the English from becoming more Irish than the Irish themselves, the Penal Laws aimed to separate the Irish from every aspect of their identity with the only hope of a better life coming by becoming more English than the English themselves. The Penal Laws desired the cultural genocide of the Irish and they made a very good go of it.

Under the Penal Laws, all Catholics were barred from holding public office or a position in the civil service. They were barred from the army as well as legal and medical professions and were not allowed to own weapons or a horse worth more than £5. These laws aimed to neutralise native Irish political power, crush the educated and mercantile classes and remove the possibility of military uprising by forcing military recruits abroad to the great armies of France and Spain to gain employment. Those educated and upper-class natives with the means to emigrate to the continent did so, following the native nobles who had supported James during the Williamite Rebellion. Ireland's best and brightest fled in great numbers.

The Penal Laws aimed to capitalise on the capitulation of Ireland's fleeing nobility and make a definitive land grab. After the Cromwellian wars, the Irish nobility was forced to Connaught and Clare but still maintained roughly 20% of the land of Ireland. After the Williamite Rebellion, that figure was reduced to less than 10%.[3]

The Penal Laws dictated that all Catholic landowners had to bequeath their lands equally between all male heirs. This had the effect over two or three generations of turning the largest remaining native estates into subsistence farms. When the son of a Catholic landowner converted to Protestantism, he was given all of his father's estate.[4] To prevent any expansion of native estates, Catholics were forbidden from purchasing land and leases were negotiable to a maximum length of 31 years.[5] As a result, by the start of the 19th century, the native noble class was dead as a political force, their lands bequeathed any number of ways into tiny subsistence plots.

Catholicism at the heart of hidden Ireland

During the Cromwellian wars the position of the Catholic Church took on more than a simply spiritual dimension in the popular Irish psyche. After the massacres of clergy at Drogheda and Wexford as well as the execution of the Bishops of Clogher, Ross, and Emly from 1649-1653, Catholicism became utterly entwined with Irish identity. This standing was enhanced during The Penal Laws. The 1697 Banishment Act banished all Catholic clergy from Ireland, making the practice of the Catholic faith illegal for natives. It was hoped that without Bishops to ordain new priests, the Catholic faith would wither away organically and force the natives to convert to Protestantism out of fear for their souls. Transportation was provided for the banished and while two out of eight Bishops voluntarily left along with approximately 400 clergy, six Bishops remained along with a majority of priests who continued to practice their duties clandestinely. However in 1709, all Catholic clergy were forced to take an Oath of Abjuration renouncing their faith, effectively making practising the Catholic faith an illegal act.[6]

To hasten the Anglicisation of the native Irish, Catholics were forbidden from teaching and Irish children were forbidden from going overseas to attain an education, meaning that native children would have to attend Protestant schools where they would be educated in English, learn Protestant morals and see the world through the lens of the coloniser. This would have the effect of separating the native from his language, religion and knowledge of his own history, culture and customs. The severity of the penalties imposed on clergy found to have provided religious services, as well as teachers who were found to have taught class, gives a sense of how motivated the Protestant Parliament of Ireland was to cleanse the Irish of their identity. For both priest and teacher caught practising their profession, the punishment was the same. For a first offence, the priest or teacher was sentenced to life penal servitude on the agriculture, cotton, tobacco and sugar plantations of Carolina, Virginia or the West Indies. If the convict escaped and returned to Ireland, he would be executed. In Co. Limerick alone from 1711-1724, nineteen teachers were indicted which, in the courts of the day, meant convicted.[7] As with the clergy, the laws, despite their punishments, simply drove educators underground where they continued to teach in the Irish language.

The Penal Laws were most easily enforced in heavily planted Ulster and in urban areas throughout the country, where the colonial apparatus was strongest. However, throughout the 18th century, the most isolated and rural areas, particularly on the barren western coast, became sanctuaries for Irish identity, hidden from view, a fiercely guarded secret. Priests were forced to give mass and sacraments undercover with invitation spread by word of mouth. Writing in 1714, Dr Hugh McMahon, Bishop of Clogher and later Archbishop of Armagh recounted that mass would be said in secret with attendees covering their faces with veils so as not to be recognised and reported by spies. Despite the dangers involved, he reported, "people were so fervent that they would often rise in the middle of the night, even in winter, in frost and snow, and attend early morning masses in secret."[8] Across Ireland mass rocks became a powerful means of worship but also a defiant declaration of identity. As of 2014, the National Monuments Service listed 272 mass rocks and a further 36 penal mass stations across the island of Ireland.[9] These were heavily concentrated in Cork and Kerry with secondary concentrations up along the west coast to Sligo. As the Penal Laws were relaxed in the

later 18th century and through Catholic Emancipation in the early
19th century, mass rocks fell out of favour and communities began to
provide—often pitifully impoverished—structures for worship.

Like priests, teachers were also forced into providing their
services in secret in hidden places in the landscape. In the early 18th
century, classes were often held outside in fields, under the cover of a
hedge, in caves, under overhanging rocks or whatever natural shelter
could be found out of sight of the state. Of course, there was no standard curriculum and students were reliant on the education of whatever itinerant poet, writer, or learned man they could get their hands
on. Often these educators were outstanding. Brian Merriman, one of
Ireland's most celebrated 18th-century bards and author of the fairy
epic *The Midnight Court*, was a hedge school teacher in Feakle, east
Clare, before moving on to teach mathematics in Limerick. And like
priests, hedge school educators attained an exalted status in their
communities and were often relied upon by the wider population to
act as community bureaucrats in helping deal with official registra-
tions and documentation. Though the conditions for education were
pitiful, the standard of education was often excellent and by teaching
students in their native tongue and preserving the link to native
music, storytelling and poetry, the educator became a vital custodian
of the cultural flame throughout the 18th century. Like attendance at
mass rock services, attendance at the local hedge school became an
act of defiance against the Anglicisation process and it worked so well
that by the end of the 18th century, there were an estimated 9,000
hedge schools in the country with 400,000 students in attendance.
Even after Catholics were allowed to teach following the relief act of
1793, hedge schools continued to be the dominant form of education
in Ireland.[10] As with the priest, from the end of the 18th century,
educators were able to move in from the wilds to any usable cabin,
shed or available building. They were able to advertise their services
openly and become, alongside the local priest, a prized figurehead in
the community, though usually abysmally paid and often paid in
meat, dairy and other dietary supplements. For all hedge schools,
reading, writing and arithmetic were the fundamentals of all learning

though teaching materials varied considerably. Alongside the history and folklore of Ireland, the hedge schools provided a curriculum more varied and colourful than that on offer in puritanical state schools.

The Statistical Survey of Co. Clare from 1808 by Hely Dutton paints the picture of an adventurous and inspiring curriculum. Pupils were encouraged to read Moll Flanders, Irish Rogues and Rapparees, Freney the Robber (the story of a highwayman from Kilkenny), a History of Witches and Apparitions among others. An outraged Dutton wrote of the curriculum on offer in Co. Clare, "Whilst these are the books, from which our poor have their education, it can hardly be expected, that the lives of pirates, dexterous thieves, witches, smugglers, and illustrious prostitutes, can have any but the very worst tendency. The fault must be in a good measure attributed to the total neglect of the Roman Catholic clergy."[11] Aside from Dutton's moral outrage, he would also, no doubt, have been fearful that such a curriculum would fan the flames of Irish identity and a spirit of rebellion.

The feeling that the hedge schools were inculcating a sense of rebellion and anti-Protestant moral sentiment was echoed in the 1825 Commissioners of Irish Education Report which provided a major review of Irish education on the eve of the Famine. The report states, "whence it frequently happens, that instead of being improved by religious and moral instructions, their minds are corrupted...to incite the lawless and profligate adventure, to cherish superstition, or to lead to dissension or disloyalty."[12] What both surveys show is that despite the best efforts of the Penal Laws, the priest and teacher had, for over 100 years, in field, ditch and mud cabin, kindled the coals of Irish identity. But just as Irish identity was to emerge from its hidden places with the easing of the Penal Laws, the Famine did its best to finish the cultural genocide that the Penal Laws had started.

A genocidal Famine

In 1835, the French political thinker and historian Alexis de Tocqueville travelled through Ireland and recorded his observations in letters home and in his travel diary. His writings give an essential insight into just how effective the Penal Laws had been in their aims to reduce the Irish to a state of eternal peasantry, a people broken and removed from their land. When visiting an unnamed Poorhouse, de Tocqueville observed "the most hideous and disgusting aspect of wretchedness. A very long room full of women and children whose age or infirmity prevents them from working. On the floor the poor are seated pell-mell like pigs in the mud of their sty. It is difficult to avoid treading on a half-naked body...They sit on wooden benches, crowded close together and all looking in the same direction, as if in the pit of a theatre. They do not talk at all; they do not stir; they look at nothing; they do not appear to be thinking. They neither expect, fear, nor hope anything from life." Leaving the Poorhouse, de Tocqueville concluded, "If you want to know what can be done by the spirit of conquest and religious hatred combined with the abuses of aristocracy, but without any of its advantages, go to Ireland."[13]

Throughout his journey he witnessed an impoverished people, though most pronounced the further west he went. Travelling between Dublin and Carlow he observed "Most of the dwellings in the country seem very poor; a large number of them wretched to the last degree. Mud walls; thatched roofs; one room; no chimney; smoke comes out of the door. A pig lies in the middle of the room. It is Sunday but the population looks very wretched. Most of them are dressed in clothes with holes or very much patched. Most of them are bare-headed."[14] When journeying from Kilkenny to Cork he observed a settlement consisting of "Mud houses, thatched roofs, often broken down. No chimney, or such an inadequate one that almost all the smoke comes out the door. No windows. A little dunghill by the door; a pig in the house. Labourers in rags."[15] He was surprised to find out that this wasn't a settlement of beggars but a community of tenant farmers. Most impoverished of all were the settlements he found on his visit to Tuam, Co. Galway. Just outside of the town was a village he only refers to as 'X'. The village was completely hidden from the outside world accessible only via a dry riverbed. The houses of the village were built into the hills on either side of the stream. He recorded, "I quickened my pace to hurry through this unhappy village whose look repelled me...All the houses in line to my right and left were made of sun-dried mud and built with walls the height of a man. The roofs of these dwellings were made of thatch so old that the grass which covered it could be confused with the meadow on the neighbouring hills...The houses mostly had neither windows nor chimneys; the daylight came in and smoke came out by the door. If one could see into the houses, it was rare to notice more than bare walls, a rickety stool and a small peat fire burning slowly and dimly between four flat stones...The pig in the house. The dunghill. The bare heads and feet."[16]

In village X, de Tocqueville spoke at length with a priest who took him on a tour of the settlement. Though the houses were pitiful and young fit men had no hope of finding work, the village maintained a house for a priest and a small one-roomed hut which served as a school. The teacher wore rags and was barefoot as were the 30 children crammed in to learn. De Tocqueville was amazed to find "an eagerness to learn which is not always found in the rich English Universities".[17] The priest took de Tocqueville to the ruins of an ancient stone church on whose remains the community had built a small new chapel and said, "The ruins you see, Sir, are the only remains of one of the most beautiful churches built by the piety of our fathers; the Protestants destroyed it. But it is easier to knock down stones than to drive out a religion from the hearts of men."[18] What de Tocqueville found even in the poorest and most isolated of Irish villages was a profound desire for education and religious devotion. On a visit to Ennis, Co. Clare, he further remarked on the richness of folk memory and local history. Speaking to an old man he was amazed with the detail with which he was able to recount the various divisions of land in the locality from Cromwell to William III to the present. In Galway, de Tocqueville remarked on a conversation with a local judge that knowledge and memory were high-status traits among the natives. Throughout his journey in Ireland, de Tocqueville was struck by the good manners of the poor and their high morals. De Tocqueville's visit to Ireland on the eve of the Famine tells us that despite the bloody-minded efforts of the Penal Laws, which had indeed reduced the native to a landless impoverished group on the whole, Irish identity and culture were still alive and vibrant in the smoke-filled mud huts of the rural poor. And more, de Tocqueville clearly identifies religious devotion, a passion for education, a strong moral code, particularly in familial affairs, and a veneration of memory and oral custom as defining features of the Irish. Unfortunately, it was these impoverished rural settlements such as village X which were hardest hit by the Famine. It delivered a devastating blow to living and inherited culture.

The 1841 census of Ireland recorded a population of 8,175,124 people. This had dropped to 6,552,365 by the time of the 1851 census. These official statistics have been disputed by historians as being underreported. Attempting to accurately count those poor people who de Tocqueville encountered on his travels, hidden in their sod-thatched mud cabins far from the view of official Ireland, would be a fool's errand. Kelly[19] has placed the number who died of starvation and disease at 1.1 million with another 2 million lost to emigration by the end of the Famine, meaning that it had claimed one in three people dead or gone. In the west—the cradle of Irish culture and colonial resistance—the Famine was hardest felt. Mayo, Sligo, Roscommon, Galway, Leitrim, Cavan, Cork and Clare all suffered the highest annual rates of excess mortality from 1846-1851. Importantly, the decline in population didn't stop once the Famine itself ended. Emigration continued apace until the beginning of the twentieth century, leading to a drop to 4.4 million in 1911.[20] Throughout post-Famine emigration, the largest numbers of those leaving came from Munster and Connaught, from settlements like Village X. In Co. Roscommon, in the townland of Ballykilcline, an entire ancient settlement of 500 people was wiped out, with the last inhabitants leaving for Liverpool in May 1848. With them went the stories, customs, memories and local knowledge accumulated over centuries.[21] Across thousands of townlands, local identity and memory suffered catastrophic losses as people were removed from their communities. Aside from death and emigration, an estimated 250,000 families were evicted from their homes in brutal fashion during the 1840s and 1850s.[22]

Added to the loss of community, memory and identity through death and displacement during the Famine and its aftermath, the trauma of everyday encounters with the Famine was enough to kill off culture. While culture and identity come to the fore in times of hardship as it did during the Cromwellian and Williamite wars where people rallied around their Irishness in response to an outside threat, the Famine presented an enemy that didn't care for culture or identity. It presented an existential crisis so grave and humanity-stripping that thoughts of culture or identity were disregarded luxuries. There are endless accounts of the daily horrors of the Famine. The soulless vessels which de Tocqueville described in his 1835 visit to a Poorhouse, human skeletons waiting to die, were now no longer confined to the Poorhouse. The whole country was an open Poorhouse. The Cork Examiner reported on Skibbereen in 1846, "The general feeling among the people was that they were doomed, that they would be found dead in the fields or on the mountains without either the consolation of religion or the comfort of friends."[23] Kelly[24] recounts a particularly grim scene where in January 1847, a gentleman pulled up to the cabin of a small farmer in the area and handed him a box. Inside was the badly mutilated head of his wife who had recently died and been buried in a shallow grave. The gentleman's dogs had rooted it up and chewed on it and he was returning it for burial. Nicholas Cummings, a Cork magistrate who visited the area in December 1846, famously wrote an open letter published in the Times of London on Christmas Eve in which he recounted, "In the first [cabin] six famished and ghastly skeletons, to all appearance dead, were huddled in a corner on some filthy straw, their sole covering what seemed a ragged horse-cloth, naked above the knees. I approached in horror, and found by a low moaning they were alive, they were in fever—four children, a woman, and what had once been a man...in a few minutes I was surrounded by at least 200 of such phantoms, such frightful spectres as no words can describe. By far the greater number were delirious, either from famine or fever. Their demonic yells are still yelling in my ears, and their horrible images are fixed upon my brain." His letter went on to describe how that same morning police broke into a house to find two corpses being devoured by rats. Later that day a mother, herself weak from hunger and disease, was seen burying her young daughter beneath a pile of stones.[25]

The rate of death across the country in 1847 was such that corpses were buried close to the surface so that they could be easily reopened to bury more family members who were certain to follow. Family members were too weakened to dig proper graves and the rate of death had led to such a general desensitisation of the soul that seeing the remains of the dead piled up outside a church graveyard or half disinterred by wild animals had become an all too common sight.

In Co. Clare, Captain Kennedy, who did a great deal to alleviate the horrors of the Famine in west Clare as Poor Law Inspector for Kilrush, reported in 1847 of the Kilrush workhouse, "Such a tangled mass of poverty, filth and disease, as the applicants presented, I have never seen. Numbers in all stages of fever and smallpox mingling indiscriminately with the crowd and all clamouring for admission." Kilrush saw particularly gruesome scenes of prolonged death as local landlords, chief among them Col. Crofton Vandeleur, took the opportunity the Famine presented to engage in mass land clearances. Vandeleur alone is responsible for removing 180 families—more than 1,000 individuals—from his lands. Captain Kennedy estimated that from November 1847 to December 1848, he witnessed the eviction of more than 10,000 individuals in the Union of Kilrush and most of those impoverished ended up in the workhouse waiting to die. Cruelly, upon entering the workhouse, families were broken up by gender and parent from child, severing the family unit. Most striking among the deaths recorded throughout the Famine in Ennistymon and Kilrush is the number of children. For example, of the 213 deaths in April of 1850 reported in the Kilrush workhouse, 167 were children under the age of 14.[26] By 1851, there were 91,000 children under the age of 15 in workhouses across the country, making up 45% of all inmates. Between 1848 and 1849, 20,000 young girls were shipped to overseas colonies where workers were in short supply.[27]

Land clearances which broke up historic settlements, mass death from hunger and disease and displacement through emigration as well as the routine break-up of the family unit had a traumatic effect on Irish identity during the Famine. Had de Tocqueville revisited Ireland twenty years after his initial visit, he would, most likely, have found village X abandoned and the poor and ragged that remained elsewhere a traumatised people, their oral customs and historic memory scattered or lost. The two defining features he would be able to objectively assess—language and religion—had undergone radical change.

Just prior to the Famine in 1845, out of a population of 8 million, there would have been between 3.3 million and 4 million native speakers. The census of 1851 which officially recorded the number of Irish speakers for the first time, shows that only 300,000 individuals spoke Irish only, with 1.5 million speaking both Irish and English.[28] In 1851 then, 29% of the population spoke Irish. By 1861, this figure had dropped to 24.5% and by 1871 only 19.8% of people spoke Irish. In 1926, while 18.3% of the population spoke Irish, the population as a whole was much reduced and that figure accounted for only 543,511 people, less than a third of the number who spoke it in 1851. Much of the cause of this decline of the language was the emptying out of traditional native speaking settlements in the west and south of the country. As emigration became the norm in the decades after the Famine, so did English become a necessity.

The decline in the use of Irish had begun before the Famine however. Daniel O'Connell, father of Catholic Emancipation in 1829 which allowed Catholics to take their seat in Parliament, helped cement an attitude that Irish was the language of the poor, the peasant and the past. Throughout his political career, O'Connell distanced himself from the language. In 1833 he went so far as to declare, "the superiority of the English tongue, as the medium of all modern communication, is so great, that I can witness without a sigh the gradual disuse of Irish".[29] When the Catholic Church took on the role of overseeing the national school system after 1835, the primary language of instruction in state schools was English and despite the attempts of successive governments, it would remain that way outside of Gaeltacht and Gaelscoileanna into the present.

Catholic Emancipation and institutional control

The fate of the Catholic Church would be much different but it too would undertake a radical transformation from the church de Tocqueville witnessed in his travels. The failure of the United Irishmen's 1798 rebellion, which had begun as a non-sectarian rebellion with the aim of establishing an Irish republic inspired by the Scottish Enlightenment as well as the French and American Revolutions of the day, ended with sectarian acts of violence on both sides and massacres of Protestant loyalists in Wexford which drove a permanent wedge between Catholic and Protestant groups. While both groups would never again fight together for Irish independence, the failed rebellion awakened a sense of national identity among Catholics. The 1801 Act of Union abolished the Kingdom of Ireland and its parliament and fully incorporated it into the United Kingdom. Crucially, King George III refused to combine the Act of Union with Catholic emancipation, which gave the increasingly nationally conscious Irish rebels a cause to rally behind. Catholic emancipation became the driving force behind Irish nationalism. Catholics had been allowed to teach again since 1793 and while the rural populations continued to prefer hedge schools, in the early 1800s Catholic religious orders began to establish schools across the country, chiefly in urban areas. Among the most celebrated of these early pioneers is Nano Nagle who bravely set up seven clandestine schools across Cork city in the 1760s while the Penal Laws were still in effect. As a child, Nagle had been secreted away to Paris to receive an education —again against the Penal Laws—and had planned to commit herself to a life of enclosure and worship before returning to teach the poor in Cork. She died in 1784 before the end of the Penal Laws but by that time she had bought a convent building in the city which would become the home of the Presentation Sisters which prospered after her death. Similarly, Waterford merchant Edmund Ignatius Rice opened the first of what would become the Christian Brothers and Presentation Brothers schools networks in 1802 on Waterford's New Street. In 1814, the Jesuit order opened Clongowes Wood College in Clane, Co. Kildare. This explosion of Catholic schools helped create and nurtured a new native Catholic middle class, largely in the east of the country, who would go on to dominate Irish economics, politics and nationalist thinking until the founding of the state and beyond.

Just as the Catholic Church came to be the driving force behind the nationalist movement in the early 19th century, it also took control of education out of the hands of the hedge school masters after the establishment of the Irish national school system in 1835. By 1900, the Catholic Church presided over 8,684 schools catering to 770,622 pupils in every village and townland in Ireland.[30] Their institutional control of education was complete but it came at a cost. While Catholicism and education continued to be a defining part of Irish identity into the 20th century, it was now no longer of the people. Faith and education became regulated and standardised matters. While that helped promote a sense of a shared national identity, that was achieved by greatly narrowing the sense of regional identity. Throughout the Penal Laws and the first half of the 19th century, the priest and the hedge school master were financed directly by the impoverished natives of a townland. Driven underground, both faith and curriculum were idiosyncratic and responsive to local needs. Education was a private transaction between a community and an itinerant scholar. Similarly, the priest, an outlaw, was as likely to be as ragged and poor as his parishioners and understood that he relied upon his flock for survival. They were all in the same boat so to speak. That changed rapidly in the first half of the 19th century.

As the Catholic Church cast off its mass rocks and mud huts, an

astonishing rate of church building took place. By the beginning of
the 20th century, 24 major cathedrals and more than 3,000 churches
had been built.[31] In this same period, the church began to embrace
clericalism, focusing on church hierarchy and dominion over its flock
rather than service. At the Synod of Thurles in 1850, Archbishop Paul
Cullen led the synod with an ultramontane agenda. He reformed the
Irish church in line with the church of Rome with a strong emphasis
on Papal authority. Cullen would play a leading role in drafting the
dogma of Papal Infallibility for the First Vatican Council in 1869.
Aside from standardising church organisation, and establishing a
vast bureaucratic apparatus for the Church in Ireland, the Synod
demarcated clear boundaries between clergy and laity. Clergy were to
be dressed formally with collar at all times so that they clearly stood
apart from the public. Being an ultramontane, Cullen demanded an
absolute adherence to the rules of Rome, casting the folk traditions of
the native church aside. There was a heavy focus on penance and
special days and holidays were set aside for the laity to fulfil their
obligations of penance. The aftermath of the Synod was that the new,
standardised Catholic Church, under a Roman centralised bureau-
cracy, was a powerful political machine. The Synod of Thurles and
Cardinal Cullen established the Catholic Church as an absolute and
top-down authority on education and moral matters until its
authority loosened in the 1970s.

By the end of the 19th century, Irish identity had undergone a
profound transformation. The Irish language was seen as a language
of failure and backwardness. Schools and politicians promoted
English on utilitarian grounds and as the language of success that
could grant access to the middle classes for the better-off and a ticket
to the New World for the emigrant. The church had extracted itself
from the people and went about enforcing the church of Rome with
the vigour of a colonising administration. Their relationship with the
people shifted from one of mutual survival to one of dominion.
Importantly, many of the local customs, traditions and folklore that
had managed to survive the murderous Famine were now the enemy
of the ultramontanes who did not tolerate cultural variance. At the

dawn of the 20th century, Ireland's unique cultural identity had been all but extinguished. The process of Anglicisation was nearing completion with most Irish towns and cities looking and sounding increasingly like their British contemporaries.

The Celtic Revival

From this nadir sprang the Celtic Revival which would lay down the key identifying features of Irish identity for a century. In May 1798, the year of the United Irishmen rebellion, Daniel O'Connell was called to the bar to practice law. While he agreed with the aims of the United Irishmen, he was opposed to their ends and was profoundly impacted by the bloodshed of the failed rebellion. A barrister and gifted orator, he believed in achieving Irish independence through political means and so largely eschewed cultural nationalism as seen in his indifference to the death of the Irish language. When O'Connell died in 1847 with the Famine at its height and his great political goal of repealing the Act of Union looking destined to fail, a new wave of revolutionary nationalism took form, once more taking inspiration from the United Irishmen. The Young Irelanders were to lead a failed rebellion in 1848 but through their highly influential newspaper, The Nation, they set the blueprint for later revolutionaries by coupling cultural identity to revolutionary nationalism by extolling Irish language, poetry and literature. This would find full voice with the establishment of the Gaelic League in 1893. Under its first president, Douglas Hyde, the son of a Protestant rector from Roscommon, the Gaelic League established its own paper *An Claidheamh Soluis* where it published original stories and plays in Irish and English. From 1903 to 1909, the paper was edited by Padraig Pearse. Unlike O'Connell, Hyde understood the importance of cultural nationalism. In his famous lecture, 'The Necessity for De-Anglicising Ireland', delivered to the Irish National Literary Society in November 1892, he asked what would be the point of achieving independence were the people to ape their coloniser, culturally and linguistically post independence. In it he states, "In order to de-Anglicise ourselves we must at once arrest the decay of the language...In a word, we must strive to cultivate everything that is most racial, most smacking of the soil, most Gaelic."[32] Hyde's words would be echoed by de Valera in the 1930s when he said, "We cannot fulfil our destiny as a nation unless we are an Irish nation and we can only be truly that if we are an Irish-speaking nation."[33]

The Gaelic League aligned neatly with Yeats' Literary Revival which also found inspiration in the lead of *The Nation*. While the Gaelic League and the Literary Revival played an important role in romanticising the cause of armed rebellion in the run-up to the 1916 Rising, they were both destined to fail to leave a lasting impression on Irish identity. Their vision of Irish identity was simply the product of an eastern and, more specifically, a Trinity College and middle-class Catholic elite. This weakness was exemplified when the opening night of J.M. Synge's *The Playboy of the Western World* at the Abbey Theatre in January 1907 was met with riots. Synge's depiction of Christy Mahon as a coward who would murder his own father and Pegeen Mike as a woman of questionable morals who would run off with said cowardly murderer outraged nationalists. So soon after the Famine and so shortly before 1916, nationalist ideals couldn't allow such denigration of the idealised western community. The Playboy struck at the heart of the idealised Irish man and woman. The nationalists of 1916 revered the impoverished, yet noble and morally superior peasant de Tocqueville found in village X, unbowed by the horrors of the Famine. Synge did not receive criticism for being a Protestant and a Trinity-educated, wealthy urbanite but for poking at the root of idealised Irish identity—the western smallholder—he unwittingly laid bare the east/west socio-economic divide that had formed over centuries of Anglicisation and which had accelerated with the emergence of a robust urban Catholic middle class.

By comparison, Seumas O'Kelly, who was born in Loughrea, Co. Galway, steeped in the local folklore and recounting of stories of land agitation, was able to deal with incendiary topics in his writing such as sexual abuse and bribery because it came from a perceived place of authenticity. In 1903, O'Kelly, who was a journalist, became editor of *The Southern Star* based in Skibbereen. He would have seen first-hand the cultural and political aftermath of one of the worst-hit scenes of the Famine. He was a friend of Arthur Griffith and guest edited his journal *Nationality* when Griffith was imprisoned in 1918. It was while acting as editor that the offices of the paper were raided by the British army and during the event O'Kelly collapsed and died, making him a republican martyr.[34] In his best remembered novelette, *The Weaver's Grave*, O'Kelly recounts the fictional story of two old men who bicker as they try to remember where to bury the recently deceased weaver, Mortimer Hehir. The novel pokes fun at the two old men as they fail to remember the exact location of the weaver's grave and as they strike out at one another with fearsome barbs as each one, in turn, gets the location wrong. It is a battle for supremacy—which elder is the true custodian of the oral history of the locality. Here O'Kelly is tapping into what de Tocqueville observed across the west of Ireland, the high cultural value placed on oral history and intimate knowledge of the landscape. For the old men, knowledge of every grave and the story of who occupied it going back generations is a mark of rootedness in the landscape that defines one's belonging to a place.

At the end of the play, the weaver's widow falls in love with one of the young gravediggers to discover that a relationship need not only be a contractual matter. This was a direct attack on established rules of courting and matrimony in the west of Ireland—a theme just as scandalous as Synge's depiction of female immorality. However, O'Kelly gets away with it because while his characters are imperfect, they are each heroic in the way only the impoverished can be. He never threatens the root of Irish national identity.

Much like Synge, Yeats too misunderstood the intricacies of Irish identity that he undoubtedly contributed to forming. Like Synge, Yeats wove Romanticism through Irish scenes of gritty realism and did essential work in both bringing literary pride to Ireland while also fuelling the nationalist cause through an abundance of heroic poetry and plays, not least, *The Countess Cathleen* with its theme of self-sacrifice in the pursuit of idealism which was easily absorbed into the nationalist struggle. Much like Synge however, Yeats wasn't of the idealised western peasantry he wrote about. He too was a wealthy Anglo-Irish Protestant, and when residing in his Anglo-Norman towerhouse at Thoor Ballylee in Co. Galway, close to Lady Gregory's Coole Park estate, he resembled more the landlords of old than a fellow nationalist. Yeats was deeply fascinated by Irish folklore and did important work in promoting it, not least in his Celtic Twilight series of essays which show that a wealth of folklore had indeed survived the Famine. His writing was inspired by the occult and pagan practices as well as wider literary devices fashionable to the well-educated in the Romantic period. Yeats thus removed the folklore from the fireplace of the poor country cottage and instead gave it back as the sanitised expressions of the learned gentry. The hauntingly beautiful *The Stolen Child* could not have come into being without the stories told to him by the western peasantry, but equally it could not have come into being without his upper-class and Romanticist sensibilities. Yeats was a firm believer in fairies and in this he was influenced by the intellectual fashions of the day wafting over from England. For those with artistic sensibilities, time and money, fairy hunting had become a craze as scientists, anthropologists and artists raced to find evidence of their existence.[35] Sir Arthur Conan Doyle was also a firm believer and in 1904, J.M. Barrie's Tinker Bell, the winged fairy who appeared in Peter Pan, was a hit on the London stage. In Britain, the fascination with fairies was largely seen as a romantic reaction to the intense industrialisation of the landscape. For Yeats, a man of his class with time and money at his disposal, fairy hunting was a folly that did produce some poetry and plays that served as useful fuel for the nationalist movement but ultimately belonged to an elite literary movement removed from the peasant classes who inspired it in the west of Ireland. The Literary Revival was, to its detriment, a middle-class movement for eastern intellectuals and nationalist leaders who drew on the symbolism and experiences of the noble peasant in the West to forge a national identity that could serve as a recruitment for rebellion. In this regard, the Gaelic

Revival was destined for long-term failure. It would quickly lose relevancy in times of peace.

The most successful element of the Revival was the establishment of the GAA in 1884. Hurling and Gaelic football had been popular pastimes before the Famine but as cricket, rugby and soccer began to gain a foothold in the upper and middle classes from the 1860s, it became necessary to codify hurling and football to offer a nationalist alternative to English sports. Hurling, in particular, became an instant cornerstone of Irish identity and nationalism with references to it going back to Brehon Law and the great mythological cycles of the Táin Bó Cúailgne. Michael Collins famously played for and was club secretary for Geraldine's GAA club in London while he lived there. Collins worked alongside Sam Maguire and it is said that Collins was introduced to the IRB via the two men's connection to the GAA. Aside from its overtly nationalist principles, it was because the GAA struck out at the middle-class sensibilities of the Trinity elite, Catholic as well as Protestant, that it became so successful. Of all of the movements of the Gaelic Revival, the GAA was the most inclusive of the people it drew inspiration from as clubs rapidly spread throughout the country. On the morning of the 21st of November, 1920, after Michael Collins' daring coordinated assassination operation of British intelligence officers across Dublin which left 11 dead, British army auxiliaries retaliated by driving onto the field at Croke Park and opening fire on a crowd who had come to watch Dublin play Tipperary in a game of Gaelic football. They shot indiscriminately into the crowd leaving twelve dead. From that moment, the GAA was an unshakable part of Irishness and Croke Park became less a stadium and more a monument to Irish cultural identity.

Slow death of the Church

In 1943, an ageing Eamon de Valera—arguably the man who had done more than any other to engineer Irish identity—looked back on the era of Irish revolution and laid out his vision in his *Ireland That We Dream Of* St. Patrick's Day speech. In it he envisioned,

"The ideal Ireland that we would have, the Ireland that we dreamed of, would be the home of a people who valued material wealth only as a basis for right living, of a people who, satisfied with frugal comfort, devoted their leisure to the things of the spirit – a land whose countryside would be bright with cosy homesteads, whose fields and villages would be joyous with the sounds of industry, with the romping of sturdy children, the contest of athletic youths and the laughter of happy maidens, whose firesides would be forums for the wisdom of serene old age. The home, in short, of a people living the life that God desires that men should live."[36]

De Valera's romantic Ireland was a pre-Famine dream, the vision of the Gaelic Revivalists, the home of the idealised noble western peasant. He had done a great deal to exact this vision by giving special status to the Catholic Church in the 1938 Constitution and by handing moral, spiritual and academic education over to the church. And while he continuously extolled the importance of the language, it continued to decline under his stewardship in the absence of any direct intervention equivalent to the special status given to the Church. His inward-looking economy did hold off the inevitability of industrialisation and with it the intrusion of foreign cultural norms but with economic stagnation and collapse in the 1940s and 1950s and a return to mass emigration, de Valera's Ireland was dead and buried with the only pillar emerging unscathed being the Catholic Church. But that wouldn't last either.

Rather presciently, the priest in impoverished village X that de Tocqueville spent time with in 1835 foresaw the weakness of the new Catholic Church introduced by Cardinal Cullen at the Synod of Thurles in 1850 and which flourished in de Valera's Ireland. It was a church that claimed dominion over its flock rather than service to it. When de Tocqueville suggested to the impoverished priest that it would be better if the government were to fund church construction and clergy, the priest stated "The day I received government money, the people would no longer regard me as their own...We would lose by the change...It is among the people that the roots of belief are to be found...Any religion which broke away from the people would move away from its source and lose its main support."[37]

In de Valera's Ireland, the church achieved a level of institutional power unimaginable across the continent. In 1951, the ambitious Dr Noel Browne, as part of the first inter-party government's attempts to modernise the Health Ministry, attempted to introduce legislation that would provide free antenatal and postnatal care for mothers and free medical care for all children up to the age of 16. The Catholic Church and the powerful Archbishop McQuaid of Dublin saw this as the state setting foot on Church territory—family affairs. The clash represented the first time that the Church and State came into serious conflict, a conflict the Church easily won. Browne, who had been incredibly successful in stamping out TB and opening up more beds in Irish hospitals, was removed from his position and the fallout was such that the government itself collapsed later that year. It was a stern warning for all politicians to keep in line.

By the 1970s, with Ireland opening up to the world via the Lemass FDI economy and with an emergent college-educated middle class in urban areas, the Church faced its first popular revolts. The Second Vatican Council which ended in 1965 saw a radical modernisation of the Church which attempted to redress the clericalism of the church, introduced Mass in vernacular language and demanded that clergy engage with members of the church on matters of concern to them. In the Irish context, key emerging issues were contraception and divorce which were fiercely debated throughout the 1970s and 1980s. In 1973, the *McGee vs Attorney General* case ruled that the ban on contraceptives in Ireland interfered with the plaintiff's right to privacy in marital affairs as laid out in the Constitution. The ruling opened the door to securing the general sale of contraceptives. In 1979 the Family Planning Act[38] allowed individuals to purchase contraceptives with a prescription and in 1985, the amended Family Planning Act[39] allowed people to purchase contraceptives without prescription. In 1996 the Divorce Act[40] marked the beginning of secularisation of the Irish state.

However, it wasn't the removal of the church from the organs of political power that ended its role as a crucial part of Irish identity, rather a series of sex scandals dating back to the 1960s that began to be made public from the 1990s. The Ryan Report (2009) uncovered a massive scale of physical, emotional and sexual abuse at Church-run residential industrial schools and orphanages throughout the 20th century. The report concluded, "Physical and emotional abuse and neglect were features of the institutions. Sexual abuse occurred in many of them, particularly boys' institutions. Schools were run in a severe, regimented manner that imposed unreasonable and oppressive discipline on children and even staff." The Ferns Report (2005) and The Murphy Report (2009) detailed how senior clergy helped to protect clergy who had been credibly accused of sexual abuse. Most notably, The Murphy Report detailed how Archbishop McQuaid, a principal advisor to de Valera, had covered up sexual abuse in his Dublin Diocese. The report stated that "Archbishop McQuaid was familiar with the requirements of canon law but did not apply them fully. It is clear that his dealings with Fr Edmondus in 1960 were aimed at the avoidance of scandal and showed no concern for the welfare of children."[41] This was the Archbishop who helped bring down Dr Noel Browne's Health Department and government because it intruded on 'family affairs'. In each of the major reports, the deference the state showed to the Church was identified as a key enabler of the systemic abuse that took place over decades.

The massive scale of abuse and cover-ups between church and state that came out at the start of the 2000s fundamentally shattered the nation's trust in the church. It also sullied the romantic image of de Valera's Ireland, presided over as it was by McQuaid who had set in motion the pattern of suppressing the voices of the victims of clerical abuse. At the height of the Celtic Tiger, the nation turned away in shame from the Catholic Church—the one constant pillar of Irish identity. As the canny priest from Village X had warned 170 years previously, "Any religion which broke away from the people would move away from its source and lose its main support." Since the Irish Catholic Church had broken away from the people in 1850, the relationship between clergy and laity was one of dominion based on the clergy's claim to moral guardianship. Once it became clear that the Church had violated that trust to such a staggering degree, there was no organic relationship between church and laity from which to rebuild. In the 1990s, 80% of Irish people attended church once a month or more. By 2020, 28% of Irish people did.[42] This stunning collapse paved the way for gay marriage (2015) and abortion referenda (2018) to be passed by massive margins and with all major parties supporting and the church having no say in the matter.

Loss of community and identity

Arguably the least valued element of identity throughout Ireland's recent history has been the relationships between people, their landscapes, the oral tradition and how they blend to form binding communities. While language, religion, literature and sport were, from the late 19th century on, co-opted for political purposes, the one constant that remained organically of the people, was their fireside habits. De Tocqueville was not granted access to the social interactions of the people of hidden Ireland. He did a good job of describing the layout of their villages, their social conditions and the political conditions under which they laboured. Understandably, eye-witness histories of the Famine by visiting scholars and politicians concern themselves with the horrors of the starving and those lucky enough to emigrate. Despite the best efforts of Synge, Yeats and Lady Gregory, their collection of folklore took it from its native setting, the cabin fireside, and found itself, largely, reworked into their literature and poetry.

From 1937 to 1939, the Irish Folklore Commission under de Valera undertook the national Schools Manuscripts Collection project in 5,000 primary schools across the nation. The project, while an invaluable act of curation, did nothing to slow the removal of these stories from their roots, the fireplace, the farm cabin, the local landscape. Instead it helped hasten them into dusty archives for academics to interpret and reinterpret for their own purposes. Culture and identity are living things. Once they exist in museums only, they cease to be influential and a new culture will occupy the vacuum, creating a new identity.

The Famine laid waste to much of Ireland's folklore and fireside culture. Fortunately, a few outstanding texts grant access to what this Ireland may have looked like. The most celebrated example of pre-modern Ireland is the Great Blasket series of biographies. Sadly, generations of Irish students have been turned off of these invaluable ethnographies having been subjected to them in Irish language class in school. From 1962 to 1995, *Peig*, the autobiography of one of the island's most famous residents, Peig Sayers, was compulsory reading material for the Irish language senior cycle curriculum. While invaluable to the ethnographer, the recounting of struggle, emigration and death was widely mocked by pupils who felt it was depressing and made many, no doubt, feel embarrassed of their culture. In a 2006 Seanad Debate[43] on how the Irish language should be taught in schools, Progressive Democrats Senator, John Minihan, summed up the sentiments of many when he said, "No matter what our personal view of the book might be, there is a sense that one has only to mention the name Peig Sayers to a certain age group and one will see a dramatic rolling of the eyes, or worse." He had a point. *Peig* begins, "I'm an old woman now, with one foot in the grave and the other on its edge. I have experienced much use and much hardship from the day I was born until this very day. Had I known in advance half, or even one-third, of what the future had in store for me, my mind and heart wouldn't have been as gay or as courageous as they were in the beginning of my days."[44] It is a stunning opening but one that bore heavy on the shoulders of successive generations of Irish teens.

Maurice O'Sullivan, also an islander, wrote his autobiography, *Twenty Years a-Growing* in 1933. It begins, "I am a boy who was born and bred in the Great Blasket, a small truly Gaelic island which lies north-west of the coast of Kerry, where the storms of the sky and the wild sea beat without ceasing from end to end of the year and from generation to generation against the wrinkled rocks which stand above the waves that wash in and out of the coves where the seals make their homes."[45] Aside from its starkly upbeat tone compared to

Peig, it is rich with descriptions of everyday life on the island. One memorable chapter recounts how O'Sullivan and his neighbours would celebrate Halloween by going on a thrush hunt. O'Sullivan brings the island's beaches, pathways and coves to life as he recounts small acts of bravery as he and his best friend descend a cliff to find some thrush. "The cove looked mysterious in the dead of night. You would think the living and the dead were below with the roar of the waves breaking in among the rocks and the hiss of the foam through the cracks in the stones."[46] This is a man rooted in and intimately connected to his landscape, reverent of its power and how it provides. When he recounts his first season lobster potting with his father and uncle, he is recounting every boy's entry into the world of men in that place going back hundreds of years. A thrush hunt, a day lobster fishing, scavenging the booty of a sunken ship, all these stories are in turn told to family and neighbours around the fire at night where they become myths added to the countless stories of bravery and survival handed down the centuries.

This connection between experience, landscape and fireplace marks the passing of everyday events into myth and shared identity. Great Blasket is now abandoned. The houses of the great biographers are in ruins. One can see the skeletal remains of the home of Maurice O'Sullivan on YouTube videos and documentaries. It looks no different from the countless abandoned Famine villages across Connemara and Mayo. Looking at the ruins it is impossible to imagine that within living memory, that house was alive with dancing, music and stories of thrush hunts and children playing snap apple on Halloween evening. A whole world existed in that cottage and now that world is lost. A whole world of culture existed in every cottage across the west of Ireland and the loss of every house through migration or death during the Famine marks the death of countless stories and experiences and intimate knowledge of and relationships with these landscapes.

In 1937, the American anthropologist Conrad Arensberg, spent time in the village of Luogh, in Co. Clare. In his seminal study, *The Irish Countryman*, Arensberg analysed the role of folklore in everyday life and how it wove the key elements of the countryman's life together to root him in his community. Unlike the work of the Gaelic Revivalists who viewed the stories of the countryman in isolation looking for mythical and nationalistic properties, Arensberg uncovered how the folklore of the countryman played a role in regulating interactions and behaviours and kept up standards in rural communities. He identified religious belief and fairy belief as two separate and unshakable pillars of identity in these traditional communities. "First, one must notice that the Irish countryman is a very devout man. His life is ordered in adherence to his religion. Much of his habit of mind and his view of the world respond to his faith. He is a devout and practising Catholic. But he is also devout in another direction too, very often. Just as there is room in his mind and heart for patriotic fervour along with religious zeal, so is there room for fairy belief."[47]

Arensberg goes on to identify how just as the countryman's actions are dictated by religion, so too were they dictated by his belief in the fairies. For example, each night food and water would be left out for the fairies in case they were hungry while passing on their night rambles. Dirty water was never thrown out at night in case it landed on them. What Arensberg came to realise is that these rituals were actually basic household management tasks draped in folklore. Throwing out dirty water in the yard was seen as unhygienic and it was the community who would frown on it as much as the fairies. Arensberg found that what made the fairies angry aligned neatly with what the community found unwelcome and the maintenance of a strong belief in the fairies was a means of indirectly keeping high personal and communal standards in a village.[48] This is the crucial nuance that the Celtic Revivalists lost—the regulatory effect of folklore. They were not simply stories, they were an essential means of binding a community.

Beginning in the 1970s, folklorist and storyteller Eddie Lenihan attempted to find and record the remnants of the world Arensberg witnessed in Co. Clare. In his book *Meeting the Other Crowd* he confirmed Arensberg's observation that fairylore acted as a vital driver of social action. One story that Lenihan gathered, *The Bush that Bled,* recounts the building of a road near Lough Bunny, close to Gort, Co. Galway in the 1950s. The storyteller—a ninety-year-old man— worked for the council at the height of the de Valera economic collapse when people like him were grateful to have a job to save them from emigration. One morning, the storyteller and his brother arrived to work to find a stand-off between the foreman and the workers. There was a fairy bush on the proposed route and the workmen refused to remove it for fear of offending the fairies and the bad luck that would follow. The foreman threatened the men's jobs and reluctantly, two stepped up and began to saw at the limbs of the tree. The storyteller said that blood started to flow out of the cut limb and nobody would touch the tree after that.[49]

This might simply sound like a quaint tale to enthral the tourists. But in 1999, as the Celtic Tiger was reaching its pinnacle and vast infrastructural projects ploughed their way through the Irish land- scape in the name of modernisation, during the construction of the M18 motorway which linked Galway to Limerick, Lenihan brought it to the attention of the county engineer that the proposed motorway risked disturbing a fairy bush in Latoon, just outside of Newmarket- on-Fergus, Co. Clare. After Lenihan warned the engineer that there would be accidents and bad fortune for those travelling the road should the bush be removed, the engineer made the decision to alter the route of the motorway.[50] It was the first time in the history of the State that a major construction project made way for a folk—not archaeological—artefact. While Lenihan's unlikely success at Latoon marked a victory for Irish folklore and identity, unfortunately, it was an exception.

When the American travel writer Lawrence Millman travelled through Ireland in 1975, he astutely pointed to the devastating role television had on Ireland's unique fireside culture. RTÉ began broad- casting to the whole nation on New Year's Eve 1961 and after only fourteen years, Millman observed, "audiences were treated to the spectacle of glossy, fantastic images from outer space for the first time, and it didn't take them long to decide that they preferred American situation comedies over programs having to do with their own culture. It was like opting for cleanliness over dirt and grime."[51] Millman skilfully—for an outsider—detected the handed-down embarrassment and sense of backwardness and poverty that people had come to associate with hidden Ireland from the age of O'Connell. Television coincided with Lemass' economic opening-up to the world and Ireland's rapid emergence as an economic powerhouse. By the time Lenihan saved the Latoon fairy bush he was very much a man out of step with time. Even in the west of Ireland at the turn of the Millennium, jobs were increasingly in factories, not on the land, social lives were spent in the pub, not by the fireplace, and those who did stay home were more likely to watch British soap operas and reality TV or American movies. Culture became radically more passive to the detriment of community as one need only switch on the TV for a night's entertainment and even when one did go to the pub, it became increasingly fashionable to gather there to watch English Premier League football or international rugby. Where a music session broke out at a pub, it was most likely entertainment provided by the publican to lure in an audience to spend money on beer, again a passive experience for the audience, nice background ambience, but not something they themselves were a part of—except perhaps for the end-of-night well-lubricated singsong. At the height of the Celtic Tiger, it was not uncommon to see a night in the pub end with a group of well-oiled young men belting out Irish rebel songs while wearing Manchester United, Liverpool and Arsenal soccer shirts. Cultural identity had become a confused mix of Anglo-American pop and social culture churned up with vestiges of the native. Still, particularly in rural areas, there was an enduring devotion to the GAA and a solid, if consciously unexamined, sense of ethnic identity that hadn't yet been challenged by a shift in demographics. That changed radically under Fianna Fáil's Celtic Tiger building boom.

As outlined in the last chapter, between 1996 and 2006 the Irish economy was propped up by a building boom which peaked at a record 90,000 houses being built in 2006.[52] Huge numbers of these houses were placed into ancient villages all across the country, induced by subsidies and tax incentives, particularly in rural areas. Because the majority of people taking up residence in these houses were Irish people looking for affordable housing in rural areas close to urban hubs where the FDI economy was based, little consideration was given to the long-term effects such a massive internal migration would have on community cohesion. There was a general sense that it would take care of itself within a generation as the children of the new arrivals would seamlessly integrate once sent to school and to do sports with the locals. That didn't happen.

Fr Harry Bohan, a priest and sociologist from Co. Clare is widely celebrated in the county for his pioneering social housing projects in rural Ireland. Growing up in the 1950s he saw firsthand the devastating effects mass migration had on rural communities. He left to work and study in Cardiff and upon his return, he set up the Rural Housing Organisation (RHO) in 1972. The model has been considered to be a success and Bohan, up to 2002, had secured housing for 2,500 families in 120 rural communities. Why did he succeed in settling people in historic parishes without disturbing the fabric of community while the Celtic Tiger failed? Bohan points to a number of factors. RHO communities were small-scale settlements so they did not threaten the local and established community structure. More importantly, the bulk of these settlements took place in a time when Ireland was poorer and so community was, by necessity, stronger. As Bohan put it, "In poorer times, the real definition of community was not just family but groupings of families and neighbours that helped one another socially and economically. More recently there has been a general move away from community towards this emphasis on self...The man used to know his neighbours but his son doesn't know them at all. In other words, an important part of identity has been broken." [53]

The difference between the settlements of the RHO and the Celtic Tiger wave is that the people dwelling in the former belonged to a time when community and 'putting down roots' were driving motivators, not simply proximity to a job. The Celtic Tiger, rooted in the FDI economy, largely reduced these new satellite settlements, wedged into historic villages, to a place to sleep but whose occupants work, socialise and shop elsewhere. Parallel societies grew up between locals and interlopers and while some will have managed in the intervening years to bridge the gap between, many more, having no incentive to do so in the individualistic, secular, FDI economy, bear no deeper roots than having a bed to sleep in and a TV to watch at night after a hard day's work at the multinational factory. In other words, the Celtic Tiger marked the moment in the FDI economy where people became transient, atomised commodities whose principal purpose was to man multinationals. The connection between people and community was severed and the connection between people and landscape was shattered. Irish fireside tradition was uniquely predicated on people's intimate knowledge of one another, the landscape and a high social value placed on continuity or rootedness via oral communication. Celtic Tiger Ireland was individualistic and anonymous. Social value was placed on TV and, shortly thereafter, on social media and virtual communities.

The severance of people from the land didn't just happen in the private sphere. Fianna Fáil, the party of de Valera, undertook an unprecedented assault on Ireland's historic and archaeological landscapes. The number of recorded archaeological excavations in Ireland increased from between 50-60 per year in the 1980s to 932 in 1999. There were almost 2000 licences issued for archaeological works in both 2003 and 2004, while in both 2006 and 2007, there were more than 2000 licences issued. By 2006, there was an estimated backlog of 3,000 to 4,000 unpublished excavations many of which would never see publication.[54] The sheer scale of destruction of Ireland's archaeological landscapes would, of course, have a profound effect on any attempts to protect, resurrect or rekindle Irish fireside culture, reliant as it was on these monuments to act as totems or physical anchor points in the landscape for stories to take place.

Fianna Fáil had taken credit for putting Ireland on the path to globalism via the FDI economy and EU integration under Lemass and later, under Ahern, they would send a powerful message that de

Valera's Ireland was dead and gone. In 2003, planning permission was granted to build the M3 motorway linking Dublin to Cavan and to newly expanded commuter villages and towns in Meath. The pathway of the M3 went through the archaeological landscape of the Hill of Tara, arguably the most important archaeological landscape in Ireland, destroying more than 28 sites and monuments in the immediate vicinity of the Hill.[55] Monumental activity at Tara dates back to the Neolithic period with the 5,000-year-old Mound of the Hostages on the hill. During the Iron Age, Tara became the seat of the High Kings of Ireland. St. Patrick came to Tara in the 5th century as part of his Christianising mission and, long after the site had passed into ruin, it remained a powerful symbol of Irish identity.[56] In 1798, the United Irishmen chose the Hill of Tara to make their stand against the British and in 1843, Daniel O'Connell chose the site for one of his most famous 'monster meetings' to rally the Irish behind his cause of Catholic emancipation. Despite protests from local groups, academics both at home and abroad—notably Conor Newman, the future head of the Heritage Council of Ireland—as well as a range of international celebrities, the motorway went ahead.

On the 11th May 2005, Minister for the Environment, Dick Roche gave permission for the route to progress. The government drove a motorway through the heart of the most important historic landscape in Ireland, a vessel that held more than 5,000 years of Irish archaeology, folklore, struggle, continuity and identity. This was the date that the Irish state in effect announced that nothing would stop 'progress'.

In 2005, when the state went to war on Irish identity, the ethnic Irish still comfortably made up a supermajority of the population. The 2006 census showed that there were 420,000 non-nationals[57] living in Ireland out of a total population of 4.4 million.[58] 9.5% of the population was non-national. Only a year before, the EU had admitted ten eastern European nations including Poland, Czechia, Latvia, Lithuania and Estonia who made up a significant percentage of Ireland's migrant population during the later Celtic Tiger years. While 9.5% represented an extraordinary increase in the non-native population since virtual homogeneity a decade before, there was not yet a sense among the wider Irish population that those coming to Ireland for work would represent a permanent demographic shift. There was a sense, much like Germans had in the 1950s and 1960s under their guest worker schemes, that non-nationals would come, work and then return home with their earnings. Because of this, there was no perceived threat to national identity caused by demographics. By 2024 it had become apparent that non-nationals were not 'going home' and moreover, they were arriving in such numbers that integration or assimilation was not possible even if there was political will for it to happen, which there wasn't. By March of 2024, 22% of the population of Ireland was non-national. Further, there was a generation of children born and coming into adulthood belonging to the Celtic Tiger non-nationals who had integrated with varying degrees of success. As the public became aware of the depth and speed of legal and illegal immigration into Ireland and as, for the first time since the end of the 19th century, Irish society was in upheaval, Irish people felt an existential threat but when they went looking for a sense of shared identity, the old reliables were no longer to hand, they had died off somewhere along the way.

If you were to ask an Irish person in 2024 'What does it mean to be Irish?' they would struggle to give a coherent answer. The Irish are no longer a church going people—only 28% attend mass once a month or more. They are no longer an Irish-speaking people, they hadn't been since before the Famine. Irish music and folklore are for tourists or passive interaction on a night out at the pub. The Irish are no longer a close-knit, community-oriented people with a distinct fireside culture. Their connection to the land is gone and if their homes are based in an ancient village they, most likely, play no significant role in it. It is a bed and a base for work in the FDI economy. Their social lives are increasingly individualised and supplied by a screen, and the pop culture they consume is increasingly Anglo-American, their preferred sports also. What makes an Irish person uniquely Irish, and is there even such a thing as being uniquely Irish in a secular, post-Catholic, post-community, multi-ethnic, globalised nation? For too long, Irish people tried to escape what they saw as the backward elements of their identity or they simply didn't need to consciously reflect on it. And now, as Ireland burns amid unprecedented demographic change and political parties close ranks to ensure the country's rapid integration into the global economy, a group of well-funded NGOs and academics have stepped into the identity gap to forge a new, post-nation globalist identity for Irish people. It begins by making the Irish 'white'.

4

MAKING THE IRISH "WHITE"

As frustration turned to arson over the 'no veto, no consultation' placement of groups of single male immigrants into close-knit communities across Ireland throughout 2023 and 2024, time and again politicians invoked historic Irish emigration as grounds for Ireland's moral obligation to accept these new arrivals. In March 2024, as part of his St. Patrick's Day tour of America, at a gathering of Irish-Americans in Boston, Leo Varadkar told his audience that St. Patrick was a "single, male, undocumented" immigrant who brought some "dangerous foreign ideas" such as Christianity to Ireland before concluding that "The story of St Patrick teaches us that migration is nothing new. It has always been part of our national story."[1] Varadkar had a long track record of claiming that his migration policy was justified by historic Irish emigration. At a November 2019 speech at a National Immigrant Council of Ireland Conference, he said, "When we look at those who come to Ireland seeking a new life we need to ask ourselves do we see strangers, or do we see ourselves? Our global diaspora includes the children of economic migrants, the grandchildren of exiles, the great-grandchildren of refugees. There was a time when we were 'the tired, the poor, the huddled masses who yearned to breathe free'. The words inscribed on the Statue of Liberty are part of our historical DNA."[2]

Similarly, at the 175-year National Famine Commemoration in Strokestown, Co. Roscommon, in May 2022, Micheal Martin took the opportunity to draw parallels between the death, cultural destruction and mass emigration of the Famine and the experiences of the Ukrainians then fleeing war with Russia. Using the sanctity of the Famine Commemoration, Martin ginned up support for the government's disastrous Ukrainian refugee programme by concluding, "Ireland has opened its doors to the people of Ukraine at their time of need and that crisis has brought home the importance of those who can help others, doing whatever they can to aid those in dire straits."[3]

At the 102-year commemoration of Michael Collins' assassination at Béal na Bláth in August 2024, Taoiseach Simon Harris stated, "Misinformation and lies are the greatest risk to democracy and peace in our time. Nowhere is that more evident than in the area of migration. There is a small group of people who want a country whose history has been woven by mass emigration to diminish the value of migration. They seek to create a division among those who were once forced to leave their home in search of a better life with others who are now seeking to do the same."[4]

In each case, Varadkar, Martin and Harris chose sacred landscapes, totems of Irish identity, to advocate for their mass migration policies. The settings for these speeches were not accidental. Just as O'Connell and the United Irishmen drew on Tara to rouse feelings of national pride and imbue their actions with direct authority from one of Ireland's most sacred landscapes, so too did Varadkar, Martin and Harris carefully draw on the cultural and historical authority imbued in Boston, Strokestown and Béal na Bláth to sell their immigration message. In doing so, they attempted to redraw Irish emigration history and present it not as a heroic and inspiring story of survival and a hard-fought right to self-determination, rather as a debt that needs to be paid off in the present. As discussed in the last chapter, as Ireland's identity crisis deepens with the loss of language, church, community, collective memory and folklore together with their places in the landscape, the government, among other opportunistic groups, will insert their own narrative into the void to suit whatever agenda is fashionable or profitable. In the case of Fianna Fáil and Fine Gael, generating a sense of guilt or unpaid debt for historic emigration is essential in selling mass inward migration in support of the FDI economy and for their no veto, no consultation IPAS centres across the country.

The notion that Ireland's historic emigration story incurred moral debt is an extraordinary claim and one that merits examination.

Irish emigration history

Prior to the Famine there were several major waves of emigration from Ireland. These can be attributed to various phases of colonial expansion as well as penal policies that resulted in the forced transportation of the Irish to different parts of the British Empire. On September 4th, 1607, after the defeat of the Ulster nobles in the Nine Year War which paved the way for the Plantation of Ulster, a Spanish vessel carrying notable nobles and their entourage left Lough Swilly, Co. Donegal, destined for Spanish Netherlands. The aim was to raise an army to reconquer Ireland and restore the church of Rome. However, the 90 who left would never return and though their number was small, it marked the beginning of a pattern of war-related emigration for the coming centuries. After Cromwell's conquest of Ireland there were 34,000 to 40,000 Irish soldiers in captivity. Cromwell had wished for them to be sent to Barbados as slaves but such numbers would have outnumbered the Anglo planters two to one. So instead, Parliament decided to allow them to go and serve in the armies of Europe, not then at war with England. So they were spread out among the armies of France, Spain, Austria and Poland.[5] In 1691, after the failure of the Williamite rebellion and the Treaty of Limerick, Patrick Sarsfield left for France with 15,000 soldiers and their families.[6] These military-related migrations, along with the scattering of fighting men from Ireland after the United Irelanders rebellion, left the native Irish without protection after each phase of British colonial expansion. This, in turn, allowed successive Parliaments to enforce an agenda of Anglicisation, displacement and impoverishment of the natives that culminated in the Famine that would lead to the migration of millions up to the end of the 19th century.

After Cromwell deported the remnants of the native fighting forces, he was free to begin deporting the defenceless citizenry to underpopulated colonies on mainland America, mainly Virginia and Maryland, and in even greater numbers to the Caribbean. Throughout the 17th century thousands of vagrants, impoverished, and suspected rebels were sent to Monserrat, Barbados, St. Kitts, Nevis and Antigua. The 1678 Census for Montserrat showed that 50% of the population, 1,900 men, women and children, were Irish. On Antigua, 26% were Irish, 10% on St. Christopher and 22% on Nevis. They arrived as voluntary and involuntary indentured servants, meaning they worked for a plantation master for a set number of years. Voluntary indentured servants were then, upon the end of their contract, to be given the means to establish themselves and given the status of freemen. The term voluntary makes the experience sound consensual, but in reality, most of those Irish who left voluntarily during the 17th and 18th centuries did so as a matter of survival due to the ravages of colonial rule, especially under the Penal Laws, at home.

It is estimated that 50,000 Irish people in total entered into indentured servitude in the Caribbean, 10,000 of them involuntarily. The treatment of the Catholic Irish indentured servants in the Caribbean was notoriously brutal. Irish Catholics suffered terribly under their Anglican plantation bosses with floggings and long hours under the Caribbean sun leading to a high mortality rate. Punishment for attempted escape included being branded on the forehead with the letters 'FT' for Fugitive Traitor. When John Scott, an English adventurer visited the West Indies, he saw Irish indentured servants and black slaves working alongside one another and remarked, "Without stockings under the scorching sun...[the Irish] were derided by the negroes, and branded with the Epithet of 'white slaves'."[7] While indentured servitude is not the same as the chattel slavery which brought Africans to the West Indies, the former having a set term of contract, it was common for the Irish upon release, to be denied the terms of their contract—a sum of money or a plot of land—leaving many of those who survived their contract destitute.

With the loss of the American colony in the 18th century, Irish indentured servants were increasingly sent to Australia. From 1787-1853, 26,500 poor Irish were transported to New South Wales as convicts.[8] For those in involuntary servitude in Australia, their lot was similar to those of the Caribbean. If they survived their penal sentence, they were released as freemen but none had the price of passage home, making their exile a permanent one. Indentured servitude, voluntary or involuntary, was essentially a life sentence in exile for those who survived it. Catholic Irish indentured servants were particularly brutally treated due to their religion and for fear of rebellion and treason among their ranks. After the United Irishmen rebellion of 1798, thousands of rebels were sentenced to be transported to Australia though only between 400 and 800 have been accounted for in official records. Veterans of the rebellion staged Australia's first convict uprising in 1804. The Castle Hill Rebellion was led by Philip Cunningham and did not gather the numbers hoped for. The rebellion was swiftly put down with five ringleaders hanged on the spot. Cunningham was hanged from the Government Store in Parramatta as a warning to other would-be convict rebels.[9] Throughout the 19th century, Irish political prisoners would be sent to penal servitude in Australia. After the Young Irelander rebellion in 1848, William Smith O'Brien and Thomas Francis Meagher were transported. While in exile in Tasmania, Smith O'Brien would become a fierce critic of Britain's role in the Famine.

The mass starvation and emigration of the Famine were caused by a blight, by the social structures that took shape after Cromwell's land clearances and the Penal Laws and, importantly, by the British Whig Government's response to the blight. While Smith O'Brien, writing in penal servitude in Tasmania didn't go so far as to label the Famine a genocide, he unequivocally blamed the British for the "premature extinction" of one million Irish.[10] It is a sentiment echoed by Miller in his definitive study of Irish emigration to America. He states, "The potato blight was unavoidable, but the Great Famine was largely the result of Ireland's colonial status and grossly inequitable social system."[11] Also in prison in Tasmania, it was the summation of Smith O'Brien's fellow Young Irelander, John Mitchel, that has echoed longest in the Irish memory. In *The Last Conquest of Ireland (Perhaps)* Mitchel, was in no doubt that the Famine was an attempted genocide, writing, "...the loss of one crop [is] a visitation from Heaven, Irish famine is a visitation from England."[12] It is a sentiment that Coogan echoes in his study of the Famine. He concludes, "John Mitchel's stark analysis that God sent the blight but the English created the Famine rings true."[13]

The rate of emigration during the Famine and chain migration in the decades that followed meant that by 1891, the Irish made up 26.3% of the total population of New South Wales, 26.5% of Victoria, 26.1% of Queensland and 20% of the population of Tasmania.[14] The Australian government have estimated that in addition to convicts, 300,000 Irish people emigrated to Australia from 1840 to 1914, accounting for one-quarter of Australia's foreign-born population in 1871.[15] For those arriving during the Famine, it was common to face discrimination in public and private life. Females were needed for domestic service and to correct the lopsided gender imbalance on the continent. Between 1849 and 1851, 4,000 female Famine orphans between the ages of 14 and 20 were shipped from overcrowded work-houses across Ireland to Australia. They were often mocked in the media and in person for their appearance, illiteracy and lower-class status.[16] While many of these girls went on to birth notable Australian families, they arrived and built an existence from the bottom rung of the social scale in an inhospitable land.

For the first 40 years of the Australian colony, settlement consisted almost entirely of convicts and their government and prison handlers. To them fell the rough task of physically building a nation. When the first convicts arrived in New South Wales in 1788, there were no roads, no towns, no agricultural bases, nothing.

Convicts were assigned to work on building roads as well as other public infrastructure, and also for the businesses of the settler class or on their farms. By 1830, there were 15,700 free settlers compared to 61,000 convicts. By 1850, however, this ratio had shifted with over 191,000 free settlers and 144,615 convicts. The Irish made up a quarter of all convicts and 40% of all female convicts.[17] Land was in the hands of the Anglo colonial settler class and the large increase of people arriving up to 1850 was due to government bounties and other initiatives which incentivised emigrants to come to Australia rather than North America to work as agricultural labourers, farm mechanics and tradesmen. With the bulk of Irish Catholics arriving from the most impoverished parts of Ireland, they were condemned to work as unskilled labourers and so, in practical terms, their daily routine would often differ little from that of the convict.

The key point to the Irish emigrant experience to Australia during the 19th century is that it was initially compelled by the British government through convict transports; and later, during the Famine and until the end of the 19th century, the Irish who left for Australia to escape British colonial misrule at home, found themselves begrudgingly needed by that same power in Australia. Irish Catholics took up their place on the lowest rung of society in Australia and, through sheer will and backbreaking labour, not only did they play a crucial role in building a nation from red soil and desert, but many went on to become leading citizens.

Though migration to America from Ireland is most strongly associated with the Famine, between 50,000 and 100,000 arrived in the 1600s with another 250,000 to 400,000 from 1700-1776. Importantly, while about three-quarters of immigrants in the 1600s were southern Irish Catholics, in the 1700s, only one-fifth to one-quarter were.[18] The majority of emigrants were Ulster Presbyterians and other Dissenters and would later come to be known as Ulster Scotch.

This distinction is important, as we shall see later, as these Ulster Scotch were better educated and equipped with useful trades. They also possessed a religion that acted as less of a barrier to public life in America than the Catholicism of the impoverished masses of southern Catholics who arrived during the Famine and who faced discrimination much the same as they faced in Australia and the Caribbean.

This meant that often, when one reads histories of early 'Irish' political and economic power in America prior to the Famine, one is actually reading about Scotch-Irish political and economic power and not southern Catholic or native Irish political and economic power. Their experiences were very different. Much like the pattern established in Europe, migrations to America in the 17th and 18th centuries, for the native Irish Catholic, were the result of war and colonial land clearances. As in the Caribbean, the majority of southern Catholics arriving in America as indentured servants were initially sent to work for a set period on plantations, notably in Maryland and Virginia. Other Irish Catholics sailed to America as servants and labourers for Presbyterian and Anglican families leaving Ireland. Where Irish Catholics did emigrate with sound finances, these were overwhelmingly individuals who Anglicised their names and religions to climb the Colonial social ladder or, like the Blakes, Darcys and Kirwans, the so-called "tribes" of Galway, they were old Catholic English gentry who looked to rebuild abroad after the Cromwellian wars.[19] Again, to emphasise, the old class systems followed from the old world to the New World and those southern or Catholic Irish who arrived in America from 1600-1800 were overwhelmingly poor and politically powerless.

From 1815 to 1844, between 800,000 and 1,000,000 people left Ireland and again these were two-thirds Ulster Presbyterians and Anglicans. Because of the economic hardships brought on by the Napoleonic wars, they were joined for the first time in great numbers by Anglicans from the south of Ireland. The 1803 and 1816 Passenger Acts, brought in under the pretence of improving the conditions of emigration to North America, were actually a means of raising the cost of travel to the New World by restricting passenger numbers. The aim was to stop the loss of landlord labour at home and while this was somewhat successful, it did little to stop skilled workers and monied families—Protestants—from emigrating. Poor Catholic

Irishmen found their way around the exorbitant ticket prices by catching a ride—at a much reduced cost—in the hulls of Canadian timber transport ships. Government incentives such as reduced ticket fares and increased travel and trade routes between Britain and America in the 1820s saw an increase in Catholic emigration to America such that between 1827 and 1832, Ulster Protestants only made up 50% of people arriving in North America from Ireland.[20] It was only around 1835, when de Tocqueville travelled and recorded the poverty of hidden Ireland, that these same people made up the slight majority leaving the island of Ireland for America.

The period directly following the Napoleonic wars saw rapid agricultural modernisation and profiteering by Anglo-Irish landlords in Ireland. To maximise profitability on landlord estates, laws were passed that gave landlords powers to clear both those tenants in arrears and even those not in arrears from the land. Leases were reduced to a year-to-year basis and, in a reversal of the Penal Laws, strict laws were enacted which prevented tenants from subletting or subdividing holdings among their children forcing the second, third and further sons off the land and on to a ship bound for the New World. The crowded small holdings of the Irish peasants were cleared, displacing approximately 100,000 families in the period from 1815-1843.[21] If a family was 'lucky' they might avail of a government resettlement grant to Canada or a landlord would pay for the family to emigrate to Canada after being cleared from their land. So, almost thirty years before the Famine, the stark option of emigrating or going to the Workhouse was already in effect.

Between 1845 and 1855, 1.8 million Irish emigrated to North America. As in Australia, they faced discrimination and occupied the lowest rung of American society. The route to North America proved even more treacherous than that to Australia as cholera, dysentery and typhus tore through packed substandard 'coffin ships'. 20,000 died en route or shortly after arrival in North America in 1847 alone. Grosse Ile, a quarantine checkpoint for ships seeking access to Canada, bears particularly sad testimony to the horrific conditions which dispossessed Irish emigrants faced. In May of 1847, a backup of

40 coffin ships at the poorly manned quarantine island saw more than 5,000 Irish die in horrific conditions. The island hospital was so overcrowded that passengers, healthy and sick alike, were quarantined on their ships awaiting clearance. The typhus-afflicted lay in their own filth waiting to die while the healthy watched and waited their turn. When the backlog finally did clear, many of those who were given passage to Canada brought the disease with them, dying on the streets of Montreal[22] and elsewhere.

The Famine Irish, most of whom were agricultural labourers, were too poor to purchase land in America. It is an interesting twist of fate that in the New World the Famine turned Irish farmers into urban industrial workers. These impoverished wretches took up the lowest-skilled, poorest paid and most dangerous positions—railway and canal construction, dock labourers and factory positions. For the first few years after arrival in America, life was largely transient for men moving from insecure job to insecure job. This employment insecurity kept the new arrivals on the lowest rung of the economic ladder for decades after arrival. As in Australia, girls and women found work in domestic service. The living conditions of the new arrivals were horrific. New slums sprang up in New York, Boston and elsewhere to deal with the massive influx of immigrants. In the Fifth Ward of Providence, Rhode Island, in 1850, on average nine people were crammed into one- and two-bed dwellings. In New York, almost 30,000 people, largely Irish, lived in filthy, dim cellars beneath ground level which were often flooded with human waste which ran off from open sewers.[23] Between subhuman living and work conditions, it was estimated that the average life expectancy for an Irish immigrant in Boston in the 1840s was fourteen years.[24]

As a means of escaping urban slums and life-threatening manual labour, many Irish chose to join the US Army and they played an outsized role in the US Civil War. In the 1850s almost 60% of the US Army had been born in Ireland. When Robert E. Lee, leading a unit of US Marines, put down John Brown's slave rebellion at Harper's Ferry, the only marine fatally wounded was Irishman Luke Quinn. When the first shots of the Civil War rang out at Fort Sumter, 63% of the garrison inside were men born in Ireland (both Scotch-Irish and Catholic Irish).[25] During the course of the Civil War, 180,000 Irish-born men fought for the Union with a further 70,000 first-generation Irish Americans fighting. More than 35,000 of these died on the battlefields of the Civil War and hundreds more in the notorious Andersonville prison camp.[26] At least 20,000 Irishmen fought for the Confederacy. The Enrolment Act of 1863, the United States' first military draft, required that all citizens and those awaiting citizenship fight for the Union. While the Act allowed for upper-class citizens to buy their way out of service for $300 or provide substitutes, the majority of Irish Catholics had no option but to fight. And they did so with outstanding valour with Irishman often pitched against Irishman in some of the war's bloodiest battles including at Antietam. At Antietam in September 1862, the Young Irelander Thomas Francis Meagher, who had escaped penal servitude in Australia, was commander of the Union Irish Brigade which suffered devastating losses. The Irish Brigade lost 540 men on the Sunken Road on September 17th. At the Miller Cornfield, the 105th New York which had a strong Irish contingent, and the 6th Louisiana (Confederate), which was predominantly Irish, both battled for control of the field. Both units would be decimated within an hour of the beginning of hostilities at Antietam with Irishmen on both sides, no doubt, killed by their fellow Irishmen. The brigade to which the 6th Louisiana belonged took 323 casualties from 550 men sent to the cornfield.[27] Three months later at Fredericksburg, Meagher's Irish Brigade again suffered devastating losses. On the morning of December 13th, the Brigade assaulted Marye's Heights. Out of 1,200 men who led the charge, there were 545 casualties. At Gettysburg, it was the Irish 69th Pennsylvania that halted Pickett's Charge on Cemetery Ridge thus turning the tide of the battle and the war. Tales of Irish heroism during the American Civil War are too numerous to recount but their contribution is recognised by the fact that no non-American nationality has received the Medal of Honour, the United States' highest military honour, more than the Irish. 10% of the Civil War's Medal of Honour awardees, or 146 individuals, were Irish men.[28] There is no doubt that the Irish played an outsized role in securing victory for the Union and ushering in black emancipation.

Let's return then to the statements made by Leo Varadkar in Boston in 2024, Harris at Beál na Bláth and Martin at the 175-year anniversary of the Famine. These statements were designed to justify radical, demographics-altering mass immigration policies. Each of their justifications is grounded in an inferred moral debt that the Irish owe to the world. Varadkar's statement in Boston that St. Patrick was a "single, male, undocumented" immigrant who brought dangerous foreign ideas deserves direct attention because it represents a crass distortion of Ireland's Patron Saint, bordering on mockery. Saint Patrick was not an "undocumented" immigrant in the modern sense. It's so simplistic it's almost embarrassing to say it but, there was no documentation process for those entering Ireland in the 5th century. Ireland was not a centrally organised state. It was a collection of local and provincial kingdoms in strategic alliance with one another for protection and expansion.[29] While there was a High King, in the 5th century his role was largely symbolic and certainly not concerned with border control, passport production and visas. Further, St. Patrick's arrival in Ireland in 432 was not random—nor was it in search of shelter, refuge or a luxury hotel in the West of Ireland with a weekly cash allowance. In his self-penned *Confessio*, Patrick recounts how he was one of thousands kidnapped and taken to Ireland at the age of sixteen and, after six years as a shepherd, he returned home to Britain. After training to be a priest he returned to Ireland as a missionary. The point, and this is where Varadkar's caricature falls apart, is that St. Patrick did not return with dangerous foreign ideas. A year before Patrick's return, the *Chronicon of Prosper* talks of Palladius who had been sent to Ireland by Pope Celestine "to the Irish believing in Christ as their first bishop".[30] There is confusion whether Palladius was Patrick or whether they were separate individuals. However, the *Chronicon of Prosper* shows that there was an established Christian community in Ireland before Patrick arrived—most likely the result of trade links with Britain and Europe or brought by captured slaves. Patrick was the Irish church's first great missionary and helped expand the faith after gaining the trust of the Uí Néill clan whose wars of expansion also allowed Patrick to expand the faith. Far from bringing foreign dangerous ideas to Ireland, Patrick rapidly spread what had already taken root and the speed with which it spread was a testament to the enthusiasm with which it had already been greeted.

To compare St Patrick—a missionary who came to know Ireland after being kidnapped and who later became one of its greatest historical figures—to those now showing up at Dublin Airport having thrown their identity documents away is crass. Of course, there is another way of looking at Varadkar's St. Patrick analogy. He states that Patrick came with "dangerous foreign ideas"—meaning Christianity—which had taken root in Ireland before Patrick and which he helped to spread enthusiastically, to the point that it became a central pillar of Irish identity until recently. A controversial case could be made that St. Patrick was the face of Ireland's first successful colonisation—that by the Church of Rome. From this perspective, the insinuation in Varadkar's words would be that those who are now coming to Ireland "with dangerous foreign ideas" will do the same as Patrick did, that is, usher in a new age of cultural or religious colonisation. That is something the Irish people did not give Varadkar or any other politician a mandate to pursue. Yet, in the absence of a coherent national identity, as outlined in the last chapter, it is a very real possibility.

Martin, Harris and Varadkar's broader claim is that because Ireland is a nation of historic emigration, we now bear a moral burden to allow others the chance to come to Ireland. This claim is based on a cynical misrepresentation of Irish emigration history.

Colonial era emigration from Ireland is characterised by voluntary and involuntary migration. From the 17th century through to the 19th century thousands were forced from their homes forever as indentured servants. These people were sent to British colonies throughout the New World and toiled in brutal conditions. Many did not survive. Many more went to the New World as voluntary indentured servants and were treated just as poorly. It was not uncommon, particularly in the Caribbean, to be cheated out of the terms of their contracts once freed. While these Irish people technically entered into these contracts of their own volition, they were pushed to do so as a last resort and a means of survival because of colonial expansion, legal and economic repression at home. Is it correct for Varadkar, Harris and Martin to say that Ireland owes a moral debt to the world because of these people? No. Primarily any debt is owed by the British Empire to these people and their descendants.

The bulk of historic Irish emigration occurred during and in the decades after the Famine. The social organisation, economic conditions and poverty that led to catastrophic death and emigration during the Famine was the result of economic and legal abuse by the British Empire in the centuries before the blight and in their handling of the disaster. Those who fled and arrived in Australia faced conditions little different from the indentured servants who went before them. Those who left for North America took up the lowest rung of the social and economic ladder in society. Living in overcrowded and unsanitary slums and working the most dangerous and undesirable jobs, the average age of survival after arrival in Boston for the Famine Irish was 14 years. It was undoubtedly a similar age in America's other urban centres. Those Irish who arrived before, during and after the Famine and wished to attain citizenship were forced by draft to fight in the American Civil War. They died in their tens of thousands.

If culpability or moral debt is to be taken on by any party for the emigration of the Irish during the Famine and into the last decades of the 19th century, that culpability unequivocally lies with the British Empire. Importantly, those Irish who arrived in the New World did not arrive with their hand out looking for support. They were recruited to build the new nations of the Empire and the expansion of industrial era America. They expected no handouts and none were given. Those who did not secure work, died. Those who obtained work often died too because of filthy living conditions and unsafe employment. Aside from Boston's 14-year life expectancy for Irish emigrants, in New York's Five Points neighbourhood, the mortality rate for Irish children was 25% due to disease and malnutrition.[31]

Irish migration 'debt'

The question then is, do those Irish who were forced out into the New World by their colonial masters at home leave an unfulfilled debt? Obviously not. Not only did they help to build those nations that they arrived in, under horrific conditions and poor pay, but, in the American case, they played a decisive role in winning the Civil War and bringing about black emancipation. In all cases, they entered these nations at the bottom of the social pecking order, were treated with suspicion and often outright hostility and violence, and they prospered. Not only do they leave no moral debt behind, they are rightly celebrated. To compare the experience of the average Irish Famine emigrant in the slums of Boston or New York to Fianna Fáil and Fine Gael's asylum seekers who are put up with a stipend in hotels in Ireland's tourism hotspots, often in the very areas those poor Irish fled during the Famine, is to degrade their memory. It is rank political opportunism that relies on the Irish public being sufficiently ignorant or passive about the experience of historic Irish emigrants.

There is another, geographical and relational element to historic emigration that needs to be pointed out. Irish historic migration is not random. Initially in the 1600s and 1700s Irish indentured servants were given no choice in where they were sent. They were sent to whatever corner of the British Empire that needed strong backs. The British Empire planted the seeds of the Irish diaspora against the will of the Irish. And these seeds blossomed as the Irish became unwilling founding fathers of these nations, in blood and sweat, if not administration. The international Irish diaspora took root in those areas their colonial masters sent them—Australia, America, Canada —and in the UK, the headquarters of Irish displacement. Early Irish emigrants, forced out of their homeland, contributed mightily to these places and in doing so the Irish earned their place there. This is why, even today, these locations are the primary destinations for Irish economic migrants—they feel connected to them and are welcomed because of the achievements of their ancestors. In the twelve months to April, 2024, 10,600 Irish people moved to Australia, the largest number since 2013.[32] While every Irish person travelling to these places today must officially apply for a visa alongside every other immigrant, unlike other immigrants, they enter these countries with an established status. They are the personification of the old land and they keep the link between the old and the new world unbroken.

Conversely, the Irish have never settled in great numbers in Nigeria or Algeria or Pakistan. That's not accidental. Ireland does not have historic ties with such nations. Ireland was not a colonising nation so no moral or material debt is owed to any other nation. Quite the opposite. Ireland was Britain's longest-held and most brutalised colony. The Irish did not go to unfamiliar places seeking what was not theirs. The story of historic Irish emigration is one that is narrowly played out in a handful of nations. The moral culpability for that emigration is unquestionably British and any moral debt to those nations that received those emigrants is paid off with interest.

But there is another wave of mass historic Irish emigration that lies outside of British culpability. In the history of the Irish Free State and the Republic of Ireland, there have been three periods of mass emigration; the 1950s, the 1980s and the post-Celtic Tiger era. In the 1920s the US began to introduce immigration restrictions and with the 1929 Wall Street Crash, Irish emigration to the USA slowed with Britain becoming the preferred destination. Between 1951 and 1961 the Irish Free State lost 500,000 people or 16% of its population due to the failure of de Valera's protectionist economic model. Another 200,000 left in the 1980s as a result of poor management of the 1981/82 global economic crisis. Between 1976 and 1979, Ireland saw an annual GDP growth rate of 5.3%. When Fianna Fáil came to power in 1977, they employed an aggressive public spending spree though the 5.3% GDP growth rate was unsustainable. Public borrowing increased from 13% of GNP in 1976 to 20% of GNP in 1981 which triggered infla-tion. In 1980, as the economy stalled, Fianna Fáil doubled down on public spending but rather than having a stimulus effect, inflation rocketed to 18.2% as unemployment and migration grew.[33] With echoes of the 2002 and 2007 budget giveaways which overstretched the public purse, Fianna Fáil's reckless public spending prior to the 1981/82 crash and their unwillingness to make timely hard cuts for political gains, meant that Ireland took significantly longer than her European neighbours to recover. In 1989 alone, 70,000 emigrants left Ireland. Emigration on such a mass scale would not be seen again until 2010 when 27,700 Irish people left after the Celtic Tiger collapse.[34] In 2012, 46,500 Irish people emigrated from Ireland which represented a 300% increase on 2006 numbers when 15,000 left.[35] And while the 33rd Dáil of Fianna Fáil, Fine Gael and Greens boasted about being a rich nation, in the 12 months to April 2024, 34,700 Irish people emigrated.

What all three major phases of mass emigration in the Irish Free State and Republic have in common is government mismanagement. Fianna Fáil and Fine Gael have always relied on emigration to familiar destinations to act as a pressure release valve in times of economic crisis. De Valera's protectionism and unsustainable public spending in the post-de Valera FDI economy have led to cycles of boom and bust resulting in mass emigration. While few can doubt de Valera's love of Ireland and the Irish people, the transformation of Ireland by both parties since the 1960s into a low-tax, FDI economy with close links to the EU has led to an abandonment of native industrial development and the veneration of immigration to sustain productivity. In post-de Valera Ireland, Irish people have, to be blunt, become expendable to Fianna Fáil and Fine Gael. When Micheal Martin stands in Strokestown and invokes the Famine to sell mass immigration to Ireland, Varadkar doing likewise in Boston, not only are they perverting and reworking Ireland's most sacred landscapes and traditional cornerstones of identity to fit a modern mass immigration narrative, they are also directing attention away from their own very real personal and party culpability for the loss of hundreds of thousands of Ireland's best and brightest.

Fianna Fáil and Fine Gael have long shirked responsibility for their role in mass emigration and the devastation it has caused to families and communities. Fr Harry Bohan grew up in Feakle, Co. Clare in the 1950s as de Valera's Ireland fell apart. "I left primary school during that decade and watching so many of my school mates leave brought home to me the terrible reality of them having to go... There were 14 in our class. Nine had to emigrate. Within a few years of us finishing primary school, all of us were gone from the parish...I remember one morning seeing a girl from my class standing at the bridge in the middle of the village. She was standing there with her suitcase waiting for the bus. The bus would take her to Limerick and from there onto Cobh on her way to America. That meant she was going forever."[36]

In 1987, when emigration levels were peaking with no end in sight, Fianna Fáil's Tánaiste, Brian Lenihan Sr., attempted to spin the haemorrhaging of youth and talent from Ireland as being a positive thing. In an interview with Newsweek he stated, "What we have now is a very literate emigrant who thinks nothing of coming to the United States and going back to Ireland and maybe on to Germany and back to Ireland again...It's very refreshing to see it." He followed up his remarks by stating, "After all, we can't all live on a small island."[37] His comments normalising emigration as something to be expected, welcomed even, were rightly met with anger but they set an important precedent. In the FDI economy, Irish emigrants were acceptable collateral damage and those leaving were doing so for personal gain and would be back again all the better for their little professional development jaunt overseas.

When the Celtic Tiger collapsed, politicians added yet another layer of spin. As the Irish economy lay in ruins, in a Dáil debate on the 30th of September 2010, Minister of State at the Department of Finance, Martin Manseragh stated, "Government clearly bears an important responsibility, but there is also—I do not mean to include literally everyone in this—a collective responsibility. Most people bought into and benefited in some way from the Celtic Tiger."[38] The sentiment was echoed by Finance Minister Brian Lenihan Jr. who, speaking on RTE Prime Time two months later, laid the blame for the banking crisis and reckless public spending on to the public stating "Let's be fair about it, we all partied." In 2012, Fine Gael's Enda Kenny, then Taoiseach, similarly attempted to shift blame for the collapse from his own party's failures in opposition, on to the public when, at a WEF Davos forum, he stated, "What happened in our country was that people simply went mad borrowing."[39] After the Celtic Tiger then, Fianna Fáil and Fine Gael put their own spin on emigration: Not only were the thousands of Irish people forced out of Ireland going on a merry professional jaunt, they were clearing off to live in luxury, leaving poor Fianna Fáil and Fine Gael to clean up the mess they left. Whereas Lenihan Sr.'s emigrants were off getting terrific work experience to bring home, Lenihan Jr.'s emigrants were greedy hedonists looking out for themselves.

So, finally, does Ireland owe a moral debt to the world for the migration of more than a million Irish people since the founding of the State under Fianna Fáil and Fine Gael rule? No. Those emigrating have followed familiar paths to Australia, America, the UK, Canada, places where their ancestors cleared a path in blood and sweat. But this time, there is no blaming the British Empire. The blame lays squarely on the shoulders of Fianna Fáil and Fine Gael. When Micheal Martin, Leo Varadkar and Simon Harris stand at Ireland's most hallowed landscapes and talk of a moral obligation to take in the world, they are both manipulating history and also hiding in it. They are associating Irish migration with British misrule and something historic, but the reality is, Fianna Fáil and Fine Gael are responsible for the departure of a million Irish. They blame the public for their mismanagement that results in mass emigration and point to the British Empire as the emigration bogeyman, but the simple truth is, Fianna Fáil and Fine Gael have a moral debt and obligation to the million Irish they forced out of Ireland and to those communities and families devastated by those departures. Fianna Fáil and Fine Gael policy decisions should be focused solely on righting these wrongs. All immigration policy should be focused on bringing home those Irish pushed out by their mismanagement. Instead of humbly acknowledging fault and working to heal the wounds of emigration, they manipulate Irish history, exploit the landscapes of a hollowed-out national identity and blame others, even Irish emigrants themselves, as being the reason that those Irish who stayed at home are now punished with seemingly unlimited immigration.

And the greater problem is, once Fianna Fáil and Fine Gael have made Ireland into a multi-racial, multi-religious, multicultural state, what becomes of the Irish? Well, they become 'white'.

Adopting 'white privilege'

During a Dáil debate on June 4th, 2020, Fine Gael's Jennifer Carroll MacNeil stated that "it is worth putting on the record of this House the concept of white privilege and how that can be normatised in our own lives...I refer to the concept of the 'invisible knapsack', a term coined by Peggy McIntosh in 1990 with respect to white privilege. The concept is not about racism being something that disadvantages others, but the corollary that whiteness is in itself an advantage and the need to really try to understand that idea."[40] Thirteen days later at a Dáil debate on "Supporting Inclusion and Combatting Racism in Ireland", Social Democrats co-founder Catherine Murphy told TDs that "While it is true that the Irish have known our fair share of oppression, the reality is that during that oppression we still maintained our invisibility cloak of white privilege."[41] On December 18th, 2023, Green Party councillor for Cork, Colette Finn tweeted, "White people in Ireland need to understand that we have an unearned privilege simply being white. Let's examine our own biases on International Migrant's Day."[42]

The term 'white privilege' was coined by Peggy McIntosh, not in 1990 as Jennifer Carroll MacNeil stated, but in 1988. In a 1989 essay entitled *White Privilege: Unpacking the Invisible Knapsack*, McIntosh defines white privilege as being "an invisible package of unearned assets that I can count on cashing in each day, but about which I was 'meant' to remain oblivious. White privilege is like an invisible weightless knapsack of special provisions, maps, passports, codebooks, visas, clothes, tools and blank checks."[43] McIntosh came to the idea of white privilege from her feminist writings on men. "After I realized the extent to which men work from a base of unacknowledged privilege, I understood that much of their oppressiveness was unconscious...I began to understand why we [white people] are justly seen as oppressive, even when we don't see ourselves that way. I began to count the ways in which I enjoy unearned skin privilege and have been conditioned into oblivion about its existence." For McIntosh, it is essential for white people to consciously reflect on how they are unfairly advantaged because of their race and where they lie in a system of "interlocking oppressions": race, religion, gender, social class etc. Not to reflect on this "unearned privilege" is to prop up the "systems of dominance" and oppression that they are built upon and all white people must commit to dismantling these systems—our current capitalist liberal Western democracies—in order to promote "equity".

To illustrate the concept, McIntosh provides a list of 26 examples of her white privilege which she claims are racially exclusive. The issue with McIntosh's concept, as Ray[44] has pointed out, is that McIntosh's list is less a list of racially exclusive privileges and more a list of the privileges McIntosh personally enjoys as an upper-middle-class academic who has lived a life of wealth. McIntosh hails from a wealthy New Jersey family involved in information technology. She was privately educated, moved in society circles and spent her working life tucked away in the exclusive halls of Wellesley, a private, fee-paying Liberal Arts college in Massachusetts. As Ray puts it, "Peggy McIntosh was born into the very cream of America's aristocratic elite, and has remained ensconced there ever since."

In her first point, "I can if I wish, arrange to be in the company of people of my race most of the time", McIntosh is oblivious to the living conditions of less economically well-off white people. It may be possible for a wealthy white person in the USA living and working in exclusive neighbourhoods to avoid contact with non-whites but that is a scenario based on income inequality that speaks to the power structures of the rich rather than to that of all white people. Her second point, "If I should need to move, I can be pretty sure of renting or purchasing housing in an area which I can afford and in which I would want to live" also shows how out of touch McIntosh is with the normal financial situation of average Americans of any race. Only the extremely wealthy in the US do not need to worry about affording a house in a desirable neighbourhood. Her third point, "I can be pretty sure that my neighbours in such a location will be neutral or pleasant to me", doesn't just display a continued lack of understanding about her own class standing but it takes on a strangely racist undertone. McIntosh states that moving to exclusive—white in her view—neighbourhoods guarantees good neighbours. She appears to be implying that non-white and poor neighbourhoods are filled with people who are not "neutral or pleasant". Are non-white neighbours incapable of being polite? And so the list goes on.

McIntosh's invisible knapsack of white privilege is in reality an attempt by an individual who has lived at the economic and social pinnacle of American society to remove the burden of guilt she apparently feels for that position and instead place it on the shoulders of all white Americans. Added to the fact that McIntosh's essay is a personal narrative that lacks any broader social context, fieldwork, data etc., it is remarkable that the idea gained any currency in academic studies. Indeed, it is precisely because McIntosh held a position at a prestigious, fee-paying, private Liberal Arts college that she was able to circulate her work and have it accepted without needing to pass through the traditional channels of academic peer review. This was a feature of McIntosh's career and a perk of working for one of the most prestigious and expensive private schools in the country, a college that produced Hillary Clinton, Madeline Albright and Diane Sawyer among other notable alumni.

The wholesale importation of McIntosh's concept to Ireland, a vastly different society with a different history, economic and social structure as well as a radically different migration history should come with careful discussion as to whether the concept fits. When Collette Finn states that "White people in Ireland need to understand that we have an unearned privilege simply being white", that needs to be examined. When Catherine Murphy, on the floor of the Dáil makes the statement that even during the Cromwellian invasions, Penal Laws and the Famine, the Irish "still maintained our invisibility cloak of white privilege" without pushback from the chamber, there is evidence that McIntosh's imported idea has been accepted by Ireland's political class. Murphy's background as a former member of the Irish Workers' Party, a Marxist-Leninist group, gives a clue as to her enthusiastic embrace of McIntosh's ideas.

McIntosh's work is enjoying a renaissance as 'critical race theory' (CRT) has grown as a field of study in the past decade. Both Robin DiAngelo's NY Times bestseller *White Fragility* and Ibram X Kendi's *How to be an Antiracist* build on McIntosh by employing the argument that all white people unfairly benefit from how Western democratic and capitalist societies are structured and that in order to not be racist, white people need to commit to a lifetime of breaking down the social, political and economic structures that underpin that system. McIntosh makes it explicit that whiteness is inseparable from Western capitalist democracy, arguing that "It seems to me that obliviousness about white advantage, like obliviousness about male advantage, is kept strongly inculturated in the United States so as to maintain the myth of meritocracy, the myth that democratic choice is equally available to all." In order to overcome white privilege, white people must commit to rebuilding society through 'positive' discrimination or as Kendi states in his book, "The only remedy to racist discrimination is antiracist discrimination. The only remedy to past discrimination is present discrimination. The only remedy to present discrimination is future discrimination."[45] Like McIntosh and DiAngelo, Kendi does not believe in individual free will or agency, they believe that the answer to perceived inequality is equity—not equality of opportunity—equity, meaning equality of outcome. Using homelessness statistics as an example of structural racism, or white oppression, Kendi states that "Racial equity is when two or more racial groups are standing on a relatively equal footing."[46] He points out that black Americans and Native Americans are more likely to be homeless than white Americans and to solve the issue, 'positive' discrimination laws must be put in place so that these groups are brought up to the same level of homelessness as white people. A failure to do so is systemic racism propped up by white people who refuse to acknowledge their unearned white privilege and who, importantly, refuse to commit to actively dismantling Western systems of society, economics and governance. If this—the removal of individualism and individual agency replaced by discrimination in favour of certain groups to achieve equal outcomes for all—sounds like Communism, that's because the roots of Kendi, DiAngelo and McIntosh's work are directly descended from Marxist thinkers concerned with race as a social construct who linked white privilege to historical racial inequalities going back to the founding of the USA.

"Until...the 'white race' is destroyed"

The term "whiteness" was first used by W.E.B. DuBois in his 1920 essay *The Souls of White Folk*. In *Black Reconstruction*, DuBois argued that while underpaid, poor white workers received a "public and a psychological wage" by virtue of their skin colour.[47] DuBois applied to join the American Communist Party in 1961 and in his writing, he couched race relations in the context of the wider Communist struggle against Capitalism. In the Irish context, it is Noel Ignatiev, a radical Marxist activist and a Harvard academic at the W.E.B. DuBois Institute for African and African-American Studies, who is of most interest. Ignatiev committed his career to abolishing the white race. In 1992 he co-founded *Race Traitor* Magazine. Each edition appeared with the Magazine's slogan, "Treason to whiteness is loyalty to humanity" emblazoned across its cover. The magazine's mission statement reads "The white race is a historically constructed social formation. It consists of all those who partake of the privileges of the white skin in this society. Its most wretched members share a status higher, in certain respects, than that of the most exalted persons excluded from it, in return for which they give their support to a system that degrades them. The key to solving the social problems of our age is to abolish the white race, which means no more and no less than abolishing the privileges of the white skin...RACE TRAITOR aims to serve as an intellectual centre for those seeking to abolish the white race...it will support practical measures, guided by the principle, Treason to whiteness is loyalty to humanity."[48] In a 2002 essay[49] published in Harvard Magazine titled *Abolish the White Race*, Ignatiev reiterated his desire to destroy the white race. "Make no mistake about it: we intend to keep bashing the dead white males, and the live ones, and the females too, until the social construct known as 'the white race' is destroyed—not 'deconstructed' but destroyed."

Ignatiev achieved fame for his book *How the Irish Became White*. In it, he takes the example of historic Irish immigration to the USA to argue that race is a social construct and that the Irish, after a period of assimilation and separation from free black Americans with whom they shared similar social and economic status within 19th-century America, were granted access to the white race with all of its associated privileges. It is precisely this idea that Catherine Murphy is articulating when she states that the Irish possessed an "invisibility cloak of white privilege" during their colonial horrors. Of course, what Murphy is doing, much like her colleagues who talk about 'white privilege' with regard to the Irish, is importing a radical race idea from an American context and trying to force it into an Irish context where it simply doesn't work—not least because Ignatiev's work was faulty to begin with.

In Ignatiev's *How the Irish Became White*, he defines racial oppression in the same manner as McIntosh and the other authors mentioned above, not as individual acts of racism but as a "particular system of oppression—like gender oppression or class oppression or national oppression". He goes on, "The hallmark of racial oppression is the reduction of all members of the oppressed group to one undifferentiated social status, a status beneath that of any member of any social class within the dominant group."[50] Ignatiev argues that access to the white race is dependent on access to political power and labour unionisation to strengthen a group's collective bargaining power within the capitalist system. He charges that the Irish in America chose to pursue access to this dominant group and in doing so they betrayed free black Americans and those still in slavery by leaving them behind as an oppressed class to instead become 'white'.

The most glaringly obvious issue with Ignatiev's thesis is that he is imposing a modern radical Marxist interpretation of race onto the events of the past and people who did not see the world in this manner. The Irish, free blacks, Italians, Jews and others vying for their place in 19th-century American society did not use a Marxist lens to analyse race or their relations to one another. That has always been the luxury of academics distant from the brute realities of daily survival during that time. By imposing a Marxist framework on his telling of history, Ignatiev set the boundaries of this trial of the Irish so that they must be found guilty. Ignatiev uses a sly sleight of hand in assigning power to Irish Catholics that did not exist prior to the American Civil War as evidence that the Irish consciously separated themselves as a group from black Americans. Ignatiev begins his book by trying to shame the Irish in America for not supporting the abolitionist cause with sufficient zeal. He holds up the rejection of Daniel O'Connell and his 1842 'Address from the People of Ireland To Their Countrymen and Countrywomen in America!' by some in the Irish-American community as evidence that Irish-Americans as a group consciously attempted to separate themselves from black Americans. O'Connell's address passionately states, "America is cursed by slavery! WE CALL UPON YOU TO UNITE WITH THE ABOLITIONISTS, and never to cease your efforts, until perfect liberty be granted to every one of her inhabitants, the black man as well as the white man."[51]

O'Connell gathered 60,000 signatures from his Repeal Association machine in Ireland to support the document. The document itself was written by members of the Hibernian Antislavery Society and was morally righteous but abstract from the experiences and expectations of normal Irish people in America. The three men who wrote the document, James Haughton, Richard Allen and Richard Davis Webb were all wealthy Quakers. To the masses of impoverished Irish at home and abroad it was a noble but luxurious political pursuit as detached from the political needs of the poor Irish as its drafters were socially detached from the poor native Irish. This is Ignatiev's first sleight of hand. He begins his story by framing the Catholic Irish as being somehow uniquely responsible for the goal of abolishing slavery. They were, in fact, the least equipped to have any impact on the matter.

Daniel O'Connell, and through him, the Catholic Irish in America, were co-opted into the long-standing Philadelphia Quaker abolitionist movement and in doing so, O'Connell opened the Irish American community up to a great degree of danger. Much of Ignatiev's story takes place in Philadelphia, a Quaker town long invested in the abolitionist movement. Philadelphia was founded and settled in 1682 by William Penn as a place safe from religious persecution for Quakers. It was in Philadelphia in 1775 that the first abolitionist movement in America was founded and in 1780 Pennsylvania became the first state to outlaw slavery. As a Mecca for free blacks and runaway slaves the black population of the city swelled. By the 1830s however, the relationship between black and white in the city had soured. Between 1830 and 1850, though they only made up one-fourteenth of the city population, blacks were responsible for one-third of serious crime.[52] As poor Irish Catholics began to pour into the city, competing with poor blacks at the bottom of society, tensions between the two groups flared. In 1834, a mob, mainly working-class Irish, rioted for four days leaving two blacks dead and major damage to property in black neighbourhoods. A committee founded to establish the cause of the riots was sympathetic to claims that poor blacks were being chosen for jobs ahead of poor Irish Catholics. The Irish in turn were on the receiving end of violence from the Ulster Protestants who had established themselves in the city and were able to quickly rise up the economic and social ladder because of their faith and better standard of education on arrival. In 1831, Ulster Protestants and Irish Catholics fought one another in the city at a Protestant celebration of victory at the Battle of the Boyne.[53] It is into this racial pressure cooker, that Daniel O'Connell waded with his uncompromising and inflammatory attacks on America and

Irish Americans who did not vocally support his abolishment stance.

In the British House of Commons in 1839, O'Connell expressed his opposition to the US annexation of Texas, fearing that it would become a slave-holding state. He also proposed the establishment of a British colony on the Mexican border that would be a safe haven for freed slaves and would prevent further American expansion. It was a highly inflammatory call for Britain to not only interfere in Southern slavery, but stop federal expansion.[54] By holding up O'Connell and expecting all Irish Americans to stand with him, Ignatiev asks too much of those struggling to survive day to day in American slums. It's thoroughly naive. O'Connell was a radical aligned with the most fringe elements of the American abolitionist movement. This was a fine position for a man who never set foot on American soil but was a reckless position for the most vulnerable free group in American society. Regular Irish Catholics in America were morally supportive of abolition after Pope Gregory XVI's 1839 Papal Bull denouncing slavery. But where they could spare time to think of anything other than daily survival, they were much more interested in focusing their limited resources and power on repealing the Act of Union in Ireland and pursuing Irish nationalist causes. Father John Hughes, the Bishop of New York, is one of the principal villains of Ignatiev's book and one of the few actual Catholics who took a prominent stand against O'Connell. Hughes was far more aware than O'Connell of the precarious positions that the fledgling Irish Catholic community found itself in. In rejecting O'Connell's Address, Hughes made it clear that while slavery was wrong, people from outside had no right to dictate politics in America, and attempts to mobilise the Irish in America for such ends would put them at great risk of reprisal: "I am no friend of slavery, but I am still less friendly to any attempt of foreign origin to abolish [it]...The duty of naturalized Irishmen or others, I consider to be in no wise distinct or different from those of native born Americans."[55] And in the end Hughes would be proven correct. He had seen at first hand the danger of the Nativist threat to Irish Americans. For two years prior to O'Connell's Address, Hughes had been unsuccessfully lobbying New York City Hall for state funds for Catholic school children. His request had infuriated Nativist Samuel Morse who had frustrated Hughes at every step. Morse saw Hughes as an agent of the Pope and so a subversive.[56] O'Connell's antagonistic Address simply inflamed anti-Catholic sentiments and gave the likes of Morse ammunition. On November 10th 1842, the same year as O'Connell's address, Philadelphia Bishop Francis Kenrick wrote to the city Board of Controllers asking that Catholic children be allowed to use their own Bibles in school. This request was met with Nativist hostility and in May and July of 1844 Nativists rioted in Philadelphia, targeting Irish Catholic homes and the Seminary of the Sisters of Charity, St Michael's church and St. Augustine's church. Bishop Hughes responded to the riots in Philadelphia by stating that if any such attacks were to occur on churches in New York, then New York would "become a second Moscow",[57] that is, burned to the ground.

O'Connell's political moves in the US, and particularly his Address to the Irish on the abolishment of slavery were clumsy. By joining such a radical movement, he put Irish Catholics in America at extreme risk in a very dangerous moment for them. For Ignatiev to hold O'Connell, a man who himself never set foot on American soil, up as the path Irish Americans should have followed unquestioningly shows a very simplistic understanding of social history.

Another reason why Ignatiev chooses O'Connell as his model for how the Irish betrayed black Americans is that it allows him to attribute power and economic status to Irish Catholics that they did not have. Throughout his book, Ignatiev conflates Scotch-Irish, Anglo-Irish and Catholic Irish. This is most egregious when he states, "Emigrants did not represent the poorest layers of Irish society; in 1820 American port officials recorded that 27% of Irish arriving that year were farmers, 22% artisans, 10% tradesmen and professionals, while only 21% were labourers. As the *Dublin Evening Post* lamented in 1818, 'Emigration is necessarily restricted to the class immediately above the labouring poor, who cannot raise the money to pay their passage.'"[58] These well-off immigrants were overwhelmingly Ulster

Protestant and those Anglo-Irish fleeing from the south of Ireland after the Napoleonic wars. Ignatiev tars them all as "Irish". As noted earlier, Irish Catholics who did depart for America at that time largely did so in the holds of Canadian timber ships.

It is also an egregious conflation because, as noted in the case of Philadelphia, the Ulster Scots, later the Scotch-Irish, and Irish Catholics brought their class and political differences with them to the New World. Ignatiev states, "From the time they began emigrating to about 1850, Irish Protestants were known in America simply as Irish...The sharp distinction between Irish and Scotch-Irish developed in the United States in the last half of the 19th century for reasons that were primarily American."[59] This is not true. As Miller[60] points out, the division between Irish Catholic and Scotch-Irish was ever-present in America. "In the United States the native-Protestant/Irish-Catholic dichotomy was sharp and violent, exacerbated by the emigrants' own sectarian legacies. The sacking of the Charlestown convent in 1834 and the great Kensington riots of 1844—both incidents ranging native and Irish Protestants against Irish "papists"—were only the most blatant examples of the religious and ethnic animosities permeating Jacksonian America." Not only were Irish Catholics and Protestants seen as different groups by established American Protestants who favoured the latter, but individual members of the groups saw themselves as different also. Miller recounts how religious and class differences from the old world showed themselves on the journey across the Atlantic already in the 1820s and 1830s. "On some voyages 'there was scarce a day without a fight or a night without a robbery', and faction fights and pitched battles between Irish Catholics, Orangemen, and British Protestant passengers were commonplace."[61] When one ship, embarking for the New World in the 1830s, encountered a storm, "one Ulsterman denounced his 'papist' companions as a 'cowardly set of hounds' who 'in the time of danger...would do nothing but sprinkle holy water, cry, pray, cross themselves and all sorts of tomfoolery.'"[62]

Not only does Ignatiev conflate Irish Catholic and Protestant but he also attributes the actions of the ascendant Protestant Irish to all.

Chapter three of the book is largely dedicated to the case of John Binns, a Philadelphia alderman and one of the signatories of a famous letter to Daniel O'Connell telling him that his Address to Irish Americans would cause the Irish in America problems. Ignatiev uses Binns as his primary case study for how the Irish became 'white' stating; "To trace...the movement from the Republican Party that carried out the 'civil revolution of 1801' to the Democratic Party that served as the centre of parliamentary opposition to the civil revolution of 1856-77...is to explain the link between the Jacobin, agitator, conspirator, gun-runner, and jailbird who left Ireland in 1801 and the alderman who swore his allegiance to the Constitution and slavery in 1838. It is also the answer to the question, How did the Irish become white in America?"[63] The problem with Binns, which Ignatiev holds up as the example for how the 'Irish' became white, is that he was not, in any way representative of the majority of Irish people. Binns was an Anglo-Irish Protestant who was born in Dublin but moved to England at an early age where he became active in republican political agitation. He became a member of the London United Irishmen seeing common cause with English republicanism and after emigrating to America after his arrest and brief imprisonment in England for his radical activities, he became embedded in the English radical democratic community in Pennsylvania. For Ignatiev to hold Binns up as being in any way representative of the Irish Catholic experience in America is simply misleading. Binns was a friend of Irish Catholics over their shared hatred of the English monarchy. Outside of that narrow issue, Binns would have little to nothing in common with the typical Irish Catholic. His Protestantism granted him access to the upper echelons of power in America. And if Binns is the case study of how the Irish became white, then Ignatiev has made a fatal error in not distinguishing between Irish Catholics, Scotch-Irish and Anglo-Irish. He should have called his book, *How the Scotch- and Anglo-Irish Assimilated into American Society*.

There is a sense upon reading Ignatiev's book that he possesses a thinly veiled dislike of Irish Catholics. Aside from framing them for the political choices of the ascendant Anglo-Irish and Scotch-Irish in

America, his handling of the Civil War, Catholic Irish America's greatest moment, is shameful. He dismisses the Irish in the American Civil War in half a page. Most is dedicated to shaming the Irish for their role in the 1863 New York draft riots. Ignatiev dismisses the riots as Irish racism, not wanting to fight for black slaves. What he leaves out is that the Irish, among other white working-class immigrant groups, rioted because upper-class Americans could buy their way out of service and, importantly, because the draft did not include free blacks who did not have citizenship status. The Irish, who were in direct competition with blacks for the slimmest of employment pickings, didn't want to vacate their hard-fought corners of the unskilled and minimally skilled urban labour market to free blacks, just to go fight and die to free more blacks to compete with. Ignatiev concludes, "The Irish had two aims in the war: to establish their claim to citizenship, and to define the sort of republic they would be citizens of. Whether in the Army or on the barricades, they took up arms for the White Republic, and their place in it."[64]

Ignatiev reduces the Irish experience in the Civil War to a selfish act. He is correct that many fought for citizenship, many also fought for a steady job and an escape from the slums. But importantly, after 1863, they had no choice. They were drafted. Whatever their individual reasons for fighting, and despite anger at being drafted, they fought in overwhelming numbers for the Union and from 1863 with the Emancipation Proclamation, Lincoln used Irish bodies to achieve his explicitly stated aim of abolition. The historical effect of the Irish effort in the American Civil War is that 200,000 Irishmen fought and helped black Americans achieve their freedom. At least 35,000 Irishmen died in pursuit of their individual goals and Lincoln's Emancipation efforts. Ignatiev dismisses these efforts as "taking up arms for the White Republic, and their place in it." They may have taken up arms for the Union and their place in a future United States, but they also secured the black man's place in that United States and deserve credit for that achievement. The Civil War earned the poor Irish Catholics their place in American society. After the War they proved remarkably efficient at union and political organisation.

Ignatiev calls this securing their place in the 'White Republic' as though the Irish Catholics magically transformed into WASPs and didn't themselves shape American politics and culture. And that is the biggest issue with Ignatiev and proponents of 'white privilege' in general, they deny individuals and downtrodden groups any agency.

Contortions of race and class theory

Not only did many Irish remain destitute living in slums throughout the later 19th century and early 20th century, but many black Americans achieved success in the so-called 'White Republic'. By the late 19th century there was a vibrant emerging black middle class establishing itself just as Irish Catholics were. Gatewood[65] found that late 19th-century black society was markedly different "in lineage, in education, in inspiration and in character." Within the black community there were clear stratifications. Those who had been free men in the Antebellum era as well as mulatto (mixed race) moved into leading positions of power over the more recently freed slaves. The emergent new black community embraced inequality and social stratification as eagerly as did any of the emergent white groups, Italians, Irish, Jews. The stretching of the social class system for blacks mirrored the contradictions often seen in these other groups. While those on the upper end of the structure could be prejudiced towards those of their own race vying to join their exclusive status, they could also show a strong commitment to raising up the name and reputation of the race, investing in charitable organisations and political movements for the advancement of the group. Most famously, the Washington DC black elite, known as the 'Black 400', was a collection of approximately 100 old upper-class black families who toured Europe, held holiday homes in exclusive country destinations, held prestigious debutante balls and consolidated power within their elite group. It was the black equivalent of Caroline Schermerhorn Astor's 400 in New York, an exclusive social list of America's richest old money and Gilded Age families. The Black 400 placed extreme value on education with children of the elite being sent to exclusive finishing schools before attending University at Harvard, Howard, Fisk among others. Class lines were clearly enforced between elite blacks and lower classes. The New York and Newport Ugly Fishing Club founded in the mid-1860s was reserved for upper-class black men and as more blacks began streaming north after the War, elites founded clubs such as the Descendants of Early New England Negroes club which only granted entry to blacks who had lived in New England prior to 1830.

Ironically, it is W.E.B. duBois, one of Ignatiev's inspirations for his white privilege theory, who acts as one of the best examples of black social upward mobility after the Civil War. DuBois was born into a free black family in New England. He was born in 1868 and went on to become the first black man to achieve a Ph.D. at Harvard in 1895. Ignatiev's thesis that the Irish became black oppressors by virtue of self-selecting into the 'White Republic' falls down on his inability to distinguish between the different experiences of various 'Irish' people. It falls down on him conflating the assimilation of Protestant Irish emigrants in the US with that of Irish Catholics. It falls down on his cherry-picking of historical information such as the causes of black and Irish tensions in the 1830s to 1850s. It falls down because he strips the poorest of black and Irish groups of their agency. It falls down because Ignatiev invents a contrived position that starving Irish Catholics with a life expectancy of 14 years taking on the worst industrial jobs and living in the poorest slums, were somehow responsible for uplifting the black slave. Importantly, in his race-based Marxist view of society, the poorest, most illiterate and downtrodden Irishman, living in a slum in Boston, was held in higher esteem by the 'White Republic' than W.E.B. duBois as a Harvard graduate. The Black 400 of Washington DC would have laughed at the absurdity.

The issue now for Ireland is that politicians like Jennifer Carroll MacNeill, Collette Finn and Catherine Murphy are introducing Ignatiev's bad ideas to Ireland where it doesn't fit. The notion of white privilege is based on the idea that black people in particular are locked out of society because white society was built specifically to exclude them. Even if Ignatiev had proven his case against the Irish in America, how, exactly would that relate to the Irish context? In Ireland, the native Irish Catholic was the lowest rung of the ladder for several hundred years. The Irish Catholic was discriminated against, cleared from the land and came close to extermination. When Catherine Murphy says that the Irish wore an "invisibility cloak of white privilege" for those hundreds of years, what was the baseline? There were no black people or any other race in Ireland throughout its most brutal historic periods. She cruelly dismisses the suffering of the Irish by implying that if there had been black people in Ireland during the Famine, they'd have suffered even worse than the native Irish. Or of course, she means that the case has been proven in the American context that the Irish are 'white'—that is an oppressor—because they joined WASP society by paying the entry price of punching down on black people—therefore this sin allegedly committed in America must now be atoned for by the Irish at home who never left despite the horrors they endured.

As the Irish struggle to articulate a coherent post-Celtic Tiger identity, the government stands in the sacred landscapes that were once places that bound the Irish in a self-assured sense of unity. They stand there now, reshaping the past to sell open borders in the present. Fianna Fáil and Fine Gael need massive numbers of overseas workers to feed the FDI machine. And with mass migration comes great opportunity. If leftist politicians can make the Irish 'white', then there is extraordinary wealth and power to be accumulated by bullying, guilting and discriminating against the native oppressor in the name of diversity, equity and inclusion. In Ireland, universities and the NGO sector are the driving forces behind a powerful new social justice industrial complex.

5

THE SOCIAL JUSTICE INDUSTRIAL COMPLEX

Once the Irish are made 'white' then, by the rules of Critical Race Theory (CRT), they inherit and benefit most from the power structures of the international 'white' man and must commit to dismantling them by promoting other races through positive discrimination in all matters of social, economic and political 'justice' or be labelled racial oppressors. However, it isn't simply white privilege that the freshly transubstantiated Irishman must acknowledge and make way for. Once the Irish have been convinced that they're 'white', then they must acknowledge that 'white privilege' is simply the tip of the 'privilege' iceberg and that there is also 'male privilege', 'heterosexual privilege', 'able-bodied privilege', 'skinny privilege' and a whole host of others in which the heterosexual white man is most privileged and must commit to ensuring an 'equitable' Ireland. Each of these areas has its own fierce advocates, areas of study and lobbies, but they do overlap at certain junctures in what is known as intersectionality. What this means is that individuals can be profoundly oppressed by belonging to multiple intersecting oppressed groups. For example, a lesbian black woman is more oppressed than a lesbian white woman. Both are significantly more oppressed than a straight white woman who in turn is grossly more oppressed than a gay white man or, worst of all, a straight white man. Fortunately, Irish universities and an NGO sector funded by public money to the tune of €6.5 billion per year are on hand to teach the straight white man—for centuries just an Irishman doing his best to survive—how to dismantle Irish society to stop himself from being irredeemably racist, sexist, ableist and homophobic. Together, Irish university departments and the NGOs that they churn increasingly radicalised students out into, are the Irish Social Justice Industrial Complex.

Pluckrose and Lindsay[1] have sketched out the interconnections of the modern Social Justice movement identifying the key elements that unite each area. There are two principles common to all. First is that Social Justice theories emerged from the mid-twentieth-century postmodernist movement and are built on radical scepticism of any claim to objective truth. They are equally sceptical of all religions, the prominent early 20th century political theories, National Socialism and Marxism alike, but they are particularly sceptical of science's ability to uncover objective truth or knowledge. Second, retaining elements of its Marxist roots, the modern Social Justice movement adheres to the principle that all societies are made up of systems of power in which there are clearly identifiable hierarchies in which more and less privileged groups are ranged out. Pluckrose and Lindsay further highlight four principal themes that underpin—to different degrees—modern Social Justice theories. Each is concerned with 'disrupting binaries', or blurring boundaries between categorisations. This is most evident in Queer Theory's concerted effort to break down the biological realities of sex, instead prioritising gender theories that blur the distinction between male and female. This has been a driving force in the transgender movement.

In academia, particularly in anthropological and sociological studies, this blurring of identities combined with a rejection of traditional scientific methods has seen the elevation and indeed veneration of qualitative research methodologies such as 'autoethnography'. Autoethnography, as defined by the American Psychological Association,[2] is "an autobiographical genre of academic writing that draws on and analyses or interprets the lived experience of the author and connects researcher insights to self-identity, cultural rules and resources, communication practices, traditions, premises, symbols, rules, shared meanings, emotions, values, and larger social, cultural, and political issues." Such methodologies are highly subjective, almost impossible to replicate and contribute little to a broader understanding of how societies function—by design. The data-driven or quantitative-heavy scientific method accepts or rejects new knowledge formulation based on its production within a testable, replicable, logical framework. Social Justice theorists however, who use predominantly qualitative methods—like autoethnography—deem these methods useful or not based on the theorist's adherence to the principle that their subjective analysis is set within a world where Western societies—built to suit the needs of heterosexual white men —are the pinnacle of oppression. These societies need to be destroyed while simultaneously, non-Western cultures and those groups of people supposedly marginalised on the lower rungs of the Western power hierarchy are to be elevated and venerated.

As TOUCHED upon in the last chapter when observing Ignatiev's dismissal of individual agency and his crude view of 19th-century Irish and black America as groups where the least of one (the Irish) is always placed above the greatest of the other (black) in the 'White Republic' of the USA, Social Justice scholars reject individualism and meritocracy. Instead, they cleave society into different and at times overlapping identity groups which act almost as unions wherein a few theorists and figureheads will speak on behalf of and exert the collective lobbying power over all members of the group. Identity politics is, essentially, the unionisation of politics. Whereas in Marxist theory, the bourgeoisie oppressed the proletariat, the rich oppressed the poor, access from the working class to the upper classes was still possible via individual agency and meritocracy. In Postcolonial studies, CRT and Queer studies, identity is based on immutable characteristics, one cannot move from one category to another, one does not go from being gay to being straight, black to white etc. in order to reap the rewards of Western society. Therefore, the only way to effect change is through collective lobbying, harnessing the collective power of the oppressed to fundamentally change the system. Identity politics doesn't seek to reside with or 'become' the straight white man at the top of a meritocratic, capitalist society. It wants to smash the current society and build a new one on top of the rubble.

'Social Justice' in academia

In the academic context, modern Social Justice is focused on producing activists to do that smashing, and without a need for grounding in an objective, quantitative scientific framework, it becomes incredibly easy for students and teachers of Social Justice theories to achieve academic titles, writing credits and esteem. Because there are few objective measures with which to decide what is useful research and what is not, once members of the Social Justice community commit to a shared understanding of how society is ordered and use the correct lingua franca, access to the wrecking crew is granted. Modern Social Justice research is extremely seductive. For many mediocre students and academics, the thought of being subjected to the rigours of a traditional double-blind peer review by scientifically-minded and committed peers is tortuous. Applying non-replicable and scientifically minimally valid research methods undermines the peer review process by making every paper intimate and one-of-a-kind. One can cheat the peer review system— the traditional quality control safety valve of academia—and allow activists to become academics based solely on signalling to one's crew. This of course explains how Peggy McIntosh, Noel Ignatiev and many more like them have managed to secure lucrative and influential careers as academics.

The modern Social Justice subversion of the peer review system and by extension academic reliability was ruthlessly exposed by Pluckrose, Lindsay and Boghossian who, in 2018, wrote 20 fake academic papers filled with Social Justice jargon and absurd conclusions. They sent these papers for peer review in leading Social Justice journals. One paper, *An Ethnography of Breastaurant Masculinity: Themes of Objectification, Sexual Conquest, Male Control, and Masculine Toughness in a Sexually Objectifying Restaurant?* purportedly analysed sexual objectification and toxic masculinity at Hooters-style restaurants. Another, *Our Struggle is My Struggle: Solidarity Feminism as an Intersectional Reply to Neoliberal and Choice Feminism*, took sections of Mein Kampf, swapped out anti-semitic phrases for feminist jargon. *Human Reactions to Rape Culture and Queer Performativity at Urban Dog Parks in Portland, Oregon* discussed rape culture among dogs based on observations at a dog park. *Going in Through the Back Door: Challenging Straight Male Homohysteria and Transphobia through Receptive Penetrative Sex Toy Use* proposed that anal penetration by heterosexual men could help combat transphobia. Incredibly, all of these passed peer review and were published in social justice theory journals. In total, seven out of twenty papers passed peer review and were published.[3] The experiment should have seen Social Justice studies cast into the abyss, rightly derided as the lunatic fantasies of a marginal cult of 'academics'. Instead, Social Justice studies have gone from strength to strength in Irish universities.

It is now possible to undertake dedicated Social Justice electives or modules at degree level and dedicated post-graduate courses in every university in Ireland. At Trinity College it is possible to take a Black Studies elective. Elective courses are modules outside of one's core discipline and they can be completed for 5 ECTS to contribute to one's degree. A video on the Black Studies module homepage[4] states that an aim of the module is "to raise provocative questions about the experience of being black in a globalised world as well as here in Ireland". The same video offers to equip partakers with "the language and skills that you need to discuss the challenges and criticisms that combine in deconstructing anti-blackness and blackness and anti-racism in a globalised world". This overview, with its promise to deliver "the language" of anti-blackness, neatly illustrates Pluckrose and Lindsay's characterisation of CRT as an ideology built upon post-modern word games and a commitment to the oppressor/oppressed worldview. While called "Black Studies", the course also brings together a number of intersecting areas of oppression by offering classes on "Decolonialism", "Feminist Theory", and "Queer Theory". Participants attain 50% of their grade by "journaling". Four pieces of "reflective" writing are to be handed in as part of an ongoing or formative assessment and a final, or summative grade, of 50% is given for a group project that "critically"—meaning using a social justice lens—examines a chosen study area. The intentionally opaque nature of the assessments—no objective and knowledge-based quiz or essay—is to encourage students to commit to CRT language and theory and in return a good and subjectively awarded grade awaits.

At UCD, Dr Ebun Joseph's 'Black Studies and CRT'[5] module at the School of Education is an even clearer case study on how Irish universities have become playgrounds for Social Justice Theory imported from the most radical activist university departments in the USA. The module outline is a veritable bingo card of Social Justice jargon. It opens, "The aim of this course is to enhance critical thinking devoid of Eurocentric paradigms about Blacks, their achievements and struggles. It brings together two scholarly traditions for social change; Black Studies and Critical Race Theory (CRT) which are inter[multi]disciplinary approaches to studying and understanding the experiences of people of Black African descent across the Diaspora, and challenging social hierarchies." The freshly minted "white" Irish person needs to de-centre their "Eurocentric paradigms" about Africans because they now, according to the rules of "whiteness", hold the same oppressive views of Africa as do colonial oppressors, and Africans in Ireland are as oppressed as those in Antebellum America. Most importantly, after acknowledging personal and systemic moral culpability via CRT, Irish students will be challenged to upend the institutionalised racism inherent in Irish society because of its unbearable 'whiteness'. In a June 2020 interview with Hot Press Magazine, Joseph stated, "We don't teach our students, our nation, that once Ireland gained independence...we became white and we became white on the backs and the necks of

Africans. When we ticked that box of whiteness, we began enjoying our white privileges".[6] It is an astonishing statement, one that directly draws from Ignatiev. But whereas Ignatiev limits his bad recasting of the Irish American experience to the American context, Joseph imports the concept wholesale and applies it directly to the Irish context.

In her teaching materials also Joseph makes little effort to hide the fact that she is simply copy/pasting radical CRT ideas of American origin onto the Irish context as though the histories, experiences and worldviews of both groups were interchangeable. "Black studies which has its origin in higher education grew mainly out of demands made by Black students, their allies and supporters on campuses during the mass protest movements of the late 1960s and early 1970s. Its main aim is to transform higher education, especially to address the over-reliance of traditional curricula on Eurocentric paradigms." Disturbingly, in the outcomes section of this Black Studies and CRT module, Joseph states, "This module will provide students with a theoretically informed understanding of these movements, and historical and contemporary attempts to unsettle whites' dominance over Blacks." The module, as advertised, is based on American society and American race relations. It is intentionally provocative and focuses on points of conflict between black and white and explicitly aims to "unsettle whites' dominance over Blacks". Again, Joseph is leaning into the supposed hierarchical nature of race relations in 'white' nations and the need for revolutionary overthrow of that system...in Ireland. In the Approaches to Teaching and Learning section of the module, Joseph writes that, "Depending on where you stand, the number 3 can be perceived as the letter M, W or E." Students can expect that there will be little data-driven overview of the subject matter, as well as little attempt to appeal to objective realities. Even if they are mentioned, they will be blurred through a 'critical' analysis.

This intention is further made clear as she continues, "In this module, you are likely to encounter ideas and perspectives, which may challenge your thoughts, values and present understanding.

Although this might sometimes feel uncomfortable, it can also be an exciting opportunity to see the world from another's perspective and exposure to other truths." In a classroom where appeal is made to logic, reason and analysis of data, there is no need to feel 'uncomfortable', one simply follows the evidence and accepts or rejects it based on the data at hand. The tell as to why students may feel uncomfortable is where Joseph talks about "other truths". By foreshadowing that students "might sometimes feel uncomfortable", and by relying on incendiary case studies like BLM and the American Civil Rights Movement, Joseph appears to indicate that students will be expected to submit to CRT through 'white' guilt.

Joseph's academic publishing record is awash with a superimposed labelling of 'white' onto the Irish. In her 2019 offering, *Making Sense of Race in Global Justice Education: Insights from a Radical Stratification Project in Ireland*, Joseph lumps Ireland in with the 'Global North' as a racist state. She states, "Ireland like most countries in the Global North has been found to be a racial (Goldberg, 2002) and a racist state (Lentin & McVeigh, 2006), and also a heavily racially stratified state with a white over black dichotomy (Joseph, 2018). What this means is that Whites are stratified at the top and Blacks at the bottom."[7] As is a trend in her work, there is no analysis of Ireland's unique history of Colonialism nor is there an acknowledgement that permanent black migration to Ireland is an entirely new and complicated phenomenon.

Prior to the Celtic Tiger there was virtually no permanent black immigration to Ireland. From the mid-1990s to 2007 there was a radical shift in immigration patterns. As reported by the Irish Human Rights and Equality Commission in 2018, in Ireland no group other than black people have problems accessing or advancing in the Irish labour market. The report states, "Some ethnic groups, such as those who identify as Asian-Irish or White EU-West, are at an advantage in the Irish labour market, both in terms of access to employment and progression."[8] The study identified black non-Irish individuals as being more likely to be unemployed than native Irish and less likely to hold management positions. For black-Irish individuals the study showed that there was no difference between native Irish in employment rate but they were less likely to hold a managerial or professional role than the native population. Ebun Joseph takes this discrepancy between black and native—and presumably Asian and other EU whites—as evidence that Ireland is a "racist state". The true answer is far simpler.

While immigration rates to Ireland rocketed during the Celtic Tiger, non-EU visas were tightly controlled and granted to high-skill and priority candidates only. The vast majority of Ireland's economic needs were made up by relying on EU migration. Annual immigrant numbers went from 60,000 in 2002, peaked at 150,000 in 2007 and fell to 52,700 in 2012. Prior to 2002, the majority of immigrants to Ireland came from the UK, many being returning emigrants or descendants thereof. Of those legal economic migrants arriving at the peak of the Celtic Tiger, the new accession eastern bloc EU states made up a majority of immigrants, these migrants having the right to move freely and work within the EU. In 2011, 74% of legal economic migrants were European and the single largest group was Polish, accounting for 23% of the non-Irish population at that time.[9]

The origin of black 'disadvantage' in Ireland

Outside of EU or EEA travel rights, it was difficult to enter the Irish labour market legally, study visas and access through marriage being typical options. For Africans then, excepting outstanding visa candidates, there was limited legal access to Ireland. And some highly qualified Africans did arrive and contribute to Irish society. From 2000-2010 there was a critical shortage of doctors in Irish hospitals leading to international recruitment to fill the deficit. While one of the lesser nations involved in the scheme, some Nigerian doctors were brought to Ireland towards its end. In 2010, 8.2% of non-Irish doctors in Ireland were Nigerian and 8.3% were Sudanese.[10] Still, professional paths to employment in Ireland were limited and this period coincided with an unprecedented abuse of the asylum system, particularly by Nigerians. In 1991 there were 9 claims—in total—for asylum in Ireland. This spiked to 1,170 in 1996 and increased rapidly year-on-year thereafter to a peak of 11,634 in 2002 before dropping slowly to 956 in 2012. In every year of the Celtic Tiger, according to records by the government Reception and Integration Agency, Nigerians, by some distance, represented the largest group of asylum claimants. In 2003, Nigerians made up 39.4% of all applications. This shows that the first wave of permanent black residents in Ireland came via the asylum system. The abuse of the asylum system was so great that in 2004, after a referendum, the Irish people voted overwhelmingly (79% in favour) to end birthright citizenship by introduction of the Twenty-Seventh Amendment of the Constitution Act, 2004[11] to prevent the phenomenon of so-called 'anchor babies'—that is individuals showing to claim asylum, then having children while in direct provision awaiting a ruling on their application, thus making it significantly more difficult to deport them once it had been found they entered the asylum system under false pretences.

The overriding issue with Nigerian asylum claims since the Celtic Tiger Era, and a continued source of considerable tension, is that few in Ireland consider Nigeria to be an unsafe land, that is a land from which Ireland should accept asylum claimants at all. This has come to the fore once more as Nigerians were again the largest single asylum group in 2023 (15.7% of all applications) amidst a surge in overall numbers. In response, in November 2024, the Nigerian ambassador to Ireland stated that there "is no doubt" that Nigeria is a safe country and should be added to Ireland's list of safe countries.[12] It was also understood among prominent Nigerian figures during the Celtic Tiger that Nigerian asylum claims were bogus. In 2000, The Irish Times published an article by a Nigerian priest visiting Ireland from Rome to pursue studies who couldn't believe that Nigeria wasn't deemed a safe nation. He poured scorn on his fellow Nigerians for abusing the Irish asylum system, stating, "Many of the stories told about Nigerian oppression are lies and fabrications...by falsely declaring themselves refugees they insult themselves and embarrass everyone else who is a Nigerian."[13] In 2005, then Minister for Justice, Michael McDowell stated that politicians were unwilling to acknowledge that more than 90% of asylum claims at the time were "unfounded".[14] It is then accurate to say that the majority of the original wave of Nigerian and African settlement, more generally, was based on bogus asylum claims. On March 4th, 2025, after years of denial and overseeing a de facto open borders system in coalition with Fine Gael, Taoiseach Micheal Martin stated, "The majority [of asylum applicants] who do apply are economic migrants."[15]

Overwhelmingly fake asylum applications is the original sin of black settlement in Ireland.

The differences in labour force participation between native Irish, Asian-Irish, whites from Western EU nations and Black workers are that black non-Irish individuals, particularly Nigerians, came to Ireland in great numbers posing as asylum seekers. In response to this abuse of the system several attempts were made to make Ireland less attractive to asylum abuse. Ireland, which went from almost no asylum claims before the early 1990s to thousands per year suddenly over the Celtic Tiger years, had to invent a system to deal with the influx on the hoof. The result was a Direct Provision system that placed claimants in one of a number of centres around the nation on a full board basis with a weekly allowance, while being afforded various forms of social welfare including child support and disability allowance. Applicants were to remain in this Direct Provision while their claim was being processed but because of the strain put on the system by overwhelming abuse, processing of claims slowed to a trickle with a backlog of years for some to receive a decision. It wasn't until June 2018 that asylum seekers were granted a conditional right to work in Ireland while awaiting a decision on their asylum application.

When Ebun Joseph claims that Ireland is a "racial and a racist state" in which "Whites are stratified at the top and Blacks at the bottom", she is leaving out key facts. Original black settlement in Ireland is intertwined with mass abuse of the asylum system. The effect of that abuse is two-fold. Because black non-Irish disproportionately entered the asylum system, they were obviously going to have less labour participation than other groups. The fact that black-

Irish, so the children of this first wave, are employed at a similar rate to native Irish shows that there is no systemic racism in the labour market. The other key effect of the original sin of black settlement in Ireland is that there is a mistrust of black settlers that results in stereotyping. Ebun Joseph herself has strongly vocalised this, stating, "From the beginning, the society and education system is socialised by the racial order in the country which teaches and reinforces the deficit model of not only having Blacks at the bottom but also expecting them to be there as a subservient group of aid/welfare recipients."[16] The issue is that, in the Irish context, the stereotypes exist for a reason. Blacks did, more than any other group, enter Ireland under false pretences and they did exist off the social welfare state.

Thus, Joseph's focus on the American context when attempting to introduce guilt by CRT into the classroom grows more understandable. As outlined in the last chapter, in Ireland, there is no history of colonialism and there is no history of black oppression. Quite the opposite. Ireland, not least the state's Justice Department, has proven to be remarkably tolerant of a community of which a very large number entered the state under legally dubious circumstances. Any community activist working on behalf of black Ireland would surely understand this delicate situation and engage with the natives with a sense of gratitude or in a conciliatory fashion. Joseph has chosen to incorporate Ireland into the Global North to obscure this origin story, deny Ireland's unique history and to push the perceived sins of America in particular onto Irish people by making them 'white'. Another reason for Joseph's whitewashing of the Irish is to be found in her relationship with her former supervisor and now colleague at UCD, Dr Alice Feldman. Many of Joseph's rhetorical turns and ideas are taken directly from her mentor. In her UCD biography, Feldman states that her research "currently involves troubling Irish and European colonial amnesias, particularly when it comes to migrants arriving from the Global South, by re/entangling Irish and Nigerian diasporic histories through a synthesis of decolonial aesthetics and arts-based research practices". She is the director of UCD's MA in

Race, Migration and Decolonial Studies. Ironically, Joseph, with her colleague and mentor Alice Feldman, is distorting historical realities of black settlement in Ireland by recasting the Irish as just more 'white' members of the Global North, using radical Social Justice theories from the US. By importing CRT and Black Studies wholesale from America, complete with American case studies, UCD and Joseph are imposing an internationally fashionable series of Social Justice theories onto Irish students who are forced to submit to being 'white'. To be blunt, Joseph and Feldman are simply the latest in a long line of colonisers. Theirs is simply a colonisation of the mind.

In July 2024, Green Party TD and The Minister of State for Community Development, Integration and Charities, Joe O'Brien, announced that Joseph would be the first National Action Plan Against Racism (NAPAR) Special Rapporteur—a position with a stipend of €100,000 over four years and access to staff. The NAPAR was put forth in 2023 as a "coordinated approach to eliminating racism in all its forms in Ireland". Along with Joseph's position, O'Brien also committed one million euros to be doled out in lump sums up to €50,000 for anti-racism projects across the country. The project is a thinly veiled power grab for the Social Justice Industrial Complex. It is built around five pillars: "Being Safe and Being Heard (Supporting people who experience racism and protecting people from racist incidents and crimes)", "Being Equal (Addressing ethnic inequalities)", "Being Seen (Enabling minority participation and Taking Part)", "Being Counted (Measuring the impacts of racism)" and "Being Together (A shared journey to racial equality)". The first measure, "Being Safe and Being Heard", established a relationship with Coimisiún na Meán, Ireland's online and media regulatory body, to clamp down on supposed "hate speech". The plan further mandates that the Gardaí gather "hate crime" data and forward it to the specialist Garda National Diversity Forum. To assist in compiling this new hate crime database, the NAPAR names 15 NGOs including LGBT Ireland, Islamic Foundation of Ireland, Muslim Sisters of Éire, and Gay Project who will have special status to act as third-party referrals to the Gardaí. All NGOs are encouraged to take part in the programme. While this NGO and Garda special relationship sounds reasonable on the surface, the government is creating a network of public and NGO bodies which privilege certain potential victims based on their standing within the Social Justice hierarchy of oppression. And more, the government is making vast sums of money available to these bodies through associated grants to find victimisation. Where there is a financial incentive and privileged access to government and law enforcement, there is motivation to find never-ending cases of racism, homophobia, sexism etc. This privileged status was cemented in October 2024 when the government forced through the Criminal Justice (Hate Offences) Act which codified in law, for the first time in the history of the state, privileged status for victims of 'hate crimes' based on "certain characteristics (referred to as protected characteristics)."[17] This law came into effect in January 2025.

The second pillar of the NAPAR, "Being Equal", aims to "address inequality of outcomes for people experiencing racism, including in employment, education, health and housing". This brings to mind Ibram X. Kendi's line, "The only remedy to present discrimination is future discrimination." The NAPAR commits to "Develop and adopt a training, expertise and employment strategy to increase the employment of groups experiencing racism". The wording here is important. The government categorically states that certain groups are experiencing racism, and their measure for that is a disparity in employment, educational and health outcomes. As explained above, the disparity between black and other groups in Ireland is based on a difference in the type of migrant entering the state—legal medium and high-skilled workers versus those who entered through abuse of the asylum system. In order to rectify this disparity, the Public Appointments Service (PAS), or Civil Service employment body, has "committed to increasing the number of job applications from, and the hiring of, candidates with an ethnic minority background...PAS... commits to delivering a 20% increase in applications from and assignments of ethnic minority candidates." This should be cause for outrage. The government aims to enforce a quota system for minorities in public employment which undermines the idea of meritocracy and, with it, professional excellence. The third pillar of the NAPAR, "Being Seen", reinforces this government-mandated 'positive' discrimination, aiming "To support the representation and participation of minority ethnic people in all aspects of life in Ireland, in particular where they are currently under-represented".

As special rapporteur for the NAPAR, Ebun Joseph is responsible for implementing all elements of the plan. As her academic work and public comments have shown, she is a radical Critical Race Theorist who superimposes US-derived ideas onto the Irish context where they cannot work. She had stated that Ireland is a racist state, that the Irish have had their knee on the neck of Africans since becoming 'white' after Independence and she has misrepresented the experience of black people in Ireland to foster a sense of grievance which can be leveraged to force 'positive' discrimination in public life—all while making a tidy sum from taxpayer funds herself. She is the most high-profile example of the Social Justice Industrial Complex in action but deeper concerns exist.

Social Justice Theory and public education

Throughout the NAPAR document, reference is made to the need to overhaul all levels of public education. Action 2.5 of "Being Equal" aims to "take steps to strengthen inclusion and anti-racism at all levels of the education system, including through addressing any bias embedded in the curriculum, and to support approaches that are fully intersectional and intercultural". It is the explicitly stated approach of the Irish government that it intends to embed intersectionality—CRT, Queer Theory, Decolonialism—into every stage of a child's education. This work has already caused public controversy. In August 2024, in a heavy-handed attempt to teach students about diversity and inclusion, the Irish Social, Personal and Health Education (SPHE) textbook manufacturer Edco were forced to defend a book for Junior Cycle students titled *Health and Wellbeing 1*. In a section titled "All Different, All Equal", two families are portrayed.

One is of a wildly stereotypical Irish family of four all dressed in Aran jumpers and standing in front of a thatched cottage. The children are performing an Irish dancing routine while the father embraces the mother in a paternalistic fashion and holds a pitchfork. An extremely bored-looking cow oversees proceedings. The text that accompanies the image begins, "We do not like change or difference. All our family members are Irish. We do not have a single relative living abroad..." It portrays the traditional Irish family as being aggressively inward-looking and resistant to change. The father is a cardboard cutout patriarchal tyrant. "Noirín would like to be a yoga instructor but my dad said it's not a proper job and she must stick to what she knows." The stereotype goes from insulting to outright absurd where it states, "We eat Irish food and have potatoes, bacon and cabbage every day because it is Irish and it is our tradition." The text rattles off several more stereotypes to make the family look insular, backward and bigoted. The children are not allowed to play foreign sports or instruments. They can only watch Irish shows on television. They can only go on holiday in Ireland. The text ends, "We get told off if we mix with people with a different religion from ours as they would be a bad influence on us."[18] In contrast to this, a multiracial family are presented in front of the Colosseum in Italy enjoying pizza and the buzz of international travel. The accompanying text is fast-paced and exciting. The world is your oyster if you just embrace diversity and inclusion. It is so exciting that the boy in this family was partially-sighted but was able to fundraise in his community and with the help of an Irish-American society he was able to fly to the US to fix his sight before flying to Syria to volunteer for the Red Cross. Why couldn't the Irish family get their son's eye fixed if needed? Bigotry and the fear of the Atlantic no doubt. Of course no traditional Irish families ever went to America before diversity. The historical illiteracy is almost as offensive as the overt social engineering.

Images of the text were shared online with many angry parents voicing their concerns. It sparked a flurry of social media anger, and Independent TD Carol Nolan wrote to the National Council for Curriculum Assessment (NCCA) and the Minister for Education

Norma Foley to demand an explanation. Nolan commented, "The typical 'Irish family' is lampooned as insular, angry, petty and let's be honest here, xenophobic and racist while the contrasting family in the presentation is apparently filled with outward-looking insight, tolerance, and intelligence...The (not-so-subtle) messaging here is that any preference for your own cultures, music and sport, for example, is now being depicted a marker for racism. This is extremely dangerous territory."[19] Indeed it would make the rabidly anti-Irish, 19th-century Punch Magazine blush. It is no accident that the caricatures presented in the text echo the idealised west-of-Ireland family, Dev's Ireland. As mentioned in the last chapter, Ireland is undergoing an identity crisis. The traditional pillars laid out in this image—the self-sufficient farming family authentically preserving Irish culture—dance, music, sport, vernacular architecture and a close connection to the land—are all but lost. That self-assured Ireland is diminished and in that gap, new identity shapers—Social Justice engineers—have begun to squat, attempting to lay a final blow, if needed, to traditional Ireland.

Not long after the public outrage and Nolan's intervention, an apology was given by the publisher and it was announced that the book would be withdrawn from Irish classrooms. While a victory for students, families and those concerned about the destructive influence of Social Justice theory in education, it was not the first controversy relating to SPHE and it will not be the last thanks to NAPAR and the deep embedding of Social Justice Theory across school curricula.

Irish Minister for Education, Fianna Fáil's Norma Foley, was particularly permissive in allowing Social Justice Theory to be embedded in Primary and Secondary Curricula over the course of the 33rd Dáil from 2020 to 2024. The Junior Cycle SPHE Curriculum that led to the "All Different, All Equal" fiasco was introduced under Foley's watch in February 2023.[20] The 'Learning Outcomes' of the document afford extraordinary latitude for schoolbook publishers to embed Social Justice Theory into textbooks. For example, in "Strand 3: Relationships and Sexuality" of the document, it is a stated goal that students should be able to "appreciate the breadth of what constitutes human sexuality, and how sexual orientation and gender identity are experienced and expressed in diverse ways." In response to these guidelines, leading SPHE book publishers Edco and Educate.ie both produced First Year textbooks (ages 12-13) which presented gender identity on an equal footing with biological understandings of sex. The Edco text *Health and Wellbeing* introduced students to ideas such as being 'non-binary', 'cisgender', 'transgender', while presenting a diagram of a 'gingerbread person' which placed 'sexual expression' and 'gender identity' alongside 'anatomical sex' as equally valid understandings of human sexuality. The Educate.ie text *You've Got This* introduces students to 'androgyny', 'cross-dressing', being 'cisgender', 'transgender', 'transitioning', 'genderqueer', 'gender fluid', 'third gender' among other highly controversial and non-scientific ideologies.[21] All ideologies are presented in affirming language in the textbooks which, depending on the instructor, encourage students to explore these avenues or at the very least, accept the confusing mess of Queer Theory as being normal and vaguely scientifically valid. Again, the issue here isn't simply these two textbooks—which should be pulped—but the underlying embedding of Social Justice Theory in the Curriculum by Norma Foley and its wider support in interconnecting pieces of government legislation such as NAPAR.

Foley's commitment to Social Justice Theory in Irish Education was also evident in all third-level institutions. Foley oversaw the Higher Education Authority's (HEA) Race Equality Implementation plan which ran from 2022-24 and resulted in the publication of principles for "Race Equality: Anti-Racism Principles for Irish Higher Education Institutions"[22] in every Irish third-level educational institution. The preamble to the document specifically cites the National Action Plan Against Racism as a key driving factor for the document. It states; "Another important reference point is the forthcoming National Action Plan Against Racism to be published by the Department of Children, Equality, Disability, Integration and Youth, which contains actions assigned to the HEA and higher education sector."

The document is a radical Social Justice Theory manifesto. It defines racism in a CRT framework stating, "We understand racism to mean the power dynamics present in those structural and institutional arrangements, practices, policies and cultural norms, which have the effect of excluding or discriminating against individuals or groups, based on their identity". It goes on to demand that all institutions take a proactive 'anti-racist' position, citing four areas. The document demands that higher education institutions (HEIs) take "responsibility, accountability and ownership of race equality issues", "actively acknowledge that race inequality exists" in their institutions, acknowledge "that Irish HEIs are not keeping pace with wider demographics and action is required to catch up", and "acknowledge the power of HEIs to influence Irish society in general". The document, signed off by Norma Foley and underpinned by the work of NAPAR, seeks to actively reform Irish HEIs in accordance with Social Justice Theory principles. These four principles are not best practice recommendations, they are genuflections. They demand that Irish HEIs 'acknowledge' their complicity in the perpetuation of white supremacy, colonial attitudes, racist, sexist and homophobic abuse in Ireland. This is why each point begins with "acknowledging" their failures. After the genuflection comes the penance, or 'commitments' as the document calls it, to the restructuring of Irish universities, and by extension, Irish society, into one which embeds Social Justice power structures.

Just as NAPAR provides a legislative authority for 'positive' discrimination in Civil Service employment hiring for minorities, the HEI Race Equality similarly demands positive discrimination. Among the 'commitments' all HEIs are required to undertake is one which states, "We will address questions of race equality within the strategic plans of our institutions." It seems rather innocuous, positive in fact. However, when one reads the glossary of terms that accompanies the document, one finds that "race equality" is actually a definition for "equity" as understood by CRT—"Race equality is defined as equal representation, equal experiences and equal outcomes of staff and students from minority ethnic groups." When this definition is understood, then the 'commitment' every Irish HEI must make is to ensure that positive discrimination takes place so that any student who is a protected minority is guaranteed at least the same outcome as the average "white" Irish student. This is made explicitly clear in another 'commitment' which states, "We will address race equality issues in relation to progression and retention of students and staff from minority ethnic groups including Travellers." The new document makes clear that any student who identifies as a minority will not be allowed to fail, or achieve grades significantly below the average. If they do, then the HEI is at fault for not correctly providing a sufficiently 'anti-racist' learning environment for them to succeed. This can only lead to a form of affirmative action which will result in a dramatic dumbing down of the curriculum and grading process either for all students, or just for those with minority status, which will again lead to long-term resentments between them and non-minority students who value meritocracy and academic excellence.

Outside of the Social Justice Theory coding in Primary, Secondary and Third-level education by NAPAR and Norma Foley, and the embedding of SJT modules within broader areas of study, it is increasingly common in Irish HEIs to have stand-alone certifications and postgraduate courses in specific areas of SJT which are designed to provide employees for Ireland's burgeoning Non-governmental Organisation (NGO) sector. For example, at UCD, students can complete an MA in *Gender, Sexuality and Culture*.[23] The course description states that students will be "able to understand, analyse and critically evaluate cultural production and cultural theory in relation to gender and sexuality as well as in relation to other intersecting power structures, such as race, ethnicity, class and migration." Work for "charities/NGOs/International Aid" are listed among the career opportunities for those graduating with the degree. In Trinity College's *Race, Ethnicity, Conflict* M.Phil.[24] there is a heavy emphasis on CRT through promotion of race as a 'social construct' and the programme promises career opportunities in "NGOs", "migrant and traveller rights" groups and as "political activists" among others.

Maynooth University's MA in *Social Science (Rights and Social Policy)*[25] offers students a programme that has "equality and inclusion" as the basis of all teaching and learning, with students learning about "critical social policy theories" and "how to write and influence policy and advanced policy analysis". The course is again targeted at students hoping to work in the NGO sector and is notable for having had Dr Rory Hearne among the teaching staff before he was elected to the 34th Dáil as a member of the leftist Social Democrats.

In 2021 there were 34,331 registered nonprofits operating in Ireland, employing 164,922 individuals and receiving €6.2 billion in state funds.[26] The sector accounted for just under 7% of the entire workforce of Ireland in 2021. While the number of nonprofits seems staggering, Ireland's political history explains its unusual dependence on the NGO sector. As explained in Chapter Two, both Fianna Fáil and Fine Gael were, for decades, happy to allow the Catholic Church to take on the role of silent government partner, outsourcing matters of education, health, spiritual, moral and social development to the church. Elements of that role are seen in the nonprofit funding data as various church bodies still receive millions in funding each year. In 2021, there were 4,647 Religious nonprofits operating in Ireland, making it the fourth largest NGO sector after Local Development/Housing, Recreation/Sports, and Education/Research.[27] It is worth pointing out that of all NGO sectors, though Religious nonprofits were the fourth largest, they received the least amount of public funding out of all (12) sectors. Many of these religious bodies will be older and representative of the state's reliance on the church prior to the Celtic Tiger. Also included in the figures are essential bodies such as schools. 3,965 primary and secondary schools are also classified as nonprofits, as are thousands of sports organisations across the country. It should be pointed out however, that teachers are not included in the nonprofit employment figures as they are technically government employees. So while 34,331 nonprofits may seem staggering, many of the groups involved do essential work that the government is not willing or able to do.

In the Irish context, 'nonprofit' is an umbrella term that includes charities, social enterprises, schools, volunteer organisations and more. The terms 'nonprofit' and 'NGO' are largely interchangeable though there are legal differences. For example, to register as a charity with the national Charities Regulator, and qualify for state funding and tax exemptions, certain criteria must be met which includes ensuring that all profits go to a stated charitable purpose and all tax records and financial transactions are kept in a transparent manner and inspected by the Revenue Office. Political parties, union groups or other political pressure groups cannot apply for charity status but can attain NGO status and with various restrictions, attain public funding.[28] The last of these, overtly political pressure groups, have become contentious in recent years, and these are the NGO groups increasingly embedded in legislation and in receipt of large sums of taxpayer money for progressive causes.

Because Fianna Fáil and Fine Gael have a longstanding tradition of outsourcing social policy to other bodies, in the 33rd Dáil, The Greens, with their NGO partners, became the de facto guardians of social and cultural identity as well as national moral arbiters. The Greens were handed the Department of Environment, Climate and Communication, the Department of Transport, the Department of Tourism, Culture, Arts, Gaeltacht, Sports and Media and, importantly, the Department for Children, Equality, Disability, Integration and Youth. The destruction of the tourism industry by handing over hotels in Ireland's most economically valuable tourism destinations makes sense when one realises that The Greens ran the Department for Tourism. The NAPAR overreach into education makes sense when one realises that The Greens were responsible for Children, Integration and Youth. And importantly, the elevation of the NGO sector to silent government partner during the course of the 33rd Dáil makes sense when one realises that The Greens, as a minority voice in government and a radically progressive political outlier, needed a powerful lobbying sector to engineer perceived wider public consensus for their policy ideas. They found a natural ally in the post-Celtic Tiger NGO sector.

A 2021 Benefacts report found that the Irish nonprofit sector boomed in the Celtic Tiger period "as special purpose vehicles to provide job creation, local development, social supports and other arms' length services on behalf of the state". While there had been a steady increase since the 1980s which aligns with the Catholic Church's dwindling influence in public life, secular NGOs boomed at the turn of the Millennium. The collapse of the Church did not just mark a collapse in faith, it marked a radical though little commented-upon changing of the ethos, ideology and direction of the Irish nation. The Catholic ethos that permeated the NGO sector was replaced by an increasingly politically progressive one, grounded in Social Justice Theory with a bloody-minded focus on obtaining institutional power and reshaping Irish society. Just as wholesale abuse of the Irish asylum system began to take root at the start of the new millennium, several immigration NGOs sprang up to facilitate it. In 2000, Nasc, the Irish Immigrant Support Centre was founded. In 2001, the Immigrant Council of Ireland, the Migrant Rights Centre of Ireland and Doras were all founded. All four of these immigrant rights NGOs have played a major role in making Ireland an attractive location for anyone looking to legitimately or illegitimately make use of the asylum system.

The privileged role of the Immigrant Council

The Immigrant Council of Ireland is primarily an advocacy group that specialises in providing legal assistance to asylum seekers and to international protection applicants who have had their claim for asylum rejected. They also advocate for the dismantling of Direct Provision and the broadening of immigration rules to widen access to family reunification for all migrants. These are all policy issues that are central to the Green Party platform. According to the group's website, since 2001, they have helped over 120,000 immigrants with their claims in Ireland and while they began with a focus on immigration reform, they now work with other groups around Europe on migrant rights projects, act as a pressure group on the government to "help shape public policy and discourse" and "to monitor and provide support to victims of racist incidents."[29] Through their Independent Law Centre, the group is involved in hundreds of legal cases on behalf of migrants.

Few bodies show the absurdity of the modern Irish NGO system quite as well as the Immigrant Council. As the Council has developed and expanded away from its initial focus on Celtic Tiger era immigration reform, it has taken on a leading advocacy role for immigrants lobbying the government for ever greater migrant rights and it takes legal cases against the state on behalf of rejected asylum applications. That would be fine except that on average, according to financial reports lodged with the Irish Charities Regulator, the Council receives 40% of its funding from the state. In 2023, the Council received €453,600 in state funding out of a total annual income of €1.1m. The money received from the state is ostensibly allotted to specific programmes within the Council that do not directly conflict with the state but in practical terms, without state funding, the Immigrant Council would collapse or at least have vastly reduced lobbying potential. In effect then, when the Immigrant Council lobbies the government on asylum reform and takes the state to court on behalf of rejected asylum applications, it is the state—well, the taxpayer—that is sponsoring it. The Irish government is paying the Immigrant Council to lobby them. That is obviously a profound conflict of interests and one the government can use as a powerful consensus-forming tool.

If the government wants to push through deeply controversial, divisive or otherwise unpopular immigration policies, because of their financial dependency on the state, ministers need only have the Immigration Council, among other state-funded immigration NGOs, advocate for the desired government policy changes in the national news media. The government can then point to that as evidence of legislative demand. In April 2024, Joe O'Brien gave the Immigrant Council a bumper grant of €730,567 as one of 17 Asylum, Migration and Integration Fund (AMIF) grant awards. That sum represents three-quarters of the total funding the Council normally brings in per year. By this point, the Immigrant Council hardly even qualifies as an arm's-length government body anymore and they most certainly cannot claim to be an NGO. The line between NGO and government departments has become too blurred. And the Immigrant Council isn't alone. Fellow immigrant rights NGO, Doras, received 80% of its budget from the state in 2023, while Nasc received 70%. Both of these groups, alongside the Migrant Rights Centre of Ireland which was 33% state-funded in 2023, also received substantial grants from the AMIF fund making them overwhelmingly funded by the state as of 2024 and as such, completely unfit to carry out lobbying and political activities with any degree of independence.

When NGOs are overwhelmingly reliant on the state for funding, then a quid pro quo relationship is inevitable. When devising controversial legislation, ministers can rely upon having sympathetic—in other words well-funded—NGOs in place who can be pointed to as evidence that an exhaustive public consultation process has been undertaken on behalf of said legislation. NAPAR is a good example. Minister for State Joe O'Brien was a chief architect of the NAPAR and is a former employee of the Immigrant Council. As already outlined, the NAPAR granted privileged positions to a slew of NGOs, giving them unprecedented access to the Gardaí in fighting against racism, homophobia etc. 24 NGOs were further given access to extra government funds for the undertaking of the plan as part of the accompanying Ireland Against Racism Fund and these included Doras, the Immigrant Council and the Migrant Information Centre. During the planning process for the NAPAR which ran from March 2021 to July 2022, 83 public bodies and NGOs made written submissions to the planning committee. These were, overwhelmingly, bodies that received all or significant public funding and included the Immigrant Council, Doras, Nasc and the Migrant Information Centre. So, as part of the NAPAR public consultation process, NGOs that are overwhelmingly propped up by state funds were asked for their input and after the NAPAR was successfully launched, these same groups were among the primary beneficiaries of the funding associated with the project as their briefs expanded. That is not a consultation process. That could more accurately be described as a cash-for-lobbying support transaction.

And while Fianna Fáil and Fine Gael were happy to offload social policy to The Greens and the NGOs, it is important to stress that the latter did not simply run roughshod over Fianna Fáil and Fine Gael with their progressive agenda in the 33rd Dáil. Charlie Flanagan, the Fine Gael veteran who retired at the end of the 33rd Dáil run, commented that there is currently no room for conservative or more centrist voices in the Irish government, indicating that members of his own party and that of Fianna Fáil were happily in thrall to the NGOs. Speaking to The Irish Times in September 2023 he said, "I do find that the plurality of voices long evident in Leinster House are not as evident now. There is a dangerous intolerance of any view that is not being pushed by vociferous, well-financed and well-funded non-government organisations." Referencing the power of NGOs surrounding recent progressive causes such as abortion, surrogacy and LGBTQ issues, he went on to state, "But I have said to colleagues that I would have more influence on Government policy if I was a middle-ranking official with an NGO than I have as a Government backbencher." And while his Green Party colleagues were fierce progressive advocates throughout the 33rd Dáil, so too were many of Flanagan's own party colleagues and those of coalition partners Fianna Fáil.

Among the most controversial of Irish NGOs is the National Women's Council of Ireland (NWC). While the Council was formed in 1973, under the 32nd and 33rd Dáils it has come to behave less as an NGO and more as a government department. A 2024 in-depth report by Gript found that over a ten-year period from 2014 to 2024, out of an income of approximately €9.2 million, €7.4 million came from public funds—notably the Department of Justice. In the three years prior to 2024, public funding accounted for 96% of staffing costs.[30] According to NWC's website, the Council's stated aim "is to lead action for the achievement of women's and girls' equality through mobilising, influencing, and building solidarity", and in this regard, their impact has been immense. The NWC has been instrumental in embedding Social Justice Theory in primary and secondary education and influencing wider legislation.

Politicising the murder of Ashling Murphy

On January 12th, 2022, in a case that traumatised Ireland and made international headlines, the talented young musician and teacher Ashling Murphy was brutally murdered by a Slovakian immigrant to Ireland, Jozef Puska. Ashling had been out for a jog in broad daylight along the banks of the Grand Canal in Tullamore, Co. Offaly when she was attacked, overpowered and stabbed eleven times in the neck. In the days after the attack, the NWC played an instrumental role in diverting a national bout of soul searching away from a conversation about migrant crime and government migration policy and instead diverted the blame for Ashling's murder onto all Irish men and a culture of misogyny. Three days after the murder, The Irish Times printed a piece that blamed "an epidemic of femicide" and "a culture of misogyny" in Ireland for Ashling's death.[31] Similarly, The Guardian asked if Murphy's murder would change Ireland's "culture of misogyny".[32] Reinforcing the narrative, in the days after her murder, the NWC organised dozens of vigils around the country and laid the blame broadly on 'violence against women'—a narrative that was parroted by government officials. Speaking to a crowd of thousands outside of government buildings in Dublin two days after the murder, the head of the council, Orla O'Connor, stated, "The death of Ashling Murphy must be a watershed moment to end violence against women."[33] That same day, Minister for Justice, Helen McEntee, tweeted, "We must come together to demand zero tolerance of violence against women." In an official statement on the 19th of January, then Taoiseach Micheal Martin said, "We have spent much of the past week ... questioning our attitudes towards women. Are we doing anything to help? Are we doing enough to help? Are we part of the problem?"[34] The narrative was complete. The blame for the murder of Ashling Murphy was laid at the feet of Irish men, not Puska and not decades of government immigration policy malpractice.

It didn't matter that it later emerged that Puska had a juvenile criminal record of sexual assault in his native Slovakia and was a person of interest in two assaults, one in Czechia and one in England, before arriving in Ireland.[35] A diligent government would have spotted this and not have allowed him entry based on that information alone. Though a citizen of a nation within the EU—which allowed Puska to enter Ireland under the right of free movement— Ireland was under no obligation to allow him, his broader family and dependents to stay in Ireland funded by state benefits. He had been unemployed for at least five years prior to the attack. The right of free movement within the EU is dependent on individuals seeking gainful employment and individual states are only required to provide protection for the first three months of an individual's stay. The 2004 Freedom of Movement Act,[36] which governs the movement of EU citizens within the EU, specifies that after the three-months protection period, an individual cannot be deported "As long as the beneficiaries of the right of residence do not become an unreasonable burden on the social assistance system of the host Member State." The Act gives several examples of when an individual has a right to be reliant 'temporarily' on social welfare for an extended period, including injury. It emerged during the course of Puska's trial that he had been unemployed and on disability payments for more than five years and should have been repatriated to his home nation long before he had the chance to murder Ashling Murphy. The fact that his social welfare abuse wasn't identified by the state raises serious questions about the degree of social welfare fraud that is ongoing in Ireland. Further, the 2004 Act specifies that a nation has the right to prevent the entry of any EU citizen if there is "a real and sufficiently serious threat to the public order, affecting the basic interests of society". While Puska's conviction in Slovakia may not have been disqualifying under the terms of the Act in and of itself, combined with his other involvements in assault cases in Czechia and England, he should not have been granted the right to reside in Ireland based on his likely risk to public safety. As noted in Chapter 2, because of poor vetting over years by the Department of Justice and others, it is unknown how many more like Puska—long-term unemployed EU citizens with criminal records for serious criminal activity in their homeland or elsewhere—are currently living in Ireland. Ashling's murder should have prompted a massive and immediate retroactive screening process of EU citizen criminal records, a review and repatriation programme of long-term unemployed EU citizens living in Ireland living off social welfare, and a rigorous new border control programme. Instead, the 33rd Dáil, with help from the NWC, distracted from the root cause of the murder.

At the sentencing hearing for Puska on November 17th, 2023, Ashling's longtime partner, Ryan Casey, read out a deeply moving victim impact statement in which he pointed to these exact failings on the part of the government. He stated, "It just sickens me to the core that someone can come to this country, be fully supported in terms of social housing, social welfare, and free medical care for over 10 years – over 10 years – never hold down a legitimate job, and never once contribute to society in any way shape or form...this country is no longer the country that Ashling and I grew up in..."[37] Four days later, when Gript journalist Ben Scallan asked Micheal Martin to comment on Casey's statement, Martin stated, "Within the European Union, we have free mobility...that's the context in terms of the free mobility of people and their various entitlements...in Ireland as you know we have one of the highest employment rates." Through vagueness, Martin's comments led the public to believe that Puska and the government had acted properly in allowing him to be in the country at the time of the murder. The national media took the cover-up further. Newstalk and The Irish Times omitted Casey's "ten years" comments from their reporting. National broadcaster RTE initially included the comments in their reporting of events but then removed this section in later reports that day.[38] As word of the censorship of a distraught boyfriend's impact statement began to gain traction on social media, Irish Times correspondent Kitty Holland went on the BBC's "The View" to discuss the matter. When asked to comment on the censored sections of Casey's statement, Holland responded, "I think elements of them were not good frankly. I think they were incitement to hatred...He is being held up as a hero of the far right."[39] The message from the government and the media was clear: misogyny killed Ashling Murphy and anyone, including her own partner, who challenged that narrative was going to be cut down.

When questions continued to be posed regarding Ashling's murder, even questions from individuals who accepted the government/ICW line that misogyny was the root cause, the government aggressively shot down any hint that their management of migration was a factor. On January 24th, 2024 during a Dáil Debate, Deputy Marian Harkin addressed then Taoiseach Leo Varadkar, "Taoiseach, last November I asked you as Taoiseach, as leader of our country, to lead what I hoped would be an open, honest, factual and respectful debate on immigration. So far this has not happened...Just two years ago, thousands of visceral statements from so many Irish women followed the horrific murder of Ashling Murphy...The Dáil was also told that 'By simply existing, women's lives are at risk from men whom they know and men whom they do not know'. Taoiseach, we believed women two years ago when they made these statements about Irish men. Why do we not at least entertain those statements from women now when they speak about the idea of 30, 40, or 50 single asylum seekers arriving in their town or village, living three or four to a room with no family connections and nothing to do most of the time? Why do we not take on those concerns as genuine?...I am asking you to have the debate, warts and all, and to manage this in a reasonable and rational way so that we can...bring communities with us."[40]

Deputy Harkin pointed to the murder of Ashling as evidence that migrants are just as likely—she stressed no more likely—than Irish men to commit violence against women, so placing IPAS centres into small communities would significantly increase the risk of women and girls in those areas. A logical argument. Varadkar responded, "I really think that to connect that [Ashling's murder] to a debate about international protection and migration is really wrong... It is really wrong. The evil person who killed poor Ashling Murphy was an EU citizen who had been in the country for the best part of ten years, working and paying taxes. That is how he acquired his rights to social welfare and other things...To connect that to international protection and refugees coming to this country, whether they are genuine or not, is really wrong. Really, Deputy, do not bring our country down into that spiral. Please do not." Aside from attempting to shut down Deputy Harkin's legitimate questions about the mass importation of single unvetted men into small communities and away from unpopular government policy by twisting her words to make her sound racist, Varadkar also misrepresented Puska's right to be in the country. Varadkar's words led the Dáil to believe that Puska had been in employment and an upstanding, taxpaying member of society before the murder. This, as had been made clear by evidence given and reported on at his trial months before Varadkar's statement, is not the case. Puska had been on long-term disability payouts beginning shortly after arrival and he and his family, an unreasonable burden on the state, should have been removed from the country before having the opportunity to murder Ashling Murphy.[41] Ashling Murphy's murder was a direct result of the failure of successive Fine Gael governments, but it didn't matter. The narrative surrounding Puska had been settled in the days and weeks after Ashling's murder.

On June 28th, 2022, Micheal Martin, along with Justice Minister Helen McEntee and Minister for Children, Equality, Disability, Integration and Youth, Roderic O'Gorman, announced the Zero Tolerance strategy, a five-year plan that would, among other measures, update "school curricula to include consent, coercive control, domestic violence and safe use of the internet."[42] Supporting McEntee, on the one-year anniversary of Ashling's murder, the Irish Examiner published a lengthy piece reinforcing the government narrative, calling for the implementation of the Zero Tolerance strategy. The paper quoted NWC head Orla O'Connor, who helped gin up support. Invoking Ashling's murder she stated that "The whole country mourned the death of Ashling Murphy, and since then 11 more women have lost their lives to male violence against women in the

Republic...[W]e must also tackle the root cause of this epidemic...We must educate our children about the misogyny that underlies male violence against women. There is a gap left by our education system." O'Connor neglected to specify that in 2022, of twelve women murdered in Ireland, six—50%—were committed by immigrants, two were substance abuse related and the majority of the rest were committed by family members or individuals known to the victim in domestic disputes.[43] The data simply does not speak to a widespread culture of misogyny among Irish men. Still, O'Connor further lobbied the government, "The National Women's Council (NWC) said although the Government's zero tolerance strategy is an ambitious plan, implementation and funding are key. The NWC said violence against women was epidemic and Government must take immediate steps to address it."[44] The framing of The Irish Times article was that O'Connor and the NWC were on the outside passionately advocating for women, lobbying the government. This couldn't be further from the truth. The NWC had been equal partners with the government in devising the Zero Tolerance strategy since 2021, the year before Ashling's murder. They knew exactly what the government planned to do because they took a central role in designing that plan. The article's framing of the Council lobbying the government from arm's length was misleading and Ashling's murder was merely a selling point to push through government/NGO legislation already in preparation.

The Foreword to the Zero Tolerance strategy, written by Helen McEntee states, "I want to thank my officials and all those working in the NGO sector who co-designed this strategy in partnership with us." The executive summary stated that the Zero Tolerance document was the joint work of the Department of Justice, the NWC and Safe Ireland—another domestic violence NGO which received 81% of its €1.9 million income from the state in 2023.[45] Section 4 of the document states that work on developing the strategy began in April 2021 with all three in charge—three-quarters of a year before Ashling's murder. Like the NAPAR document, the Zero Tolerance document is awash with Social Justice Theory. As such, being a radically progressive document, it would likely have faced greater public scrutiny and pushback if it hadn't been hitched to and presented as a response to Ashling's murder.

Defining domestic violence, the document states, "Neither domestic or sexual violence discriminate based on race, ethnicity, religion, disability, or socio-economic status. Domestic violence and sexual violence impacts on the lives of women and children of all backgrounds, and some men: in contrast, society does not treat all victims or survivors of abuse equally...Intersectionality has become an increasingly relevant term and is a useful lens for understanding oppression and privilege in our society. An intersectional approach allows for a more holistic understanding...of the needs of more excluded identity groups (that includes Travellers, other ethnic minorities, migrants, individuals with disabilities, members of the LGBTQ+ communities and others...an intersectional approach ensure[s] equality of outcome for all. All actions included in this strategy are required to take a horizontal, intersectional approach, to ensure inclusion of socially excluded groups."[46]

Similarly, the NAPAR document's definition of racism "underscores the importance of intersectionality, a concept that offers a framework for understanding how different forms of discrimination interact to create further marginalisation and exclusion. The plan acknowledges the intersectionality between racism and all other forms of oppression, including the oppressions experienced by people based on gender, socio-economic circumstances, disability, sexuality, religious belief and gender identity...It further acknowledges that women, children and men experience dimensions of racism differently. Therefore...care must be taken in implementing the actions in this plan to pay attention to the intersectionality between race and gender."[47]

Just as the NAPAR document was handed to Joseph Ebun to oversee its implementation along with a large cash injection of public money to feed a plethora of NGOs, so too will the Zero Tolerance strategy provide a cash boon for domestic abuse NGOs. To oversee the implementation of the progressive Zero Tolerance strategy, a new state agency, CUAN, was opened on February 22nd, 2024. The agency was given a budget of €59 million with €47 million to be distributed to 'front line' organisations dealing with domestic abuse and €6 million for 'prevention and raising awareness campaigns'. The leading providers of frontline domestic abuse shelters in Ireland are already overwhelmingly state-funded. Aoibhneas is 95% funded by the state, Saoirse is almost entirely funded by council grants, while Dublin's biggest domestic abuse services provider, Sonas, is 80% state-funded. CUAN's €47 million allocation will offer funds for new providers around the nation to set up services.

Obviously, the provision of front-line services for victims of domestic abuse is not just vital but noble and few would argue with the state allocating funds to them. However, the Social Justice Theory and intersectional approach underpinning the Zero Tolerance strategy ensure that there is plenty of funding available for social engineering. For example, CUAN's flagship public awareness campaign launched in November 2023 was based around the divisive idea of sexual consent. Again, while seemingly positive on the surface, the concept of consent, or ongoing and enthusiastic consent to pursue intimate or sexual activities, is commonly seen as political interference in private relations. The concept of active consent was popularised by feminist writers Jaclyn Friedman and Jessica Valenti in 2008 with the publication of *Yes Means Yes!,* a play on first-wave feminism's 'No Means No!' mantra. The move led away from rape being defined by pushing past an active 'no' to requiring ongoing active and enthusiastic consent. This definition of rape gained traction during the MeToo movement and NGOs such as Amnesty International have led the charge to make sex without explicit ongoing consent an automatic rape charge in law across Europe. As of 2024, 19 out of 31 European nations now have consent-based rape laws, up from 8 in 2008.[48] These changes have led to controversy. For example, in Sweden in 2018, after the #MeToo movement, laws were ushered in to classify sex without explicit consent as rape. The new laws resulted in a 75% increase in rape convictions from 2018 to 2020.

Undoubtedly many of these convictions were just and it is

entirely likely that more women felt brave enough to come forward to report their assault because of the new laws, accounting for much of the increase. But a notable driving factor in successful prosecutions was that under the new laws, prosecutors are no longer required to prove the use or threat of violence or coercion.[49] This has led to concerns surrounding what, exactly, constitutes consent especially when alcohol is involved. In other words, at what point does one go from 'drunk and able to consent to sex' to 'too drunk to consent'? A compounding issue is that responsibility for that decision is legally placed on the shoulders of the man, thus leading to a chilling effect on men engaging women while under the influence but no such inhibition on the part of the woman. There is an obvious problem with legal grey areas and the removal of more objectively determinable means of coercion as the benchmark for rape—the alleged victim's word holds disproportionate power over the accused in legal proceedings. This opens up the door for false allegations or allegations made out of regret upon sobering up the next day, or allegations based on being caught having an affair etc. Simply the threat of such potential outcomes will have an oppressive effect on young men wishing to engage in sexual activities casually or with a committed partner when a bad breakup or jilted feelings could result in professional and social ruination or worse. While CUAN's campaign was not advocating for changes in rape laws, it is indicative of a deeply progressive, and socially divisive, vision for this taxpayer-funded government body.

The NWC played a central role in developing the Zero Tolerance strategy though in the media, as noted, representatives spoke as though they were outsiders lobbying for change. After the Council had played a central role in developing the strategy, it again stepped out of its government partner role to take up an observer role ensuring its implementation. The Irish Observatory of Violence Against Women (IOVAW) is an intersectional collective of 28 NGOs which was set up in 2002 as a lobbying collective—an NGO lobbying super union if you will—and is chaired by the NWC. The IOVAW, chaired by Orla O'Connor is not officially partnered with the government in overseeing the Zero Tolerance document so the NWC can again step out from being an official government partner in developing the document to be a loud lobbyist in ensuring it is implemented—all while the bodies involved in that lobbying are overwhelmingly funded by the government. It is the same routine of the state paying lobbying groups taxpayer money to lobby them. In December 2023, IOVAW published a comprehensive oversight report on the implementation of the Zero Tolerance strategy. Despite the NWC playing a central role in devising the strategy, the report delivered a list of grievances about its shortcomings. The report concluded, "There are considerable challenges that remain to be addressed in terms of vindicating the rights of all women and girls to live free from violence and exploitation."[50] Unsurprisingly, the solution to the failings of the Zero Tolerance strategy was a need for more funding, "stronger collaboration across the relevant government departments and bodies" to remedy the failings in the strategy's implementation, "a stronger co-design collaboration with civil society organisations to implement the Strategy", and "robust monitoring mechanisms and data collection strategies to effectively assess the extent to which the strategy was implemented as intended (involving all the relevant bodies)". In other words, the only way to implement the multi-million Euro taxpayer-endowed Zero Tolerance strategy is to give more money and power to NGOs. The report was taken on board by Minister for Justice Helen McEntee and the demands of the IOVAW union were met. On top of €7.7 million given out to various charities and NGOs in January 2024, a further €6.3 million top-up was announced in March. Half of the members of the IOVAW were included—among them, the Immigrant Council of Ireland. And their inclusion is telling.

The Zero Tolerance strategy was ostensibly designed to prevent violence against women. Because it is rooted in Social Justice Theory with a focus on intersectionality, even seemingly disparate NGOs are all given access to funds. While different NGOs may focus on different areas of Social Justice, Intersectionality is the glue that binds Irish NGOs to one another and in turn to the government purse. If there is an immigration problem, the Immigrant Council gets a cut. If there is a problem with violence against women, the Immigrant Council gets a cut. If there is a problem with homophobic violence, the Immigrant Council gets a cut. And so on. What allows the Immigrant Council to sit with the Women's Council on the IOVAW super NGO union? Social Justice and Intersectionality. What allows 169 different minor groups ranging from the *50/50 Group* which advocates for gender parity in politics, to the *Irish Farmer's Association*, to the *Abortion Access Campaign West*, to the *Amal Muslim Women Led Group*, to the *Amdalah Africa Foundation*, to the *Fine Gael Women's Network* to all join together as members of the Women's Council? Social Justice and Intersectionality. Intersectionality is what allows disparate NGOs to join together as a powerful union to make sure that ever-increasing funds are wrested from the taxpayer and spread across the NGO sector. Intersectionality allows every NGO to be part of the answer to every social problem.

The NGO Industrial Complex

What is the NGO Industrial Complex then? Irish Universities increasingly produce students who are graduating from Social Justice Theory courses such as Trinity's M.Phil. in *Race, Ethnicity and Conflict* or UCD's MA in *Gender, Sexuality and Culture* which are specifically targeted at careers in the NGO sector. Each such course might seem unique and niche. However, buried in the course content, one will find that modules across these courses bear striking similarities thanks to an adherence to broad social justice themes and intersectionality across disciplines. So while the names of courses suggest niche expertise that would limit the course holder to a handful of jobs upon graduation, in reality, the university system's commitment to general Social Justice Theory and Intersectionality in their teaching means that a graduate with a certificate in *Gender, Sexuality and Culture* is just as qualified for a role at the Immigrant Council as someone with a seemingly more suited certificate in *Race, Ethnicity and Conflict*. One must, after all, keep in mind that the point of Social

Justice Theory courses is not to produce useful and skilled workers, rather activists with a radical understanding of how society is ordered and a desire to upend the existing meritocratic, capitalist system.

As universities churn out more of these activists, there is increasing pressure to expand jobs within the NGO sector to support them. This demand is being met by the injection of Social Justice Theory and Intersectionality in government policy documents and the expansion of funding to NGOs that specialise in social justice and intersectional approaches to solving social issues. Their common grounding in Social Justice Theory and Intersectionality allows NGOs to form powerful lobbying unions from which to demand ever more funding from the government. Crucially, government policy documents—which are developed in coordination with NGOs—set unrealistic or unattainable goals—such as the NAPAR's stated goal of "Eliminating racism in all its forms in Ireland" and the Zero Toler-ance strategy's goal of "Zero Tolerance of domestic, sexual and gender based violence." This ensures that Social Justice Theory-driven NGOs never run the risk of achieving their raison d'être and can return to the well of public finances—€6.5 billion and growing—for more and more taxpayer funding and never-ending expansion.

The Irish state allowed itself to be leveraged by the post-Celtic Tiger Social-Justice-Theory-driven NGO lobby by outsourcing social projects for decades, by abandoning domestic industry in pursuit of FDI dependency, and, in its place, fostering a handout culture of charity and NGO employment that has now exceeded 7% of the total workforce. A new breed of progressive NGOs stepped into the gap left by the Catholic church. They seized the opportunity to shape the culture and identity of Ireland, and the government—or rather, the Irish taxpayer—financed it. By building NGO unions such as the IOVAW and the Women's Council's membership model, they were able to exert significant bargaining power against the government. Allying with Irish universities to tailor modules, degrees and post-graduate courses to this shared ideology gave the NGO unions an extra bargaining chip against the government—postgraduate employment options. With NGO advocates Joe O'Brien specifically and the Green Party generally, the lines between NGO and government became almost impossible to distinguish. And so, the victory for Social Justice Theory and Intersectionality as the driving forces of social change in schools, universities, in the thousands of social projects dotted around the nation run by NGOs, and government policy itself was complete.

There is one last important element that draws the government and the NGO Industrial Complex together and that is the state's complete reliance upon the FDI economy. Since the height of the Celtic Tiger at the turn of the Millennium, economic policy has been tied to massive inward migration. This rate of migration has seen Ireland move from one of the most homogenous nations in the West in 1995 to a nation in which 22% of the population was born overseas in 2024. Even if successive Fianna Fáil and Fine Gael governments had desired the integration of these massive numbers of immigrants —and they hadn't—the sheer number of arrivals would have made it impossible. Throughout this timeframe, Fianna Fáil and Fine Gael took the easy way out by simply ignoring the radical demographic changes occurring. They focused on economic matters and, in keeping with their roots, they outsourced the job of shaping new Ireland to junior coalition partners and the NGO sector. Those groups decided to make the Irish 'white' and Fianna Fáil and Fine Gael went along with that. As a result, Ireland is less self-assured. Its cultural homogeneity is shattered. The psyche of the nation is no longer defined by pride in the collective scars of centuries of survival in the face of invasion, colonialism, forced exile and famine. Ireland is a nation that is fast forgetting its unique folklore, customs, religion and identity. And waiting to deliver the coup de grâce are the Social Justice Theory wrecking crews who dream of an Ireland less like Family A and more like Family B—globalised, rootless, intersectional, multi-cultural and utterly bland. Their strongest ally in shaping this new Ireland is the national media.

6

THE NATIONAL MEDIA FIREWALL

O n New Year's Eve 1961, President Eamon de Valera was the first person to address the nation via television on the newly-founded state broadcaster Raidió Teilifís Éireann (RTE). His address was sombre, sceptical and ultimately hopeful. Warning of the frightening potential of the new medium he stated, "I must admit that sometimes when I think of television and radio and their immense power I feel somewhat afraid. Like atomic energy, it can be used for incalculable good but it can also do irreparable harm. Never before was there in the hands of men an instrument so powerful to influence the thoughts and actions of the multitude."[1] Despite his deep misgivings, de Valera understood that the new technology was inevitable and so offered optimistically, "I am confident that those who are in charge will do everything in their power to make it useful for the nation." As already noted, when the American travel writer Lawrence Millman travelled through Ireland in 1975, the devastating cultural influence of television on Ireland's unique fireside culture was all but complete as a hungry home audience devoured the slick, glossy pulp beamed in from the USA and Britain. Television made the Irish self-conscious and embarrassed of their own 'primitive' culture. So they cast it off. It would, however, take another 50 years before the corrosive effects that RTE has had on democracy would become apparent. Over the course of the 33rd Dáil, RTE would become a de facto PR arm of the state, playing an essential role in consensus forming on behalf of Fianna Fáil and Fine Gael ahead of divisive policy decisions, depriving their core voter bases, the over-65s, of access to certain information and perspectives that would allow them to make informed voting decisions. No other institution played a greater role in ensuring that Ireland's crippled democracy remained crippled and that the process of making the Irish 'white' was normalised. RTE was not alone in misleading the public. During the 32nd and 33rd Dáils, the national print media similarly acted as mouthpieces for the state.

In order for democracy to flourish, the national news media needs to be able to operate free from any attempt by the government to interfere in editorial matters. A free press then requires laws that do not encourage arbitrary clampdowns on outlets, laws that punish the state for arbitrary surveillance or intimidation of the press or individual journalists, and an economic separation of press and state to avoid conflicts of interest.

The death of investigative journalism

The Irish government has a long history of clandestine observation of Irish journalists, which has led to a chilling effect on investigative journalism. In 1982, political journalists Geraldine Kennedy (Sunday Press), Bruce Arnold (Sunday Tribune) and Vincent Browne (Magill Magazine) had their phones tapped on the orders of Charles Haughey's Justice Minister Sean Doherty. Doherty signed the warrants which authorised the tapping with the aim of finding out who within the government was leaking information from cabinet meetings to the press. Kennedy and Arnold were reporting on internal divisions and power struggles threatening Haughey's leadership while Browne was investigating impropriety between the government and certain beef barons. When Haughey's government collapsed at the end of 1982, Fine Gael's new Justice Minister Michael Noonan revealed the scandal to the public. Noonan implicated Sean Doherty and Ray MacSharry directly in the scandal but, Ireland being a crippled democracy, both received a slap on the wrist. Doherty resigned from the party before rejoining in 1984 and MacSharry went on to become a European Commissioner and Minister for Finance once Haughey brushed off the scandal and came back to power in 1987. The scandal did, a decade later, end Haughey's career when the Progressive Democrats threatened to pull out of coalition with Fianna Fáil unless Haughey quit—which he did in 1992.[2] The journalists involved won settlements against the state which set an important legal precedent for the defence of constitutional rights to privacy in the High Court and in 1993, the Interception of Postal Packets and Telecommunications Messages (Regulation) Act[3] placed seemingly strict boundaries on the limits of state surveillance. The Act required all surveillance to be signed off by the Minister for Justice with oversight by a Judge and surveillance was only allowed in cases of serious crime and threats to the security of the State. However, the Act simply proved to be window dressing to finally put Haughey and the 1982 scandal to rest. It was an empty gesture to ensure Ireland's politicians were seen to be doing something.

In 2017, the Irish Independent reported that Garda intelligence officers were alleged to have tapped the phones of innocent civilians they mistook for criminals and others in cases of mistaken identity. A Garda intelligence whistleblower told the Independent that he often felt pressured to circumvent the correct legal avenues and that many warrant applications were sloppily filled out with little supporting evidence. When he raised concerns about his orders, he was sidelined. The officer stated that these activities had been going on for almost a decade. He settled out of court with the state. In 2024, The Sunday Times reported that an unspecified number of journalists were preparing to sue the state after the state-sponsored Garda Siochana Ombudsman Commission (GSOC) accessed their phones in an apparent bid to identify confidential sources. Ironically, the GSOC was established in 2007 as an independent oversight body to handle complaints relating to the Gardaí after a string of scandals that included the initial 1982 phone tapping incident. The Times reported that GSOC accessed the phone data of several journalists even though the journalists involved were not under criminal investigation and no judge warrant was signed off. One journalist had his phone bill accessed by GSOC on two separate occasions in a bid to identify confidential informants. Even though the GSOC phone scraping activities dated back to at least 2016, the state still hasn't chaired an investigation into the matter and when the Times contacted Helen McEntee's Justice Department with inquiries, they received no answers. This ongoing culture of clandestine state surveillance of journalists has an obvious chilling effect on investigative journalism. Journalists are unable to conduct investigative research when secret informants and whistleblowers feel unsafe contacting them. Further, by acting outside of the bounds of the law with impunity, snooping into journalists' personal devices, the state is engaging in intimidation tactics to scare Irish journalists away from politically sensitive investigations.

The decline of investigative journalism in Ireland is also tied to Ireland's high-risk defamation laws. In 1996, award-winning Sunday Independent reporter Veronica Guerin was murdered by a Dublin drug cartel. Prior to her murder she had been the victim of several beatings, assassination attempts and death threats. The year before her murder, she received the International Press Freedom Award and in her acceptance address she stated, "Ireland is...a wonderful country, great place to visit, but unfortunately for journalists the most difficult thing that we have to work within are our restrictive libel laws. It's difficult for our publishers because they're the people who have to pay the lawyers the massive amounts of money on a daily basis in courts."[4] Because of Ireland's restrictive libel laws, notably no cap on defamation payouts regardless of publication circulation, Guerin's editors could not risk naming the drug lords involved in her investigations for fear of being sued and potentially putting the Sunday Independent out of business. To circumvent this, Guerin was forced to refer to the various gangland players using colourful comic-style pseudonyms; the Monk, the Coach, the Penguin. Without being able to name her sources, the Gardaí could not provide her the protection she needed to survive in Dublin's drug underworld and so she had to take extraordinary risks in face-to-face meetings with elements in the scene in a bid to obtain incriminating evidence that could stand up to libel claims should her editors print it. This certainly played a role in her death.

Little changed for investigative reporters after the death of Guerin. Ireland still boasts among the most reckless libel laws in the world. The Defamation Act of 2009[5] was the last major update to Ireland's libel laws and included no provision for an upward cap on damages awarded for defamation. The Act combined libel and slander, recognising them both as one entity—defamation—in the eyes of the law. Under the Act it is possible to sue for defamation even if one has not mentioned an individual by name but "if it could reasonably be understood as referring to him or her." Further, the Act defined a "defamatory statement" as "a statement that tends to injure a person's reputation in the eyes of reasonable members of society" while adding "defamation is actionable without proof of special damage". These parameters, especially the lack of a burden of proof for the plaintiff to show that they have endured financial or real professional loss, make Ireland a favourable place to initiate proceedings against an individual for defamation. So favourable in fact, that Ireland has become an attractive destination for so-called libel tourism for international celebrities. In 2014, Justin Timberlake and Jessica Biel sued Heat Magazine over an alleged inappropriate incident involving Timberlake in a Paris nightclub. The case was eventually settled out of court with Timberlake receiving an apology from Heat. In 2019, American lifestyle coach Tony Robbins sued BuzzFeed in Ireland over the publication of articles suggesting sexual impropriety on Robbins' behalf. Both were viewed[6] as cases where the plaintiffs chose Ireland, despite tenuous links to the jurisdiction, because of more favourable defamation laws compared to the UK or USA.

In 2014, Monica Leech successfully sued Independent News and Media, publisher of the Irish Independent, Sunday Independent and

Sunday World among others. A court awarded Leech nearly €1.9 million in damages plus fees after finding that the Evening Herald had defamed her by claiming, in a series of articles in 2004, that she had obtained government contracts while carrying on an extramarital affair with then government Minister Martin Cullen. Speaking to the International Press Institute in 2017, Micael Kealey, in-house counsel for Associated Newspapers stated that the Leech verdict had catastrophic implications for the national press; "€2 million is enough to close a number of newspapers." He continued, "You are looking at the potential of closure for one defamation case. Unsurprisingly, as a consequence, the press have become terribly risk averse, and that impacts not just on traditional investigative journalism but across the board."[7] The 2009 Defamation Act did help news publishers by allowing judges to direct the jury in relation to appropriate damages and by allowing the Supreme Court to reevaluate settlements deemed extreme. However, newspaper publishers in Ireland, the International Press Institute concluded, remain risk-averse and are more likely to settle defamation cases out of court even if they believe they have not committed defamation, rather than risk facing a jury. This means they are less likely to engage in investigative journalism.

Indeed, some of the defamation judgments, along with significant payouts, that have gone in favour of individuals who have sued media outlets in recent years seem punitive. In 2015, David Christie was wrongly identified in a nine-second TV3 news report as being solicitor Thomas Byrne, whom Mr Christie was representing during a fraud trial. Despite TV3 issuing an immediate and comprehensive apology for the mistake, a judge found they had defamed the misidentified solicitor and was ordered to pay €140,000 in damages.[8] The Sunday World was forced to pay €900,000 in damages to Martin McDonagh stemming from a libel case in 2008. The Sunday World referred to McDonagh as a "Traveller drug king" in a 1999 article while McDonagh was being held in custody over a major drugs seizure in Co. Sligo. McDonagh was later released without charge. During the case, the presiding judge found that the Sunday World had proven that McDonagh was a tax evader and a criminal but not that he was a drug dealer. The Sunday World appealed the decision to the Court of Appeal in 2015 which found that McDonagh was a drug dealer and part of the decision was overturned. However, McDonagh was given leave to appeal to the High Court which, in 2017, found that the Court of Appeal was wrong to have reversed the initial decision. Eventually, McDonagh was awarded a vastly reduced sum and both parties settled costs outside of court. The entire legal process dragged out for a decade because it represented an existential threat to the Sunday World.

Aside from the threat of personal bankruptcy for journalists and publication-shuttering payouts from defamation cases, Irish journalists and publishers face yet another chilling legal threat—the increased use of Strategic Legal Actions Against Public Participation or SLAPP lawsuits. Such lawsuits are designed to shut down investigative journalism or legitimate criticisms and are usually used by wealthy and powerful individuals and bodies against more economically vulnerable targets. A form of legal warfare—or lawfare—the aim of a SLAPP is not to win a defamation settlement, rather to drag out costly legal proceedings to financially bleed out their target. Sinn Féin in particular have been accused of employing SLAPP suits against individual journalists and their publishers. In March 2020, Sunday Life, a Belfast paper, posted an image that included Sinn Féin constituency organiser Liam Lappin. The photograph, which was taken at the 2019 Sinn Féin Newry and Armagh Christmas party, included 14 people one of whom, the focus of the story, was Frank McCabe. McCabe was described in the accompanying article as being an "Officer Commanding (OC) of the IRA in south Armagh".[9] Lappin sued Mediahuis, the publisher, for defamation, even though he was not named or referenced in the photo or accompanying article. His legal team argued that his inclusion in the photograph meant "in their ordinary meaning and innuendo…that the plaintiff is a member of a criminal and terrorist organisation operating under the name and style of the IRA." Lappin also sued the journalist who wrote the piece, Suzanne Breen, as well as Ruth Dudley Edwards who shared the article alongside a comment in a post on social media. In November 2023, the presiding judge threw out the case calling Lappin's claim "utterly unreasonable".[10]

Northern Ireland Sinn Féin assembly member Gerry Kelly sued journalist Dr Malachi O'Doherty and Ruth Dudley Edwards for claims made in two 2019 radio interviews and in print that Kelly had shot a prison guard during a breakout from the Maze Prison in 1983. Kelly's lawsuit was badly undermined by his recounting of said event in his autobiography and, in January 2024, the Master of Belfast High Court, Evan Bell struck out the case against O'Doherty stating, "rather than being a genuine attempt to defend a reputation which has been damaged by an untruth, the proceedings are what has been referred to as a SLAPP, namely an attempt to silence two bothersome journalists with the threat of legal costs. The proceedings appear to be a strategic effort to intimidate them, to deprive them of time and resources, and ultimately to silence them."[11] Bell's ruling was supported by the fact that Kelly sued the journalists personally and not the news outlets on which the comments were made.

In November 2023, Sinn Féin TD Chris Andrews initiated defamation proceedings against The Irish Times and political correspondent Harry McGee over an article relating to Andrews's October 7th Hamas-Israel tweets. In an Irish Times article in the days after the attack, McGee wrote a piece which analysed the response of several left-wing politicians who seemingly refused to condemn the attack outright. In it he included a tweet by Andrews which stated, "It seems that according to the EU and Ireland only Palestine has no right to defend itself against murder, torture and apartheid." Details of how Andrews believes he was defamed are unclear at this point. The author of the piece simply provided Andrews' own tweet, apparently without additional commentary, making it difficult to see where any claim for defamation could be made. In April 2022, Sinn Féin leader Mary Lou McDonald initiated legal action against RTE for defamation. The claim relates to statements made on Morning Ireland in February 2022 about how women who were the victims of sexual assault by members of Sinn Féin and the IRA were treated by the party. The case came a year after RTE settled a defamation case with Sinn Féin TD Donnchadh Ó Laoghaire after he took action against RTE's Liveline radio show and its presenter Joe Duffy. Disparaging remarks were made about him on the show and he received a settlement in excess of €150,000.

In November 2023, Reporters Without Frontiers (RWF) wrote an open letter to the Sinn Féin leader about the conduct of her party in the wake of the Chris Andrews affair. In the letter, RWF wrote, "You should...be aware that the legal actions that Sinn Féin's members are currently taking against the media have the hallmarks of SLAPPs... Moreover, the number of legal actions that have been filed by Sinn Féin members points to a coordinated campaign against the media in Ireland." After referencing McDonald's own legal case against RTE, the letter concluded, "We urge you to be mindful of the chilling effect that legal actions have, not only on the media, but on our democracy."[12]

The stakes then, since the 1990s and persisting after defamation law reform in 2009, are extraordinarily high for investigative journalists. A most minor and accidental error in reporting can result in personal bankruptcy or bankruptcy for the journalist and news outlet. Even where no error has occurred, because of SLAPP actions, investigative journalists can be bankrupted and journalists and news outlets can be intimidated into dropping a legitimate story due to the cost of defending vexatious lawsuits. This has made political investigative journalism extremely unattractive for Irish news outlets and even regular political journalism—simply reporting events and stated facts—can, as Sinn Féin have made clear, be extremely risky. In a Dáil debate on November 8th, 2023, then Taoiseach Varadkar addressed Sinn Féin's frequent resort to legal action stating, "To see a Member in this House not just suing a major newspaper but also personally suing a journalist is only designed to do one thing; it is designed to make journalists afraid. It is designed to make them think twice about what they write and that is wrong. There are other ways to get redress and corrections and clarifications."[13] While Varadkar's apparent defence of press freedom appears noble, over the course of the 33rd Dáil Fine Gael and Fianna Fáil enacted an equally anti-democratic method of shutting down political investigative journalism—massive state funding and top advisory positions in government for journalists. Whereas Sinn Féin used brute legal force to shut down pesky journalists, Fine Gael and Fianna Fáil ploughed hundreds of millions of euros into propping up the national media. They created a financial incentive culture for news outlets not to conduct political investigative journalism while throwing in the added incentive of well-paid advisory positions for those journalists who might otherwise do so.

A state-funded national media

Even outside of the cost of fighting legal actions, Ireland's small population—just over five million including close to a million non-nationals—makes it tremendously difficult for privately owned media outlets to survive independently. This has led to a series of consolidations and restructuring of national outlets. The Irish Times Trust collectively owns The Irish Times, Irish Examiner, Evening Echo and a string of local newspapers. They hold a majority stake in major regional radio station Waterford Local Radio and apart from owning the Times and Examiner websites, they also own the BreakingNews and MyHome websites among others. Despite all of these assets, The Irish Times Trust posted a net profit of just €2.1 million before tax in 2023 but suffered a €5 million loss before tax the year before.[14] The company recorded an operating profit of €2.9 million in 2021.[15]

Mediahuis Ireland, whose parent company is based in Belgium, bought out Independent News and Media in 2019. Alongside The Irish Times Trust, they are the other big name in Irish print media. Their assets include the print and online versions of the Irish Independent, Sunday Independent, Sunday World, the Herald, Belfast Telegraph and a host of landmark regional papers including the Limerick Leader, The Sligo Champion and The Kerryman. In 2022, the company engaged in extensive restructuring which included offering a round of voluntary redundancy after posting a loss of €5.1 million. In 2023, the company reported a net profit of €1.3 million.[16]

Irish radio is dominated by the UK-based Bauer Media Audio. Bauer bought out Dennis O'Brien's Communicorp for more than €100 million in 2021. Bauer's major assets include TodayFM, Newstalk FM and 98FM among others. Bauer has not published detailed financial records since the acquisition but previous records show the company made a loss of €700,000 in 2018 and a profit of under €1.6 million in 2019[17] though a restructuring of the company prior to the sale had led to optimism about future profitability. A surge in radio listenership during the COVID pandemic, as well as a post-pandemic sector-wide advertising revenue growth of 4% in 2023, indicates that Bauer Radio, whose flagship assets TodayFM and Newstalk have expanded their listenership, is likely a profitable entity.

Ireland appears to have an extremely diverse privately owned print, digital and radio media landscape. Yet, The Irish Times Trust along with Mediahuis and Bauer (both foreign-owned) own the vast majority of outlets. None of these three posts large or consistent annual profits. Aside from one or two legitimate or vexatious defamation lawsuits being enough to seriously damage if not force the sale of these companies, they further could not survive without government intervention. In a bid to boost print media sales, the government announced in September 2022 the complete eradication of VAT—previously 9%—on both the print and digital versions of newspapers. The change came into effect in January 2023 as part of the annual budget. Announcing the move, then Minister for Finance, Paschal Donohoe, stated that "The Government is aware of the critical role that newspapers play in our society, from reporting on local communities to holding those in power to account" before adding that the €39 million a year tax break was "in line with the Government's commitment to support an independent press". Ironically, of course, while Donohoe promoted the move as supportive of an "independent press", it actually made the national press financially viable only at the will of the government.[18] While the media was getting a total VAT tax reduction, other struggling domestic industries such as the hospitality industry were subject to a VAT increase. At the same time that VAT on media went from 9% to 0%, it was raised from 9% to 13.5% for hospitality. The results were devastating. Throughout 2023 and 2024, as the government took record numbers of hotel beds in tourist hotspots out of circulation for use as IPAS centres, the continued VAT on the hospitality industry crushed hundreds of private businesses. By August 2024, 577 restaurants, cafes and other food-related hospitality businesses had gone out of business and claims that the government chose to save the media while leaving hospitality to fail weren't long in being raised.[19] As the media VAT reduction was announced in the Dáil, Aontú party leader Peadar Tóibín tweeted, "The winks, guffaws & grins from FF & FG TDs to the Press Gallery in #Budget23 as the Minister announced a zero VAT rate for newspapers, was more than a little uncomfortable."[20] Tóibín articulated what many others also surmised, that despite Donohoe's claims that the move was to ensure an independent press, it was actually a mutually beneficial quid pro quo arrangement. Former Sunday Times political correspondent Hugh O'Connell tweeted, "Cries of 'hear, hear' from the press gallery as Paschal Donohoe announces the abolition of VAT on newspapers and digital publications"[21] before adding, "The politicians were pretty happy about it as well."[22] The move ensured that the national media would remain solvent and, more importantly, grateful to the government.

After requests from Carol Nolan on the floor of the Dáil, the government released details on how much public money it had spent on advertising from 2019 to 2024.[23] Across all departments, €23 million was spent on print media adverts and a further €14 million was spent on digital advertising—a total of €37 million over five years. While the government did not give specific details about the nature of the adverts, RTE, private print and digital news outlets and social media networks all received advertising revenue. Considering Bauer, The Irish Times Trust and Mediahuis's precarious financial position during this time period, the substantial injection of public funding makes a mockery of any claims to the national press being independent. This is more strikingly apparent with the national broadcaster.

The national broadcaster, RTE, is a statutory body, which means that while its board is elected by the state, it still has significant room to operate independently in terms of hiring practices and day-to-day management decision-making. It operates off of a dual income model meaning that it receives significant public funding and commercial revenue via advertising. It is state-regulated by Coimisiún na Meán (Broadcasting Authority of Ireland prior to March 2023). In the twenty years to 2023, RTE received more than €3.7 billion in licence fee revenue. Despite this windfall, RTE remains heavily reliant on the state to remain solvent. In 2021 it recorded a profit of €2.4 million which was wiped out in 2022 with a loss of €2.8 million.[24] This was compounded by a loss of €9.1 million in 2023 which was heavily influenced by a loss in licence renewal revenue.[25] These losses were incurred while the government provided hidden buoyancy to the broadcasters via advertising revenue. In July 2024, then Minister for Media, Catherine Martin (Green Party), announced a rescue package for the network amounting to €725 million over three years.[26] While RTE is a statutory body in law, it is dependent on the state for its survival, even more so than the nation's print, digital media and radio outlets. In Ireland, in the course of the 33rd Dáil, all news media became dependent upon the state for survival.

The 2023 eradication of VAT, injection of government advertising and RTE's three-quarter of a billion Euro bailout eased the national media's existential dread. Still, in order to profit and grow in a crowded media landscape, all would have to suckle harder on the state's teat and apply for various grant funding. An essential revenue stream for audio and television broadcasters both public and private has been the "Sound and Vision" rounds of funding provided by the state via the government broadcasting regulatory body Coimisiún na Meán and its predecessor, the Broadcasting Authority of Ireland. These rounds of funding provide cash grants for broadcasters to produce topic-specific content for air. Coimisiún na Meán is an organisation that is built around embedding Social Justice Theory into public broadcasting. The commission's website states, "We are Coimisiún na Meán, Ireland's agency for developing and regulating a thriving, diverse, creative, safe and trusted media landscape". They go on, "We are deeply committed to promoting and upholding fundamental rights, ensuring that our media landscape contributes to an open, democratic society." In their values statement, they make explicit reference to Diversity, Equality and Inclusion (DEI) as their driving principles: "Equality, Diversity and Inclusion (EDI) is at the heart of our People Strategy, a key enabler of our first Organisational Strategy."[27] This commitment to DEI as well as contributing to an "open, democratic society" is increasingly evident in their Sound and Vision funding rounds.

In May 2021, in round 38 of Sound and Vision funding, €7.2 million was awarded to 104 radio and television projects. Some of the highlighted projects on the scheme's website included *Our Unique Tales*, for Bauer Media's Spin South West Radio, which was described as a documentary that "shares the experience of high-profile Irish LGBTQIA+ figures". *Irish Women in Harmony* for Bauer's Newstalk Radio was a documentary "telling the story of how a collective of more than 40 Irish female artists came together to record one of the most successful musical collaborations of 2020 and raise over €215K for domestic abuse charity Safe Ireland." The notes to the funding round stated that aside from fostering diverse viewpoints, positive discrimination had been employed to insure that women were prioritised for grant allocation: "In recent rounds of the Sound & Vision Scheme, the assessment of applications has included consideration of the number of women in key creative roles – producer, director, writer, director of photography and editor – as a measure to support greater gender equality in the industry."[28] In round 40 of Sound and Vision, distributed six months after round 38, again the focus was on diversity as €5.9 million was distributed to 40 radio and 26 TV projects. Among the projects showcased on the scheme's website was *Sisterhood and Sanctuary* for Cork Community Television. This documentary "tells the story of the women from the 'Saoirse-Ethnic Hands On Deck' co-operative. The women will talk about their personal experiences of moving to Cork as migrants and reflect on their lived experience as migrants in Ireland and building 'Saoirse'."

The Saoirse-Ethnic NGO is an organisation that seeks to end direct provision in Ireland. *Back on Red* which aired on Bauer's Red FM was described as a series of 20-minute interviews "about newly established musicians with migrant backgrounds who are working in the Irish contemporary hip-hop, rap and soul genres."[29] Why these hungry new music acts couldn't be interviewed without state financial intervention is unclear.

€6.4 million was distributed to 48 radio projects and 26 television projects under round 42 in March 2022. Among these was the ethnically diverse casted *Twig*, an RTE adaptation of the Greek tragedy Antigone set in contemporary Dublin. *Until Death?* was a three-part documentary on the role of the NGO Women's Aid and "the issue of domestic abuse and femicide over the last three decades and into the future". It aired on Virgin Media One off the back of the Ashling Murphy murder. Commenting on this 42nd round of funding, Chief Executive of the Broadcasting Authority, Celene Craig, stated, "all TV projects recommended for funding have some female representation in lead creative roles, with just over 80% of funding for TV applications recommended going to projects that have indicated half or more key roles are filled by women."[30] In August 2022, in Round 43, €6 million was distributed to 36 radio projects and 22 television projects. *Faithless* was a six-part comedy-drama by Virgin Media One which "follows an Irish-Egyptian father who attempts to raise his three young mixed-race daughters alone". TG4 won a grant to produce *Kneecap,* a dark comedy about the controversial nationalist rap group. Bauer's Red FM won funding for a 15-part environmental show.[31] Announcing the Round of grants, Chief Executive Celine Craig again praised the Authority's commitment to positive discrimination in favour of female talent.

In December 2022, Round 44 of Sound and Vision funding was the most ideologically driven round to date. It also represented direct state interference in public and private broadcasting. €5 million was made available "specifically for programming related to climate change and climate action". The Round was co-funded by the Department of Tourism, Culture, Arts, Gaeltacht, Sport and Media

and the Department of Environment, Climate and Communications
—both departments run by the Green Party, with the latter belonging
to Catherine Martin, who would further bail out RTE. Round 44
clearly impinged upon the independence of the national media. As
noted, both public and private broadcasters were, by 2022, heavily
reliant upon government grants for survival. Ten radio projects and 15
television projects were successful. *Ours to Protect* funded a network
of 24 local radio stations to produce 1,248 programmes to use "the
power of local radio to work together to educate and empower behav-
ioural changes" relating to climate change. RTE, particularly children's programming, were the main beneficiaries with Virgin Media
One and Dublin Community Television also profiting.[32]

While DEI directed grants continued to be handed out in subsequent rounds of Sound and Vision, Round 54 in November 2024, the
last of the 33rd Dáil, was once more given over wholly to an explicit
political agenda with grants given for the "production of content
focusing on the voices of new Irish communities".[33] €3.9 million was
allocated to 35 radio and television projects. Announcing the move,
Rónán Ó Domhnaill, Media Development Commissioner at
Coimisiún na Meán stated, "Coimisiún na Meán is committed to
ensuring a diversity and plurality of content, reflective of the people
of Ireland including their languages, traditions, religious, and
cultural diversity. We are delighted to have an opportunity to support
projects which give a voice to this diversity." He further thanked
Green Media Minister Catherine Martin for supplying "an extra €2
million in funding." Among the successful grant winners showcased
on the Commission's website was *Welcome To Moore Street* which was
broadcast on RTE and described as a series "not about immigration,
rather it gives a fascinating insight into the lives of both 'old' and
'new' Irish who are fighting to make a living here in Dublin's north
inner city." *My Ireland Too,* broadcast on Virgin Media Television, was
a documentary series about "young asylum seekers and migrants in
the Cork area [who] navigate the challenges of building new lives
amidst a sinister rise of discrimination and racist sentiment, representing an honest and authentic view of the migrant experience in

Ireland". *Bia Úr,* broadcast on TG4, was a documentary series that "introduces audiences to the cultures and traditions of new and exciting foods through the stories of people who have made Ireland home". *Mo Shaol, Do Shaol,* broadcast on Cúla4, was a show where "young viewers get a taste of the major events celebrated by new Irish communities". *Mmanwu* was a radio drama broadcast by Newstalk focused on the "complexities of maternal struggle, mental health, and the clash between tradition and modernity set against the vibrant backdrop of Dublin and Onitsha, Nigeria".

Many of the radio and television stations that availed of the DEI-driven grants made available by the Broadcasting Authority of Ireland and later Coimisiún na Meán during the course of the 33rd Dáil may well have done so having the same progressive political and ideological vision as the Commission. However, as mentioned, every private and public radio and television station in Ireland was entirely dependent upon state funding for survival during this time—be it through advertising revenue or reliance on Sound and Vision grant money. With this in mind, the increased political intervention in the Sound and Vision programme, culminating in rounds of funding given entirely to government agendas, represents a profoundly anti-democratic attempt at social engineering through mass media propaganda. Radio and news stations that were reliant on Sound and Vision funding were not able to act as independent media outlets. And while the grant funding did not 'editorialise', that is make any specific content demands as a prerequisite for applying for a grant, only those which toed the government line, as well as the Commission's DEI vision, were selected for funding. Non-conformist or critical voices were tuned out.

Beginning in 2025, Coimisiún na Meán began making grant funding available to print and digital news outlets for the first time. In January 2025, €5.7 million was made available as part of a "Local Democracy Reporting Scheme" and a "Courts Reporting Scheme". Though the grants project was announced in January 2025 under the 34th Dáil, funding was secured by Catherine Martin in 2024. The funding helped create 71 new roles for journalists as well as providing job security for 30 freelance journalists. Announcing the grants, Coimisiún na Meán Media Development Commissioner, Rónán Ó Domhnaill, stated that this would be just the first round in a set of six Coimisiún na Meán projects in national print and digital media in the coming years.[34] By creating or enhancing 100 journalist roles at a time when the industry is already dependent upon state handouts for survival, the Commission is simply tying the national and local media to state funding to such a degree that any claims to Ireland having a free and independent national and local press is simply not credible. These are 100 journalist roles that cannot survive without direct and sustained state funding. Successive rounds of Sound and Vision funding have shown that projects that have a strong DEI focus and are politically progressive attain funding, while those that are critical do not. Having seen the politically-motivated content sponsored by the Commission over the course of the 33rd Dáil, it is entirely reasonable to assume that this foray into state-sponsored print and digital news will bear similar fruit.

Outside of Coimisiún na Meán, the 33rd Dáil's most overt intervention in national news has been the establishment of the Global Ireland Media Challenge Fund (GIMC) which was sponsored by the Department of Foreign Affairs. In June 2018, Taoiseach Leo Varadkar and Minister for Foreign Affairs and Trade, Simon Coveney launched the "Global Ireland – Ireland's Global Footprint to 2025" programme.[35] The purpose of the programme was to "double the scope and impact of Ireland's global footprint" internationally by 2025 in areas of trade, diplomacy, international aid and expanding Irish influence beyond traditional channels into Asia, Africa and the Middle East. In a wildly ambitious vision for tiny Ireland, the programme stated, "At a global level, it will enhance our ability to advocate for and achieve our foreign policy objectives, including international development, peace, disarmament and security, while strengthening Ireland's engagement with its 70 million-strong diaspora and bringing our rich culture and heritage to wider audiences." To support this programme, the GIMC was established in 2020 and an initial €900k was made available over two years to national media outlets. Essentially, the Department of Foreign Affairs handed out funding for the national media to perform Public Relations duties for the Global Ireland programme. Between 2022 and 2024, funding expanded to €1.65 million with The Journal receiving €180k, RTE receiving €720k, Virgin Media receiving €400k, the Business Post, Reach Media (publisher of the Irish Daily Star and Irish Daily Mirror) and The Examiner all receiving €100k, while Bauer received €50k.

In October 2024, the Sunday Independent (which did not receive funding) asked the participating media outlets for details on how they spent their funding. The answers they received were vague. The Department of Foreign Affairs had not yet published a Memorandum of Understanding detailing outputs. The Examiner did not respond to a request about spending. A Bauer spokesman replied, "Some stories covered include the UN General Assembly in New York, St Patrick's Day in the US, peace missions by the Tánaiste to the Middle East and several EU summits." RTE used the money to hire three new international correspondents, one in New York, one in Eastern Europe and one in Kenya.[36] The Independent submitted a Freedom of Information request (FoI) to the Department of Foreign Affairs seeking access to internal documents relating to the scheme. Among the internal memos it was discovered that applicants had been encouraged, among other things, to place "more emphasis on the wider topic of climate change" and to "focus on EU issues such as the rise of populism and disinformation". When contacted for comment on the scheme by the Sunday Independent, Aontú's Peadar Tóibín stated, "The idea that a government department is suggesting the agenda of a media organisation is quite shocking. It proves the adage that there is no such thing as a free lunch. Already in this country we have NGOs massively dependent on government funding. This dependency is a key part of the political media ... NGO bubble at the heart of the administration. This is not healthy for democracy."[37]

Propping up the public and private national print, digital and broadcast media via tax breaks, advertising revenue and grants in return for political messaging was not the only way that the 33rd Dáil

fostered media dependency on the state. They also forged the largest
and most lucrative political journalist-to-government advisor pipeline in the history of the state and in doing so, disincentivised investigative journalism into government affairs through the promise of a
career and salary far exceeding what any Irish journalist could hope
to earn. In February 2025, the Irish Mail on Sunday reported that the
cost of Ministerial advisors came to €7.5 million a year during the
33rd Dáil. They projected that figure to rise to €10 million per year
over the course of the 34th Dáil. These special advisors are disproportionately drawn from media circles. By the close of the 33rd Dáil, the
leadership of Simon Harris (8), Micheal Martin (5) and Roderic
O'Gorman (7) had a total of twenty advisors between them and in
total there were 69 special advisors spread out across all government
departments.[38] Taoiseach Simon Harris' special advisors cost the
taxpayer just under €993k per year without pension contributions or
further expenses. Tánaiste Martin's advisors cost more than €700k
per year. The precise figure isn't clear because one advisor, Prof. Alan
Ahearne was on secondment from the National University of Ireland
and his salary wasn't made public. Roderic O'Gorman—whose party
played such a financially proliferate and outsized role in the 33rd Dáil
—cost the taxpayer over €952k per year in advisors.

Over the course of the 33rd Dáil, there were 18 prominent former
journalists and editors employed as special advisors. 12 of these were
notable former politics journalists or editors: Sarah Bardon (€167,264),
formerly politics correspondent of The Irish Times; Ciara Phelan
(€100,885), formerly politics correspondent of the Irish Examiner;
Susan Mitchell (€121,048), formerly deputy editor for the Business
Post; Chris Donoghue (€114,347), formerly political editor for
Communicorp; Fiach Kelly (€106,518), formerly deputy political
editor at The Irish Times; Caroline Murphy (€116,634), formerly of
RTE; Juno McEnroe (€113,693), formerly Irish Examiner political
correspondent; Niall O'Connor (€117,303), formerly political correspondent with the Irish Independent; Collette Sexton (€94,487),
formerly senior political correspondent for The Irish Times; Páraic
Gallagher (€109,414), formerly chief political correspondent at

Newstalk; Paul Clarkson (€156-€178k), formerly managing editor of The Sun UK; and Michael Brennan (€98k-€122k), formerly politics editor of The Sunday Business Post. Added to this group who served at various times during the 33rd Dáil, in 2025, six more journalists were added to the 34th Dáil as special advisors. Hugh O'Connell, formerly politics editor at The Sunday Times (Ireland) and Sharon McGowan, formerly a politics correspondent also at The Sunday Times (Ireland) were both poached by the new government as was Aiden Corkery, former political correspondent at The Sunday Business Post. This grouping of political journalists and editors represents a significant talent drain from Ireland's national media landscape. But, as media outlets struggle financially, top jobs, such as a politics editor in a competitive newsroom, which traditionally could range between €80k-€100k, are increasingly insecure positions subject to pay freezes and reductions. When the government steps in with the offer of a special advisor position beginning at over €100k, it is an easy decision for most journalists to make.

The recruitment of Hugh O'Connell was seen as a coup for the government when he joined Simon Harris' team as Deputy Government Press Secretary in January 2025, not only because he was arguably Ireland's leading politics editor but because he had broken stories critical of Fine Gael earlier in his career. In 2015 he wrote a piece for The Sunday Business Post critical of Fine Gael MEPs' expenses and in 2019 he wrote a piece for the Irish Independent which criticised Fine Gael for being out of touch with young people on housing and environmental matters. Most notably, in November 2024, in the run-up to the election for the 34th Dáil, O'Connell interviewed the victim of an assault by John McGahon who would go on to lose his bid for a Fine Gael seat in Co. Louth. Getting a potential thorn in their side on board was a major win for the government and, obviously, a blow for the national media in its role of holding the powerful to account. More than that, it would have been massively demoralising for rank-and-file journalists seeing a leading talent unable to resist stepping across the aisle. It was a stark reminder for those journalists who still believed in their vocation of just who is master and who is servant in Irish politics and also a tantalising carrot. If you play your cards right, you can go from standing in the rain chasing a story outside the Dáil to shaping the story from a cosy office inside.

This raises a series of important questions: Have the government's financial and employment arrangements with Irish news outlets and journalists resulted in a discernible quid pro quo benefit on the government's end? Has the national media been reluctant to conduct investigative inquiries into government spending or other aspects of governance? Has the media engaged in consensus-forming reporting on behalf of government policies that would be deemed controversial? Has the media provided favourable coverage to the government at crucial moments, say, in the run-up to elections, either by giving disproportional coverage to the government over opposition or by outright ignoring new and alternative parties? It would appear so.

Financial scandals without consequences

The single greatest financial scandal of the 32nd and 33rd Dáil has been the construction of the National Children's Hospital in Dublin. In April 2016, then acting Minister for Health, Leo Varadkar announced that the state had acquired planning permission to build a state-of-the-art children's hospital. Speaking on RTE Radio he told the public that funding of up to €650 million had been secured and that the project would be completed by 2019 and "short of an asteroid hitting the planet" the hospital would be operational by 2020.[39] A year later, with Simon Harris at the helm as Minister for Health, and construction firm BAM chosen as the preferred bidder for the project, the projected costs had risen by €300 million, excluding the cost of IT and electronic equipment which was expected to cost another €100 million.[40] Before a sod had been turned, the price of the hospital had spiralled to one billion Euro. The completion time for the project was also revised to November 2022. This budget was quickly blown through. By October 2022 with completion nowhere in sight, €1.13 billion had been spent and the government had no firm final cost estimate except to say that it would cost more than €1.43 billion. In February 2024, then Taoiseach Varadkar told the Dáil that the cost for the project would have a hard cap of €2.2 billion but more would have to be paid out in legal disputes with the developer long after the building opened—which he promised would be October 2024.[41] Needless to say, October 2024 came and went with the opening date being pushed back to 2026 and in February 2025, the contractor, BAM, was seeking an extra €850 million to secure its completion.[42]

A scandal of this proportion should have taken down a government or two and ended individual political careers. It didn't. While the scandal was heavily covered in the national media, that coverage was largely confined to reporting ministerial comments on the matter, progress updates as well as providing timelines of building delays and costs. What was absent was any incisive investigative reports into the matter which would firmly hold politicians to account and allow the public to decipher exactly why the building took so long to complete and why it has become one of the most expensive unfinished buildings in Europe. This lack of interrogation allowed Varadkar, Harris and Stephen Donnelly, all Ministers with direct responsibility for the fiasco, to skate by unscathed. In May 2024, then Tánaiste, Micheal Martin, availed of Dáil privilege which prevented him from being sued for defamation to claim that delays on the completion of the hospital were "likely to be part of a commercial strategy by BAM to try and extract more money and more funding from the Irish people".[43] This was widely covered in the media and became the government's default position on the fiasco. As late as February 2025, at the outset of the 34th Dáil, then outgoing Taoiseach Simon Harris was still being given a free pass as he lumped the blame for the delays and spiralling costs onto BAM. Speaking about the last potential €850 million tranche of cash supposedly being sought by the developer, Harris was quoted across the national press striking a defiant tone, stating that the government would "robustly push back" on any extra demands for fees.[44] Accusations by the opposition, such as when Mary Lou McDonald told the Dáil that the project had "descended into complete farce" and that "The buck stops with you, the Government" in September 2024, were sporadically covered by the press. However, this amounted to 'he said, she said' reporting of Dáil events. Except the buck never stops with the government and nobody is ever held to account. That is the job of the media and in the absence of high-profile investigative pieces by the national press the truth of who was to blame remained unknown as the public went to vote on the composition of the 34th Dáil in November 2024, which, unsurprisingly, resulted in the lowest voter turnout in the history of the state with a 59.7% turnout.

The National Children's Hospital was only the most prominent example of the media's unwillingness to hold the government to account on its reckless spending. Several other smaller examples of extreme government financial mismanagement came to light in late 2024 and early 2025, but media coverage consisted of little more than reporting on scandals as they unfolded, taking government members' comments at face value. No investigative work was done to find out who—exactly—was responsible for the waste. In late August and early September, after widespread outrage on social media, the national press picked up the story of a compact bicycle shed outside of the Dáil which the Office of Public Works (OPW) reported cost €336k. Initial reports focused on the fantastic overspend, which included €121k on steelworks, €45k on granite, €38k on surveying and 'outerwork', €30k for 'dry work' and €23k for 'day work'. When the press asked how such an overspend could occur and who was responsible for the waste, Dáil Ceann Comhairle Sean O'Fearghail said, "I know that I speak for everyone at this house, and I say that it's a profound embarrassment, and the depth of public anger is entirely justified" before adding "lessons must be and will be learned".[45] When it emerged in September 2024 that in addition to the bike shed, a security hut outside of the Dáil had cost €1.4 million, again the media simply allowed politicians to offer a promise to do better next time. When asked about the overspend, Micheal Martin said he was "shocked to hear the figure" and that it was "ridiculous", before adding, "I think we need a fundamental review now of what's happening there, and full transparency in front of the Oireachtas in terms of the actual breakdown of costs."[46] As with the bike shed, a cost breakdown was supplied by the OPW, the media reprinted the costs, both the government and press moved on and no individual was held to account.

It was only when Peadar Tóibín, who was a member of the Oireachtas Finance Committee, looked into the matter further that he was able to confirm that the developer for the bike shed was Sensori Facilities Management (SFM). SFM was co-founded by Michael Stone. Stone was a close friend of Fine Gael minister Paschal Donohoe and the two were embroiled in controversy in 2023 when it emerged Stone paid for the putting up and taking down of Donohoe's election posters in 2016 and 2020 with the costs not publicly declared in Donohoe's election expenses. Tóibín went on to lay out how Stone sold his interest in Sensori for a tidy profit of €17 million after it had secured potentially lucrative deals with the OPW and shortly before Donohoe took charge of the OPW as Minister for Public Expenditure, National Development Plan Delivery and Reform from 2022 to 2025.[47] While Tóibín made no direct accusations of impropriety, he laid out a series of events that suggested that the massive overspend was the result of potential cronyism between government members and developers. Any investigative journalist and news outlet worth their salt would have picked up what Tóibín was laying out for them and dug deeper into the affair. Instead, Tóibín's efforts went ignored with outlets playing it safe, simply reporting OPW overspend figures and giving softball questions to government ministers to throw out cliches like "lessons will be learned". It was no surprise then when it turned out that no lessons were learned and further scandals broke. In January 2025 it was reported that the OPW paid €490k to replace a 70-meter stretch of wall around the Dublin HQ of the Workplace Relations Commission. Again, Sensori was the construction company involved. Even this led to no further digging.

Because the national media had abandoned investigative journalism, a culture of massive financial waste was allowed to go unnoticed for years. When that culture came to light, instead of belatedly investigating the individual cases to determine if it was simply government incompetence or something more corrupt, the media chose to report events as they unfolded and allow public officials to shirk responsibility by not sufficiently pushing back on their "lessons learned" platitudes. Not a single individual in any of these scandals was identified as being at fault and not a single person resigned or faced any consequences. By not holding the government to account, the media allowed a culture of overspending to fester. Eye-watering sums of public money were wasted with the government always as angry and betrayed as the public. Blame was always allowed to land somewhere far off in the ether of the government machine but never on the shoulders of an actual individual.

Alignment of NGOs, government and national media

Traditionally, the key driving force for the media to perform investigative journalism, aside perhaps from a genuine mission to hold the powerful to account, was that the buzz of an important scoop would sell physical copies of newspapers. Because Irish newspapers and media outlets now get enough money to survive, if not thrive, from the government, the motivation to publish investigations that can potentially harm the government and damage that fine economic balance is no longer there. After all, the government give them enough to survive but that could change at any time with the reintroduction of VAT, revocation of grants or the withholding of advertising revenue. The government and national media are business partners and that partnership requires that news outlets direct their investigations towards safe targets for both.

This is largely reflected in the few investigative shows and series that exist in the national media. In the first year of the 33rd Dáil, RTE's *RTE Investigates* and *Prime Time* did actually undertake a broad range of investigations related to government performance. Through the first half of 2021 there was an interesting series of stories on the Health Services Executive (HSE) dysfunction during COVID. There was an investigation into state-owned development sites lying idle that could be used to alleviate the housing crisis. There were investigations into problems with the national Charities Regulator as well as homelessness, and investigations into council-level political improprieties. Notably, in April 2021 there was even an investigation into financial waste at the OPW, titled "We're paying too much – value for money and the Office of Public Works". In the investigation, Allen Morgan, who had just retired from his position of Managing Valuer at the OPW in 2017 after 37 years, bluntly stated that "We're paying too much for what we're getting... budgeting is not at the forefront of each individual project or each individual property that we acquire or lease."[48] The interview pointed to a culture of overspending, waste and extraordinary property acquisition fees being paid out without the Managing Valuer's knowledge. The OPW had also awarded contracts to bidders without offering public tenders in breach of guidelines. While the report uncovered a culture of profound financial waste and systematic dysfunction within the OPW which should have been followed up on, it stopped short of looking deeper into potential impropriety between government ministers and individual developers. More importantly, after this report, the issue was dropped by RTE, allowing the problems uncovered to be quickly forgotten, leading to the current spate of scandals emerging. From late 2021 on there was a noticeable drop off in investigations relating to government mismanagement with reports coming to focus on social issues, human interest stories, or animal welfare stories with a sprinkling of county council-level political investigations and HSE criticism—but little that would have caused the government any major embarrassment.

Instead of investigative journalism into government affairs, over the course of the 33rd Dáil, the national broadcaster RTE and the private print and digital national news media came to the fore in providing cover and consensus-forming efforts on behalf of the government for controversial policy decisions and failures. As noted above, in the case of green and mass migration policy, the 33rd Dáil simply provided grant money to outlets to produce positive news and broadcast stories to push policy—money which was gladly accepted.

But there are other ways of manufacturing consent. For example, despite a seemingly never-ending spate of serious crime committed by migrants—circulated on social media, seen on RTE's Crime Call, reported in court cases in the local and national media—the government's, particularly Justice Minister Helen McEntee's, mantra was, "there is no link between migration and crime". Speaking to Newstalk in February 2024, McEntee stated, "There is certainly not an increase and there is certainly not a correlation between the increasing numbers [of people] that we've seen in the last two years and an increase in crime. That is very clear."[49] Despite McEntee's claims, at no point were crime figures broken down by ethnicity made available to the public to fact check, nor did any national media outlet put sufficient pressure on the government to produce such data which could easily settle the matter. Time and again McEntee was allowed to emphatically claim there was no link between mass migration and increased crime and deflect from the issue despite a widespread feeling that this was the case. In the absence of data-driven reporting by the national media, McEntee was never held to account and public frustrations and, inevitably, prejudices were allowed to take root in the absence of that clarity. Ignoring combustible topics, under-reporting on them and lying by omission became standard tools of the national media as the 33rd Dáil ground on.

Aside from deflecting from key issues, the national media skilfully assisted in helping the government by rolling out powerful human impact stories at opportune moments to sway public opinion surrounding divisive issues. During the May 2018 abortion referendum, RTE conducted a detailed exit poll of voters in association with sociologists from UCD, UCC, DCU, and KU Leuven.[50] Among the key findings of the exit poll was that the largest single 'influencing factor' in helping people make up their minds on how to vote was 'people's personal stories as covered in the media'. While campaign posters swayed 10% of people, direct contact with campaigners swayed 7% of people and 'the experiences of people I know' swayed 34%, media personal stories as covered in the media swayed a massive 43% of people. Personal stories, then, are an extraordinarily powerful tool for media persuasion and consensus-forming and have been increasingly used in recent years. As Ireland opened its doors to over 100k Ukrainians and government policy relating to them pivoted at various points, the national media could be readily relied upon to provide a human face to help shape government efforts. In March 2022, shortly after the government waived visa requirements and masses of refugees began to arrive, the national media was awash with horror stories of human misery and escape to Ireland. RTE reported on Liliia Skrypka, a nurse who escaped the war with her son. Skrypka told RTE, "My son so much afraid to die and a few days ago he said to me momma I don't want to die because I only have years old."[51] The Irish Times reported on the heroic 87-year-old Phyllis McDonagh who opened her home up to a family of four from Kharkiv. The matriarch of the family, Viktoria, explained, "From the first days, the bombs were falling and we heard the shooting...One morning, we woke up and we decided . . . we were in the basement and we decided we cannot do it anymore."[52] This was Ireland's 'Wir schaffen das!' moment. Borders and private home doors were thrown open as the nation was overcome by the images and personal stories portrayed in the media. As heroic Phyllis said, "I think we're a charitable country. It is a great country; best country in the world, Ireland."

Wonderful images of Ukrainians being put up in a tower house castle in Galway, playing GAA, dancing and speaking Irish went viral in the following months as the best of Irish hospitality was put on full display. Of course, it was easy to be hospitable because, as the national media reassured the public in their deeply personal, human-led stories, these refugees were grateful to Ireland but were excited to go back home to Ukraine. The Irish Times reported that for Viktoria, "the plan is to create a 'normal life' in Ireland and to be ready to return to Ukraine whenever it is safe." As the months wore on, more Ukrainian refugees poured into the country and the government realised that they had overpromised on housing and social welfare support. The national media once more dutifully provided human-led stories to push the government's new policy of encouraging Ukrainians into the workforce and into privately rented accommodation. Newspapers and TV reports were suddenly awash with Ukrainians desperate to show their appreciation to Ireland by making their own way. In November 2022, the Irish Independent shared how Sergey Chudaev demanded "We can't just sit around all day, we want the dignity of working."[53] Images of an earnest-looking group of Ukrainians, intermeshed with terrifying stories of their evacuation, would make the hardest opponents of such a wish change their minds. In August The Irish Times reported that 7,100 Ukrainians had found work in Ireland, largely in the food service industry. They interviewed Karina Sheludko, a refugee from Dnipro, who reinforced the Ukrainian desire to work, "It's difficult to do nothing. It's difficult to be unemployed", before reassuring readers that Ukrainian refugees still wanted to go home at some point, "Of course I want to go back home but I don't wait for it every moment."[54] Despite the push, by January 2024, only 17,000 Ukrainians had found full-time work out of an estimated 60,000 work-aged adults. The government's media push had failed with more than 70% of Ukrainians unemployed compared to a national average of 4.5% that month. To that point, social welfare payments to Ukrainians had surpassed €650 million and the government, which had signalled a shift to slowing numbers entering the country, now signed off on plans to cut welfare payments dramatically.[55] By early 2025, there were still 80,000 Ukrainians in Ireland with little sign of mass movements back to Ukraine. Employment figures remained low and the government had shifted attention away to other migrant crisis areas. As a result, the national media largely returned to generalised reporting on policy changes and overviews of developments in the war, with personal narratives largely disappearing from reporting. Of course, that did not mean retiring the tactic of using hard-hitting human stories to shape public opinion. As government attention shifted from the Ukraine and instead focused on housing international protection applicants from elsewhere, the tactic resurfaced in the media to help soften up the public for masses of immigrants from other nations.

The 33rd Dáil alongside Sinn Féin in opposition were all fierce critics of Israel's offensive in Gaza after the October 7th, 2023 terror attack by Hamas. On the day of the attack itself, Micheal Martin stated the attack was "shocking in terms of the number of rockets, taking civilians hostage and so forth. It's clearly in breach of all international law and Israel under international law has the right to self-defence and obviously that has to be exercised in a very proportionate way and I'm very concerned now about civilians both in Israel and in Gaza." His immediate call for proportionality in Israel's response struck a tone-deaf note after the worst terror attack in the nation's history and it got worse from there. A week later, longtime Palestine supporter, President Michael D. Higgins, inflamed tensions between Israel and Ireland when he stated, "To announce in advance that you will break international law and to do so on an innocent population, it reduces all the code that was there from the Second World War on protection of civilians and it reduces it to tatters."[56] When the Israeli ambassador to Ireland, Dana Erlich, responded that Higgins' comments were "misinformed" and "unhelpful", politicians closed ranks siding with the president. Enterprise Minister, Fine Gael's Simon Coveney, stated, "I don't think it's helpful when an ambassador starts to make pointed comments in relation to our president." Ivana Bacik, the leader of Higgins' old party, Labour, told The Week in Politics that Erlich's comments were a "serious matter!", and her position as ambassador was "under question".[57] In November, Sinn Féin leader Mary Lou McDonald explicitly called for the Israeli ambassador to be removed, stating that Erlich "must be sent home immediately" and that she could "no longer enjoy diplomatic status in Ireland".[58] Then Taoiseach Varadkar added, "What I am seeing unfolding at the moment isn't just self-defence, it resembles something more approaching revenge and that's not where we should be and I don't think it is how Israel will guarantee its future freedom and security". It was clear that Israel had no backers in Irish politics. The Irish media was just as unforgiving. Mary Lou McDonald was invited on to RTE's The Week in Politics on November 12th where she reiterated her call to have Erlich removed as Ambassador. In November 2023, when Holly Cairns tabled a motion in the Dáil calling for the expulsion of the Israeli ambassador due to Israel's "savagery" which she labelled "an impending genocide", it was widely and uncritically covered in the national media.[59] When Ireland officially recognised Palestine as a state in May 2024 and when Ireland formally intervened in South Africa's genocide case against Israel at the International Court of Justice in December 2024, despite these being political moves radically out of step with the majority of Europe and the USA, again there was resoundingly positive coverage in the national press. On November 7th, 2024, the final day of the 33rd Dáil, Holly Cairns, leader of the Social Democrats, tabled a Private Members Motion reading, "Genocide is being perpetrated before our eyes by Israel in Gaza".[60] The motion was put to the Dáil and was adopted by a vote of 71-61. While the motion did not mean anything in law, it was adopted as the official stance of the Irish government. Though the motion sparked controversy in the international press, it made few waves in Ireland where it was strategically downplayed in the national media as a mere formality. In December 2024, Israel announced the permanent closure of its embassy in Dublin.

The normalisation of extraordinary anti-Israel sentiment by the national media was lamented by Dana Erlich in an interview on RTE's *Six One News* in January 2025. During an uncomfortably hostile grilling by host David McCullagh, he stated, "Israel prides itself on being the only liberal democracy in the Middle East. What other liberal democracy in the last year and a half has killed 47,000 people." Before allowing Erlich to answer he demanded, "What other liberal democracy has deliberately targeted healthcare infrastructure?" Erlich calmly replied, "I think...these kinds of questions, that we've been hearing for fifteen months on Irish media, [display] the kind of closed narratives and biases, the echo chamber that Ireland ... is stuck in." In one sentence, she managed to put her finger exactly on how Ireland became so out of step with the rest of the Western world on Israel. In a crippled democracy, where the media is kept artificially alive by government handouts, the national press simply becomes a PR arm of the state and people are forced to live in an echo chamber. In an X post on February 23rd, 2025, Erlich wrote,

"No matter how many interviews I do with Irish media, I usually expect hostility, but I'm still shocked by some questions." She went on to describe how in the week that the bodies of the Bibas children who were kidnapped and later murdered by Hamas on October 7th were handed back—a story that caused revulsion in the international press—not a single Irish news outlet was interested in discussing the story with her. She wrote, "Yet, even after ALL OF THAT, on Newstalk radio the host was only interested in perpetuating the same binary and disingenuous anti-Israel narrative that exists in much of Irish discourse. Isn't it time that Irish society looked at the bigger picture?"

In keeping with the government's stance on Gaza, from late 2024 into early 2025, there was a resurgence of tragic human refugee stories focused entirely on Gazan victims of war. In late December 2024, outlets reported widely on the arrival of eight Gazan children with their carers and siblings who were granted life-saving medical care in Ireland. They were to be the first batch in a group of 30 who would be hospitalised and cared for in Ireland. The heartbreaking story appeared in all national media alongside suitably emotive images of small children hooked up to medical devices or playing amid the rubble of war-torn Gaza. Minister for Health, Stephen Donnelly, was quoted as saying on their arrival, "There is no justifica-tion for the deliberate attacks on civilians and healthcare services in Gaza and the loss of life has been devastating."[61] The stories about dead Gazan children alongside gut-wrenching images, raw emotional war porn, continued unabated into 2025. In late February, RTE reported on a Gazan family who were living in a car in Dublin.[62] Despite the father, Hazem, being granted asylum in August 2024, the family had not received a house. He told RTE, "There is no life for us back home. That's it. It is gone...And now we have to do this here. It is worse than the war. We sleep anywhere. We are in the car and thank God I have a car otherwise we would have died in the cold." Ukrainian news coverage would have taught the more observant Irish person that an uptick of such intense human stories in the national press could only mean one thing; get ready for the next great wave of asylum seekers. This time it would be Gazan. Given the support of all Dáil parties for Gaza, the media's backing of the government stance, and their orgasmic coverage of ongoing pro-Palestine demonstrations across the country, it was natural that Ireland would become a prime destination for Gazan refugees. And sure enough, from 2023 to 2024 there was a 700% increase in refugee applications of people claiming to be from Gaza. 957 Palestinians applied for international protection from January to December of 2024, up from 118 in 2023 and, unsurprisingly, single males made up the vast majority—44%. It was further reported that a "significant proportion" of the 3,285 male international protection applicants who had not been granted state accommodation in January 2025 were Palestinian.[63] All of these figures were, naturally, glossed over.

The national media did not limit its consensus-forming efforts on behalf of the government to supporting mass immigration. When Helen McEntee and the National Women's Council used the death of Ashling Murphy to push for McEntee's Zero Tolerance policy reform complete with a bumper NGO payout, the national press, as outlined in the last chapter, played a crucial role in redirecting the conversation surrounding Ashling's murder away from failed immigration policy. Instead, the finger of blame was pointed at Irish men as well as a supposed culture of 'femicide', 'misogyny' and an epidemic of 'gender based violence'. Rarely has the Irish media been so in synch in framing a story. Where the media played a crucial role in selling McEntee's policy reforms was in platforming NGO figures who were involved in writing those very policies while presenting them as independent actors. This underhanded tactic gave the public a sense that there was a passionate grassroots demand for McEntee's reforms when in fact, it was a carefully choreographed consensus-forming exercise between government NGO and media partners.

A notable example of this was a piece that appeared on the RTE News website on November 10th, 2023 titled *Murder of Ashling Murphy was a 'watershed moment'*.[64] The article by Ailbhe Conneely began by reaffirming the only acceptable narrative, "The death of Ashling Murphy resulted in a collective trauma that manifested through vigils and memorials in January 2022. Hundreds gathered at a rally outside Leinster House, organised by the National Women's Council, to call for an end to gender-based violence." The piece went on to interview the Women's Council's Orla O'Connor and Women's Aid's Sarah Benson. Benson was quoted as saying, "There seems to be a public appetite aligned with dedicated services like ourselves and the other domestic and sexual violence services and the political will to really dig in and prevent the structural inequalities." She presented herself as an independent figurehead of a grassroots demand for structural change. The article presents both women's comments as a retrospective analysis of a spontaneous event but leaves out the fact that the groups, the Women's Council in particular, with heavy media coverage, had been the ones to set that narrative in the days after Ashling's death. Having established both women as independent bystanders and simple advocates, the article goes on to explain that in a seemingly unrelated matter, "The Government had been working on a strategy to tackle domestic, sexual and gender-based violence; however, services on the front line believe that Ms Murphy's death accelerated its implementation." That, of course, would become the Zero Tolerance strategy. As explained in the last chapter, both of their organisations—Women's Aid and especially the National Women's Council—took a leading role in providing consultation and in drafting the strategy but the article goes to great pains to present all three actors, O'Connor, Benson and McEntee, as being separate from one another. The planning for the Zero Tolerance strategy had begun before the murder of Ashling Murphy but her death provided a perfect opportunity to give that working legislation a human face.

Three days after the article was written, Katie Hannon delivered her weekly *Upfront with Katie Hannon* talk show on RTE with a monologue taken straight from the title. She opened, "The man who murdered Ashling Murphy was convicted last week". From the outset, Hannon did not mention her killer by name, framing the episode as a discussion about men and not migrant crime. She continued, "Ashling's murder was deemed a watershed moment, a turning point... Tonight is not a debate. It's a conversation because we need to talk about men." It wasn't a debate because no alternative interpretations of the event had been allowed since January 2022. Hannon's deliberate use of "a watershed moment", a phrase first used by Orla O'Connor at a vigil for Ashling Murphy outside of the Dáil on Friday the 4th of January 2022, had become a rallying cry for NGOs and the national media in the days after Ashling's murder as narrative shaping focused on vilifying Irish men.

However, the most absurd twist in RTE coverage of the Zero Tolerance strategy came on the 8th of December 2023. This time Ailbhe Conneely reported that "Victims and survivors of gender-based violence are not being sufficiently considered in the State's zero tolerance strategy, according to the Irish Observatory on Violence Against Women."[65] And who are the Irish Observatory on Violence Against Women? The NGO super union chaired by Orla O'Connor of the Women's Council who co-drafted the Zero Tolerance document. As explained in the last chapter, the Observatory's criticism was a thinly veiled attempt to agitate for more funds for NGOs but RTE played the dutiful role of presenting them as independent monitors and advocates yet again. Throughout the 33rd Dáil, the national media, and none more so than RTE, played a vital role in facilitating the NGO industrial complex's infiltration of government and their ever-expanding state funding efforts by selling the illusion to the public that NGOs were independent observers lobbying on their behalf instead of policy-forming insiders aligned with progressive government interests and with their snouts deep in the taxpayer's wallet. The national media and the NGO industrial complex, both kept alive by government funding, became extremely reliable partners of the 33rd Dáil in helping to shape public opinion on government policy. Fine Gael TD Charlie Flanagan, representing the now all but extinct traditional conservative wing of the party, stated shortly before his retirement from politics in September 2023, "The liberal agenda has accelerated in recent years in a way that causes me discomfort," adding his afore quoted concern that he "would have more influence on Government policy if [he] was a middle-ranking official with an NGO than [he has] as a Government backbencher".[66]

It is a profound statement of just how aligned the NGO industrial complex, national media and government had become in crippling Irish democracy.

Lies by omission and misrepresentation

The national media played a more direct role in subverting the democratic process by stifling criticism of the 33rd Dáil's rollout of IPAS centres around the country, by underreporting on the scale of the centres, by linking local protests to 'far right' violence, and by underreporting on the true causes of public unrest in advance of the 2024 General Election. For example, in April 2024, Gript Media spoke to Tipperary TD Mattie McGrath about the proposed location of a massive IPAS settlement on a twelve-acre site in Clonmel. The proposed site was to have 82 modular homes over 12 acres placed on what was public land. McGrath told Gript that he only found out about the proposed site through a Freedom of Information (FoI) request a month previously and that the Department of Integration had proceeded with the plan while keeping him in the dark though it was a major development in the heart of his constituency. McGrath labelled it a "denial of democracy."[67] On June 11th, he expanded on his concerns in the Dáil stating that due to lack of government transparency people in his constituency "felt betrayed" after Ukrainian refugees were moved out of Dundrum House, also in McGrath's constituency, and replaced instead with IPAS applicants from elsewhere.[68] McGrath's concerns were largely ignored by the national media with the notable exception of the Irish Independent which reported on "disquiet" in the town.[69] Not only did the broader national media lie by omission about the concerns of locals and their elected representative regarding the massive development in Clonmel, they also omitted images in news articles and on news broadcasts. Drone images of the site that were widely circulated on social media gave those who saw them a true sense of the scale of the development. Just as RTE, The Irish Times and others deliberately used evocative images and personal stories of suffering and human misery surrounding their reporting on refugees and mass immigration to shape public opinion, they ensured that reporting on Clonmel did not include imagery which could shock the public into realising the true scale of the development and just how radically different it was from any of the IPAS centres they had seen before. Interviews with individuals who manned a protest camp at the gate of the site were limited.

Conversely, evocative imagery and human-facing stories from Clonmel were employed to help turn wider sentiment against local protestors. In May there was a deluge of coverage after security fences were taken down, a security guard was badly beaten and plant equipment was set on fire. Despite the attack happening during the night by unknown vigilantes, the media blurred the line between local protestors and those responsible. Immediately after the attack, RTE spoke with Green Party TD Colm Ó Mongáin who called the attack "shocking and intolerable" adding, "there is no right to attack people that you disagree with or to intimidate other people who are loosely related". The report went on to quote Independent TD Seán Canney who said, "Regardless of the issue, there are ways of actually explaining your view on something, lobbying for it, protesting about it, but to actually harm another person is actually going way beyond what democracy should afford in any country."[70] At no point in the report was any effort made to disentangle the actions of the attackers from those of the locals who had protested at the site peacefully for up to two months before the attack. Similarly, The Irish Times, in a piece titled *Security staff allegedly assaulted and vehicles damaged by fire at Clonmel site earmarked for refugee accommodation* made no effort to clarify matters while the Independent explicitly linked the local protestors to the 'far right' stating, "Detectives do not believe the Tipperary incident involved any personnel involved in previous attacks but are concerned that it may have involved advice, information or coordination from those involved in other incidents. Far-right groups have been blamed for inciting local fears over such accommodation centres." The picture that emerged from the incident for the casual reader of the national media and consumer of media broadcast material was that local protestors were likely involved in the violence and that they were, as such, a criminal and 'far right' mob. This pattern of reporting was repeated throughout the country wherever violence broke out, notably at Newtownmountkennedy, Coolock and Rosscahill.

Again and again throughout 2023 and 2024, at IPAS centres across the nation, coverage of the government's 'no consultation, no veto' rollout minimised the undemocratic nature of the government's actions and ignored the core concerns of protestors and the very few elected officials who aligned themselves with them. Simultaneously, human stories relating to centres reported by community groups welcoming migrants were amplified. At Newtownmountkennedy, where protest marches against the IPAS centre at Trudder House counted hundreds of locals, interviews with participants were conspicuously absent from media reports, yet a small group called *Newtown Together* were given plentiful coverage for their pro-IPAS and integration messaging. The Journal quoted a member of the group as saying, "protestors have disrupted events and threatened people—simply for supporting those in need" and amplified the group's call for the IPAS centre to go ahead with additional finances and public support for integration efforts in the town. The report concluded with an uplifting message from another group member, who said that Newtownmountkennedy could be an "example of what is possible when communities come together, rather than being torn apart by fear and misinformation."[71]

The issue with *Newtown Together* was that even in their own promotional photos on their Facebook site, they never seemed to number more than 10 Irish people. The group was clearly a politically motivated activist reaction to the significantly larger group that protested against the IPAS centre at Trudder House. The Irish Independent reported that *Newtown Together* partnered with *North Wicklow Against Genocide,* a pro-Palestine group in September 2024, to screen a controversial documentary in Newtown Community Centre.[72] *North Wicklow Against Genocide* was the vehicle of *People Before Profit* politician Kellie McConnell. Speaking to the Greystones

Guide in the run-up to the Local Elections in June 2024, McConnell told the paper that she was an "enthusiastic and tenacious eco-socialist" and that she "spend[s] any spare time…on *North Wicklow Against Genocide*."[73] She was also the candidate for *People Before Profit* in the 2024 General Election.

Then on August 31st, longtime local activist and founder of *North Wicklow Against Racism*, Bernadette d'Arcy, published videos and images of *Newtown Together* at a pro-Palestine rally in Dublin to X. In the videos, members of the tiny, predominantly migrant group carried a *Newtown Together* flag and chanted "Israel is a terror state" and "From the river to the sea, Palestine will be free" among other slogans.[74] The display made a mockery of media portrayals of the group being a broad appeal grassroots organisation focused on peaceful integration in Newtownmountkennedy. But of course, it didn't matter. Because the group said the right things at the right time as Newtownmountkennedy was having masses of single unvetted migrant men forced into the community, the media was more than happy to amplify their message in support of the government's heavy-handed IPAS policy. The national media portrayed a tiny astroturfed activist clique as having as much grassroots support from the Newtown community as the Trudder House protestors did and created in the minds of their readers a false sense of balance in public sentiment in the community. Further, by linking local protestors at Trudder House to fiery images of violence and outside 'far right' agitators, the media knowingly portrayed them in a thuggish light in complete opposition to the breezy and hopeful coverage of the *Newtown Together* group.

The national media firewall

The degree to which the national media acted as a de facto Public Relations arm of the government in the run-up to the June Local Elections and November General Election cannot be understated. In an era where public trust in news media is at an all-time low internationally, Ireland retains a higher level of trust in the media than many of its Western peers. In their 2024 annual report, the highly regarded Reuters Institute reported that the average trust in news of all nations internationally stood at 40% while trust in Ireland stood at 46%. Scandinavian nations had a higher level of trust in reported news with 69% of Finns trusting their news outlets, while only 23% of Greeks and Hungarians trusted the news—a continental low.[75] In the US, trust in the media stood at 32%. Significantly, that same report showed that Irish news consumers reported a very high level of trust in RTE News which received a 72% trust score. The Irish Times also received a trust score of 72% with the Irish Examiner (68%), Irish Independent (68%) and Newstalk (66%) also scoring well. RTE dominated both the online and offline ratings for news consumption, meaning they appealed to all demographics. However, in the offline ratings—TV, print and radio—RTE News dominated viewership in Ireland, with 54% of people tuning in to RTE News once a week and 41% watching it at least three days per week. This figure is important as Coimisiún na Meán's 2024 Digital News Report found that RTE News appeals to older audiences. Out of all of the major media outlets broken down by age group retention, RTE's audience by far skewed older. While only 17% of 18-24 year-olds and 15% of 25-34 year-olds tuned into RTE TV News, 47% of 55-64 year-olds did and 57% of those aged 65 and over. To give a sense of how dominant RTE is in that 55+ slot, Newstalk only attracted 12% of the 55-64 year-old audience and 14% of the 65+ audience.[76] In other words, for the 55+ age groups in Ireland, RTE is absolutely dominant in providing them with their TV and radio news.

This RTE News capture of the 55+ audience is crucial because both Fine Gael and Fianna Fáil, more than any other political parties in the country, draw their core base from the 50+ range with the largest demographic vote for both parties coming from the 65+ age groups. In the 2024 General Election, Fianna Fáil took 27% of the 65+ vote and 22% of the 50-64 year-old vote. Fine Gael took 28% of the 65+ vote and 26% of the 50-64 vote. Together as coalition partners Fianna Fáil and Fine Gael took 55% of the 65+ vote and 48% of the 50-64 vote.[77] Additionally, in the past decade, the 65+ age group in Ireland has increased by 35.6% while the under 65 cohort only grew by 15%, much of it buoyed by immigration and individuals not eligible to vote in General Elections.[78] What this means is that Ireland is—and will remain for several more political cycles—an ageing population in which the 65+ cohort in particular holds significant electoral power. Both Fianna Fáil and Fine Gael are keenly aware of these statistics. They are also aware that their ageing bases overwhelmingly consume RTE TV and radio news media with secondary support from local and national print and digital media and are more predictable in their news media consumption habits than younger cohorts. This is why RTE has and will continue to be generously bailed out by any Fianna Fáil and Fine Gael-led government.

Whereas government outsiders Sinn Féin, in the absence of direct access to the levers of political power and, most importantly, the public purse, have adopted an adversarial role with Irish news media choosing lawfare to shut down investigations into the party's activities, Fianna Fáil and Fine Gael choose a wholly more cunning and destructive approach. By keeping the national media afloat financially through VAT reductions, advertising revenue and grants, particularly through Coimisiún na Meán, they have effectively turned the national media into a public relations wing of the government. While the government may not directly interfere in editorial decisions, by providing grants for broadcast and media stories on government policy issues such as green initiatives, anti-populism, pro-mass migration and DEI stories, they are de facto interfering and using the media to shape public opinion in return for badly needed cash. Like Sinn Féin, they too have helped to cripple investigative news reporting by creating an extremely lucrative political journalist to government advisor pipeline. Today in Ireland, a young investigative journalist doesn't know which way to turn without being personally sued into bankruptcy on one side and depriving himself of a well-paid, high-powered career in Leinster House on the other. Crucially, Fianna Fáil and Fine Gael have carefully focused all of this accumulated media influence on erecting an information firewall around their core voter base, the +65s.

With their Media partners by their side, Fianna Fáil and Fine Gael are able to spin half-truths and alternative realities to their ageing voter bases. Why wouldn't these people believe Helen McEntee when she appears on RTE News to tell them, without evidence in hand, that there is no link between migration and a spike in crime? Were they to cross-check the claim, they'd find it repeated as fact in all of the daily broadsheets. Of course they will think that protestors at the few IPAS centres they're given snapshots of around the country are violent, racist thugs when they see fiery images and stern calls from trusted Fianna Fáil and Fine Gael politicians to reject the 'far right'. Bombarded with images of dead children, rubble and harrowing stories of death and survival, they would think anyone a monster for refusing asylum to anyone from—or claiming to be from —Ukraine, Gaza and elsewhere. After hearing the impassioned speeches of seemingly grassroots community organisers like Orla O'Connor amid a sea of memorial candles for Ashling Murphy, it would appear an obvious solution to introduce new school curricula and hate laws and to give millions to NGOs to protect women and girls from an epidemic of male violence.

It would be impossible for the greying heads at home to understand the profoundly cynical theatre playing out before their eyes when an RTE journalist presents the spokeswoman for The Irish Observatory of Violence Against Women as an outside lobbyist who seems to passionately criticise the government's inaction, when they are already following guidelines she herself has helped draft. The canny older viewer would think you a conspiracy theorist if you told them that media, NGOs and government are all in cahoots and use the national broadcaster as simply a consensus-forming vehicle. The constant bombardment of lies by omission, underreporting, amplification and gaslighting in print and broadcast media on behalf of the government is so all-encompassing that Irish grandparents can wave their grandchildren off at the airport as they emigrate to Australia because they can't afford a home in Fianna Fáil and Fine Gael's Ireland but then dutifully go vote for Fianna Fáil and Fine Gael to fix the problem without seeing any logical flaw. The Irish government, in collusion with a financially dependent national media, have so thoroughly and skillfully cocooned Ireland's 65+ political kingmakers behind an information firewall of government-approved narratives that they live in an Ireland completely parallel to their children and grandchildren. It is impossible not to hear Eamon de Valera's warning to the nation on RTE's first broadcast echo, "Never before was there in the hands of men an instrument so powerful to influence the thoughts and actions of the multitude". And it is impossible not to conclude that his prediction, "I am confident that those who are in charge will do everything in their power to make it useful for the nation", has not come to pass.

7

IRELAND 2.0

I reland is a crippled democracy. Since 1958, Ireland has grown addicted to a high-risk foreign direct investment economic model that has, in conjunction with an abandonment of domestic industrial development, taken Ireland's economic destiny out of its own hands. Despite the 2008 global economic crash, which contributed to the nation being forced into a humiliating bailout that should have signalled the need for a radically different economic model, all three major Irish political parties are committed to the low-tax FDI economic model. Domestically, all three parties' policies are virtually indistinguishable. Fianna Fáil and Fine Gael are parties without meaningful ideological and policy platforms. They are floating parties. They go where they believe the votes are. Throughout the one hundred years of Irish independence, it has been difficult to tell one party from the other and in 2020 when they finally gave up the charade and went into coalition together, it was utterly unsurprising. Over the past decade Fianna Fáil, Fine Gael and Sinn Féin's healthcare, housing and social welfare plans are simply a case of looking into one another's notes and promising a few more or less hospital beds, a few more or less government funded houses per annum, a spread of taxpayer money on child support, pensions, unemployment benefits which, when all is totted up, amount to almost the exact same financial outlay. All three major Irish political parties agree on all major social issues of the day from abortion to surrogacy, to gay marriage. While Sinn Féin have been the major party in opposition to Fianna Fáil and Fine Gael over the past decade, they are de facto silent partners. Where they did manage to influence Fianna Fáil and Fine Gael's policy decision-making, it was to coax them further and further left than they already were, pushing for more government intervention on housing, health, social welfare. The two floating parties, parties without ideological anchoring, were happily coaxed left by Sinn Féin and the plethora of leftist micro-parties that have completed the Irish political landscape for the past decade, the big two greedily believing that's where the culture and the votes were.

Because all three parties have an unshakable commitment to the low corporation tax FDI economic model, all three have been enthusiastic supporters of mass immigration on a scale unprecedented in modern Western European history. In the space of twenty-five years, Ireland went from among the most homogenous of Western nations, to a nation in which close to 25% of all residents were born overseas. In that period of time, all three parties committed to forcing this radical social engineering project on the Irish people. No party was ever given a mandate by the people to utterly change the demographics and cultural identity of Ireland. In the early years of the FDI economic model it served the people of Ireland well, with pharmaceutical and early tech companies proving a good fit for Ireland's semi-skilled and graduate profile. Up until the mid-1990s a balance was maintained. Since the hedonistic years of the late Celtic Tiger, that balance has been completely upended. All three big parties maintain an insatiable greed for GDP growth which has seen an expansion of the FDI economy far beyond the supply of the native workforce. Their addiction to corporation taxes is such that entire sectors, especially big tech, now scarcely employ any Irish people and are simply tax-shy industries squatting in Ireland giving meagre corporate tax returns while recruiting overwhelmingly from non-EU nations. Irish people are a distant afterthought in the current FDI economy and the social footprint of these sectors is now overwhelmingly negative. Increasingly, those non-EU immigrant workers are pricing young native workers out of the housing market. Big Tech and the government are causing the rapid growth of ethnic enclaves which pose a serious threat to social cohesion and native identity. Fianna Fáil, Fine Gael and Sinn Féin's economic model is reducing Ireland, an ancient and world-respected nation, to a faceless, globalist packing station for US multinationals.

In the midst of this overwhelming wave of immigration, Ireland is undergoing a profound identity crisis. Ireland's sudden influx of money since the 1990s in concert with a series of scandals in the Catholic Church has led to the rapid erosion of the pillars of identity and community that Irish people took for granted since the revolutionary period. A series of clerical sex abuse scandals that emerged in the late 1990s and early 2000s shattered the remaining institutional power of the Church, leaving a moral and spiritual abyss in a nation that had, more than any other Western European country, held fast to the faith in post-industrial Europe. Simultaneously, any Irish folklore, tradition and custom that couldn't be packaged and staged in the corner of a pub was dispensed with. The old bachelors who carried the fairy lore, legends and myths of the Celts unbroken for centuries were seen as backward and filthy, an embarrassing reminder of our economically impoverished history. Fireside culture, authentic, living and breathing culture orally transmitted, rooted in the community and the landscape, was forgotten with slick big-budget productions like Riverdance embraced instead, making tourists of Irish people in their own country. The economically fatal house-building bubble of the Celtic Tiger took it further, making strangers of Irish people in the ancient communities where they purchased their new homes. Community engagement, once the staple of Irish culture, collapsed as more people than ever moved into housing estates across the country but remained anonymous, simply using their new homes as a bed, their work, families and commitments lying elsewhere, their evenings spent watching UK and American pop culture on expensive flatscreen TVs.

The collapse of the Catholic Church had profound social and cultural consequences. Prior to the Celtic Tiger, the Church was the primary beneficiary of Ireland's uniquely expansive NGO sector, providing decades-long partnership to the state in managing health, education, social and cultural organisations. A Catholic ethos permeated Irish society as schools, elderly care facilities, special needs facilities etc. were managed by religious bodies. Their collapse left a gaping pastoral and cultural hole in society, and into that gap stepped a new secular faith, Social Justice Theory. Since 2004 there has been an explosion in NGOs grounded in Social Justice Theory which have been manned by radical activists churned out by Ireland's academic institutions. Arts and Humanities departments, particularly those in UCD, Trinity College and Maynooth have, for over two decades, spread the gospel of Social Justice and their disciples have penetrated politics, teaching, civil service and especially the national media. This new breed of community leaders has set about shaping a new Irish culture and society—one that stands aggressively against the Irish nation and that subverts and degrades all that came before it. Central to this new Ireland has been the distortion of Irish history to make the Irish 'white'. By diminishing the Irish colonial experience and placing it in a wider global 'white' history via Critical Race Theory, Ireland and Irish people are placed alongside their coloniser as beneficiaries of 'white privilege'. The new secular Social Justice faith is based on imposing guilt and shame on Irish people in a bid to force them into submission to politically partisan progressivism. Irish men benefit from 'male privilege', straight Irish people from 'heterosexual privilege', 'able-bodied privilege' and so on. The answer to all of these terrible injustices uncovered by Social Justice NGOs is more guilt, more shame, and most importantly of all, more taxpayer money for an ever-expanding NGO sector. Racism, LGBTQ hate, ableism, misogyny, all can be managed, monitored, reported on—never solved —for just a few euros more. The 33rd Dáil in particular, with the rabid zeal of The Greens, systematically embedded the Social Justice

NGO industrial complex at the very heart of the state and in doing so introduced 'positive' discrimination across hiring and grant-giving initiatives. By further granting a select group of politically partisan NGOs privileged access to government via initiatives such as the National Action Plan Against Racism and the Zero Tolerance Strategy, the government created a lobbyist wedge between the electorate and government and funded that group to the tune of €6.5 billion a year, in return relying on them to gin up support for divisive government policies. The embrace of the NGO industrial complex into the heart of the Irish government was complete. It was a profound perversion of Irish democracy.

Having worked hand-in-hand to cripple Irish democracy over decades, Fianna Fáil and Fine Gael have grown ever more openly anti-democratic and authoritarian in their actions. The 'no veto, no consultation' ramming of unvetted single men posing as asylum seekers into small communities across Ireland—again silently supported by Sinn Féin—marked a forced settlement programme in Ireland with parallels only in Cromwellian times. Those concerned community members who stood up for their localities were met with Garda violence in Newtownmountkennedy, Coolock and elsewhere. But the government could not have gotten away with such actions had there been an independent national media on hand to report on events in an evenhanded and neutral manner. The dual incentive of creating a politics journalist to government advisor pipeline as well as providing vital cash incentives such as 0% VAT payments for print and digital news outlets and generous advertising revenues, meant that the government placed the national media in a compromised position. The extra incentive of Coimisiún na Meán grants for producing pro-government policy content in the areas of climate, mass migration, anti-populism and Social Justice issues meant that while the government could claim that it exerted no direct editorial influence over national media and broadcast output, in real terms, it did. If news outlets wanted to survive in a crowded and changing news landscape in Ireland, they would have to take the handout and toe the line.

By building the Irish economy around the FDI economy and EU subsidies, Fine Gael and Fianna Fáil worked together to cripple Irish democracy over decades through a lack of any alternative vision. Instead of providing that alternative economic vision, Sinn Féin joined the big two, copying them down to the minutiae of their housing, health and social welfare policies. By actively encouraging a radically progressive NGO industrial complex on board as equal government partners, Fianna Fáil and Fine Gael created a wedge between the electorate and government which absolved them of accountability. And by buying off the national media, Fianna Fáil and Fine Gael insulated themselves from criticism and ensured that their key voter bases—the over 65s—remained misinformed and compliant voters. Together, the government, the NGO industrial complex and the media conspired to vandalise Ireland.

Of course, it is possible to reverse the damage done by these conspirators over the past twenty-five years.

Mostly, the solutions to the key issues Ireland faces are easy fixes. The Irish government needs to enforce existing migration laws and step up mass deportations of illegals who have cheated the asylum system over the past twenty-five years. The government could easily prune and shape the FDI economy to suit the needs of the nation and Irish graduate profiles. There needs to be a strict separation of Social Justice-driven lobbyist NGOs and government both in terms of funding, and in terms of access to government policy formation. There needs to be a strict enforcement of viewpoint neutrality in all Irish classrooms from primary school through to postgraduate courses. This needs to be extended to broader social discourse by protecting —ideally by amendment to the Irish constitution—freedom of speech online and in public. Universities need to be incentivised to produce more STEM graduates and fewer Social Justice activists in order to break the back of the supply and demand relationship between Irish universities and NGOs. Obviously, the government should play no interventionist role in propping up the national media—they should face open market pressures and sink or swim on the basis of public demand for their product. The generous incentives the media enjoys, along with the excess billions pumped into the NGO industrial complex, the IPAS contracts racket, and the eye-watering financial waste by the government on public building projects, should be refocused on boosting native industry.

But of course it would be profoundly naive to expect Fianna Fáil and Fine Gael to do any of these things unless absolutely politically expedient. Ireland didn't become a crippled democracy by accident. It was a mix of ad hoc decisions taken over time based around an unshakable commitment to the FDI economy and the EU, incompetence, naiveté and opportunism by the big two to ensure that they remained in power at all costs. To put it bluntly, Fine Fáil and Fine Gael benefit immensely from the crippled democracy they orchestrated. To expect them to give it up without a fight is foolish. To them, Ireland is perfectly broken.

No electable alternative

Ireland needs an electable and inspiring right-wing political alternative. The country has the narrowest left/right political axis in Western Europe and currently, all but the newly formed Independent Ireland Party and Peadar Tóibín's Aontú, who are still feeling out a direction, are left of centre. At present, Aontú can best be described as socially conservative but economically liberal, placing it on sound centrist footing. The party champions a pro-life position, they have been to the fore on the excesses of Social Justice Theory, for example opposing trans women in women's sports and in women's prisons, they campaigned for No votes in the 2024 constitutional referenda, but economically they are more in line with Sinn Féin, for example calling for greater government intervention in social housing schemes to help solve the housing crisis. Rather than point to the obvious root of the problem—the arrival of well over a million people to Irish shores in just 25 years—Aontú have roundly criticised the government for not ramping up social housing schemes. On the Party's website in a dedicated section laying out their vision for the 2024 General Election to deal with the housing crisis they state,

"Firstly the supply of social and affordable housing needs to be ramped up. In the 30s, the 50s, and the 80s in tough economic times social and affordable housing was built at far higher rates...We will build 15,000 social and affordable homes a year for the life of the next Dáil."[1] Much like Sinn Féin, Aontú with their motto of 'Economic Justice' have found themselves playing copy their neighbours' homework with their domestic policy approach and just like Sinn Féin, and the other leftist micro parties, Aontú have decided that greater state intervention, expanding the handout state, is the solution. With that said, Aontú are an evolving party and their leader Peadar Tóibín places pragmatism to the fore of party policy. Their 2024 economic policy was noticeably less left-wing than in 2020 and Tóibín has been the Dáil's loudest advocate for increased oversight on government spending signalling an openness to economic policy evolution.

Before the 2024 election, Independent Ireland struck a more economically conservative tone, offering a package of incentives, tax breaks and VAT reductions, and streamlined planning permissions and regulations to deal with the housing crisis with minimal state intervention. They have extended this tax break and incentive model for dealing with the cost-of-living crisis.[2] They have taken a strong line on illegal immigration but have supported speeding up visa checks and applications for legal immigrants to come to Ireland meaning that they intend to fuel the out-of-control FDI economy which will exacerbate the housing crisis and the social cohesion problems already showing themselves. Despite their positives, both Aontú and Independent Ireland's liberal legal migration policies and support of the FDI economy mean they currently have no long-term solution to Ireland's underlying issues.

Aontú and Independent Ireland are both palatable options to mainstream Irish voters. Their relative newness and feeling out of a direction could yet, with policy tweaks, lead them to resonate with a wider rightwing audience. Outside of these two, a whole plethora of independent candidates and rightwing micro-parties identifying as nationalists have sprung up in a bid to offer a new vision for Ireland in recent elections. None have achieved wide success and some have been downright destructive, salting the earth for a professional mass appeal rightwing movement. The most successful of these parties has been the Irish Freedom Party led by Hermann Kelly until May of 2025. Under Kelly, they represented a MAGA or AfD-style populist right party which placed emphasis on achieving a united Ireland with a nationalist model of economics that would prioritise Irish interests, spearheaded by leaving the EU, claiming and exploiting territorial rights to oil, gas and fishing as well as the ability to make independent trade deals that benefit the Irish nation. They pursued a non-interventionist economic model that would leverage taxation and incentives to spur domestic industry. They aimed to relieve the strain on the housing market by heavily taxing vulture funds and by reserving the right to own a house to Irish citizens only. Socially they were conservative, promoting economic models that would boost native fertility rates, sharply reduce dependency on foreign labour and prioritise the Irish diaspora to fill employment shortfalls.[3] The party has been hampered to a degree by falling between stools in the Irish political scene. Their anti-EU stance is at odds with the vast majority of the Irish public. A major 2023 poll found that 88% of people in the Republic of Ireland said Ireland should remain a member of the EU.[4] Though they are a populist party whose policies are not out of step with other major parties on the continent or indeed the US Republican Party under Donald Trump, they have been smeared and labelled 'far right' by the national media,[5] thrown in with a plethora of ethno-nationalist individuals and parties. Ironically, because they are not an explicitly ethno-nationalist party, they are considered too liberal for those other nationalist parties fighting for the same slice of the electorate. Their support for strict enforcement of migration laws, as well as the deportation of illegals and reduction in legal migration, upsets many in the mainstream. However, their acceptance of mixed-race individuals born to one Irish parent as being Irish, and recognition of the role of Ulster Protestants in the future of any united Ireland has made them prime targets for those right of them who reject these positions. While the party won a historic first councillor in the 2024 Local Elections, and were the best performing nationalist party in the 2024 General Election, they only won 0.67% of the national vote. Party Leader Hermann Kelly himself performed well in Louth achieving just short of 4% of first preference votes and he survived until the 14th count. After the election, the party faced relentless attacks from ethno-nationalist parties to their right and after infighting and defections, including their only elected Councillor, Kelly was removed as party president and the Irish Freedom Party is in disarray and seeking to reorganise.

The furthest outlier on the right wing of Irish politics is the National Party. It is an ethno-nationalist party that promotes remigration or the mass removal of non-Irish persons and non-ethnically Irish citizens from the state. It is a party with ties to anti-semitism and National Socialism. One of their founders, Justin Barrett has, according to The Irish Times, quoted *Mein Kampf* and spoken at neo-Nazi rallies.[6] The Sunday World reported[7] that his party co-founder James Reynolds disavowed him for reading *Mein Kampf* and giving Roman salutes (Hitlergruß) at party events. After a falling out with his co-founder, Barrett has gone on to found Clann Éireann while still disputing ownership of the National Party. This new party has almost identical principles to the National Party but is overtly National Socialist. In a March 2025 interview on the Logos Academy Podcast[8] Barrett stated, "Irish people are going to have to choose to live or to die...And they're going to live under National Socialism or die under the Jews." The group's Telegram channel promotes National Socialist ideology and images of the group's paramilitary wing training in wooded areas.

The National Party has attempted to reshape its image since the split with its founders, focusing on remigration and identitarianism. Where the Irish Freedom Party aligned more with populists like MAGA and the Alternative für Deutschland (AfD), the post-Barrett National Party aligns with the younger pan-European identitarian movement. This movement was popularised by Martin Sellner who founded the Identitarian Movement of Austria (IBÖ) in 2012 pushing for remigration and "ethno-cultural identity".[9] Sellner's movement

was influenced by the French 'Nouvelle Droite' or New Right movement of the 1960s and the ideas of Guillaume Faye, who aimed to
repackage ethno-nationalism in the post-World War II era.[10] To make
it more palatable to Europeans, Faye rephrased blood and soil theory
in relatable terms for modern, disenfranchised young men. Sellner's
ideas, particularly relating to remigration—or the mass repatriation
of non-Europeans to their countries of origin—have been influential
on the Austrian Freedom Party (FPÖ), the current opposition but
single largest political party in the country.

His views on remigration were even adopted by many in the
populist AfD. They gained such traction that in February 2025, the
youth wing of the party (JA) had to be disbanded and reformed under
more direct control of the AfD mother party after a German adminis-
trative court ruled that the group could be classified by domestic
intelligence services as a 'certified right-wing extremist endeavour'.[11]
In 2024 *DW* reported that Mathias Helferich, a government minister
who came through the JA, echoing Sellner, stated in internal group
messages that he was the "friendly face of National Socialism". Other
members of the JA touted him as the party's "future minister for
remigration".[12] In January 2024, AfD leader Alice Weidel parted ways
with her long-time advisor Roland Hartwig after he attended a secret
meeting in Potsdam where Sellner was a guest speaker and spoke on
the topic of remigration.[13]

The adoption of identitarian ideology is similarly playing out in
Ireland's National Party. Barrett's cartoonish National Socialism was a
profound embarrassment for many younger, more aesthetically savvy
party members and since both Barrett and Reynolds were purged, the
party has attempted to rehabilitate its brand by affiliating with pan-
European identitarian ideology. Keith Woods, the party's most prominent figure, has been instrumental in aligning the National Party
with this movement. Woods got his big break online after making
numerous video and social media appearances with prominent
ethno-nationalist influencers such as American commentators Nick
Fuentes and Richard Spencer as well as Englishman Mark Collette
and Australian Joel Davis. In August 2023, Woods spoke at the Amer-

ican Renaissance (AmRen) Conference run by Jared Taylor and in November 2024, he spoke at the Reconquista Conference in Lisbon, a conference dedicated to identitarian speakers on the topic of remigration. Woods appeared at a November 2024 Polish Independence Day celebration alongside fellow National Party members and in the company of other identitarian nationalist groups.

In accumulating his online fame, Woods has entrenched himself so deeply in the blurred lines between identitarianism and National Socialism that he felt compelled to write two articles on the distinction in March 2025. In the first, he attempted to put distance between himself as an ethno-nationalist and National Socialism by concluding "So there is really nothing especially novel from National Socialism that nationalist movements need today. And if there were, it would benefit from being disassociated with the negative stigma of Hitlerism anyway. All the political steps I see as necessary to save my people from erasure can be carried through the vehicle of a regular old ethno-nationalist movement."[14] Woods' post received so much backlash from the National Socialist element of his base that he was forced to write a follow-up in defence of drawing a distinction between the two movements. After a lengthy discussion about the contemporary significance of Hitler in international nationalist movements, he concluded, "We should want to attract reasonable people with a strong moral sense. If people don't find a movement based around winning support for nationalist policies and restoring White homelands exciting enough without an attachment to a Hitler fandom, then they simply do not care enough about the existential challenge facing our people, and should be filtered out."[15]

As idiosyncratic and crippled as Irish democracy is, certain patterns remain remarkably stable. In the eyes of the Irish public, any party that finds itself splitting hairs between their brand of ethno-nationalism and National Socialism to keep their support base happy is beyond the pale. There is simply no widespread appetite for National Socialism or pan-European ethno-nationalism in Ireland. The National Party won just 0.30% of first vote preferences in the 2024 General Election.

Guilt by association

Since the beginning of the 33rd Dáil, the Irish national media has adopted a de facto position of calling all political groups and individuals right of Fianna Fáil and Fine Gael 'far-right'. It is a cynical move to dismiss them collectively as a political movement and to impose guilt by association on all groups. For example, while Hermann Kelly has been strongly critical of the National Party, Justin Barrett and the anti-semitic and racist elements of the ethno-nationalist movement, the national media intentionally lumps him in with them. Kelly fought hard, as Alice Weidel did in Germany's AfD, to weed out any National Socialist or openly racist elements from the Irish Freedom Party but the National Party's supporters embraced the media's labels and attacked the Irish Freedom Party. The party became a victim of a two-pronged attack by the national press and the National Party. And the National Party benefits from this. They do not look to achieve major gains in the present. They are playing a long game, appealing to disaffected and angry young men in particular and waiting for the electorate to get so angry with Fianna Fáil and Fine Gael policy that when a moment of national rage or economic collapse comes, they will be the primary beneficiaries. They do not want the Irish Freedom Party or any populist nationalist party siphoning off the rage of young men by offering an alternative vision or solutions and so their strongest jabs are reserved for those on the right—not Fianna Fáil and Fine Gael, and not the left. Importantly, the national media, through dishonest coverage of the right-wing political spectrum, and the government by pursuing a radically authoritarian, open borders and 'no veto, no consultation' agenda, are creating the conditions in which the National Party may very well, over time, become a political force. If young people continue to feel that they will never own a home, will never live a lifestyle close to that of their parents, continue to see their country, culture and identity disappear before their eyes and if they feel they could lose their job or social standing for complaining, then the pull of the National Party will become irresistible for many.

While Aontú and Independent Ireland still have a chance to become influential players in right-wing politics in Ireland subject to further policy evolution, the populist nationalist scene is currently dead after the collapse of the Irish Freedom Party. At present, the choice for right-wing voters is the centrist Aontú or Independent Ireland or the identitarian National Party with little in between. Further, because of the negative publicity surrounding nationalist politics in the national press, and their cynical tactic of lumping all nationalist parties together and tarring them 'far right', any future party or independent identifying explicitly as 'nationalist' is destined to fail before launch. It is a similar story for any party identifying as 'conservative'. The word invokes images of Margaret Thatcher, the Maze Prison and British Tories for older voters, and is reviled by many younger right-wing voters. They see it as a weakling movement belonging to a Baby Boomer generation who they blame for not preventing the problems they face today. Therefore labels such as conservative, nationalist or variations of international populist and nationalist movements such as MEGA—Make Éire Great Again—are going to be pounced on by the national media or be seen as repellent by disenfranchised voters who could be coaxed into a right-wing movement. The key to success, much like Sinn Féin achieved on the left in the 1970s and 1980s, is to position overt political ideology behind a love for nation. Create an irresistible culture of national pride and then follow it with a political movement. This has, on the right, been achieved with remarkable success in recent years by the populist AUR (Alliance for the Union of Romanians).

The party was formed in 2019 and raised eyebrows when it achieved an impressive breakthrough in parliamentary elections on December 6th 2020, capturing 9% of the popular vote. It was a meteoric rise that continued in the 2024 parliamentary elections where the party became the second largest party in Romania, 4% behind the winning leftists' PSD. Significantly, AUR beat the traditional centre-right Liberal Party (PLN) by a significant 6% margin. While COVID politics, lockdowns and other internal political factors contributed to AUR's stunning growth, the party's gains were far from an overnight success story. Before there was a political movement, AUR was a cultural movement. From 2012, future candidates and leaders of what would become AUR engaged in organising a series of summer camps, demonstrations and cultural events to build a sense of national pride in a positive way. Hungary's Fidesz, the party of Viktor Orban, is also a proponent of the political summer camp concept and each year the party comes to Romania to connect with the Magyar—ethnic Hungarian—population and to boost a sense of community and national pride inclusive of its diaspora. The annual summer camp includes political speeches with a keynote by Orban himself mixed with concerts, cultural events and sports.[16] These events by AUR and Fidesz have been crucial in shaking young, disenfranchised voters out of their apathy towards the political system and making them feel part of something special. More importantly, such events identify and hone a core political base, as well as providing a pool of committed leaders from which to stock a political party with candidates. In a similar but smaller vein in the Irish context, most weekends in Dublin, one will find a pro-Palestine or pro-worker union rally organised by People Before Profit and any number of leftist micro-parties. While an annoyance or silly spectacle to many, aside from snaring news headlines, these types of rallies provide young people with a powerful sense that they belong to a movement, allow them to rub shoulders with party elites and make a name for themselves within the movement all while giving them a sense that they are forcing political change. They do not care if they are hated by some in the mainstream; that builds resolve, a siege mentality even, and drives them further into the party. While a new right-wing party in Ireland may want to avoid this degree of confrontation, they do need to observe the tactics and consider how to engage a youth vote for themselves and understand that the right wing holds more cards than any for creating a cultural base from which to build a new political movement.

A cultural revival

As pointed out, authentic, grassroots Irish culture and identity is facing an existential threat. Across the nation, communities are awash with housing estates whose Irish inhabitants are strangers in the wider village. RTE, the national media, universities, NGOs and politicians are actively delivering the death knell to Irish identity and culture by aggressively supplanting it with a punitive, divisive Social Justice Theory vision for the nation. The answer is to kill apathy and social engineering with authentic connection and a new cultural revival. A core group of individuals with aspirations to later create a political movement must take responsibility for arranging a web of small and major cultural events around the nation.

This should start at the absolute grassroots level and provide an opportunity for well-known or new individuals in communities to lead a series of events that connect people to their own locality. Every single parish in Ireland is awash with ringforts, castles, mass rocks, holy wells, ancient pilgrimage routes and more. Every one of them has a story. It would cost nothing to put a sign in the local shop window and ask the local priest to let parishioners know at mass that a heritage walk is leaving each Sunday morning from the church gates. It is a certainty that someone in the village will have stories— be they historically accurate or folk tellings—about every point in the landscape visited. If not, the local organiser can come prepared and will quickly establish a reputation as an expert. This event should be then grown into a base where there is a monthly meeting at a local community centre or home to host music, dance and lectures. This movement should focus on reigniting a rambling house culture reminiscent of the old Burren bards, a place where people can come in the evenings to experience the talents of the local community. It is essential that all of this is done voluntarily and without recourse to government grants and handouts. It is a certainty that should a cultural movement like this take root in a community, local Fianna Fáil and Fine Gael representatives will attempt to covet it and buy it out. That can't happen. These people should be welcome to join but understand that it is not the property of the government, rather the people. In the ideal scenario, the community would come together to renovate an old cottage or landmark building in the community to act as the village's official rambling house. This house would become the heart of cultural revival and sustenance for the community and a base for folklore, music, dance, handicrafts and lectures. Highlight events should be held at Bealtaine (seeding), Lughanasa (harvesting), and Samhain (Halloween) with special storytelling events, handicrafts, agricultural history and heritage walks integrated.

The great potential of an approach like this is that it allows for a big-tent right-wing movement that can accommodate traditional Catholic conservatives, a la carte Catholics, wider Christian denominations and non-religious conservatives. Aligning all of these factions in a right-wing political movement is no easy feat but it is crucial for a later broad base political party. By engaging with the landscape, with historic sites, history and culture, there is room for negotiation. A non-religious nationalist can go to a mass rock celebration and appreciate that it was a subversive act against a colonising force. It fosters an understanding that even if someone is not personally religious, they are culturally Catholic and their past is tied up with Ireland's Catholic past. For disillusioned Catholics and devout realists who understand that religion is in its nadir in Ireland, they will spot a unique opportunity for using mass rock celebrations and holy well visits to make Catholicism cool again. Not only do mass rocks, hedge services and stories of martyred clergy sent to the New World under colonialism for practising their faith make religion feel dissident, it provides a chance for the clergy and the observant to break from the Church's post-Synod of Thurles' overly-hierarchical and detached structure. A folk Catholic revival can bring the church back into the mud cabins of hidden Ireland as it were, back to the grassroots. Fostering this sense of flexibility among members is essential for later when the cultural revival moves into a political movement and has to face potentially fractious policy decisions about abortion, gay marriage and surrogacy. In a very real way, simple actions like visiting holy wells and enjoying them variously as religious, cultural or symbolic objects depending on one's personal beliefs is setting the ground for a big-tent conservative social policy capable of accommodating various degrees of religiosity.

With a successful base in several communities, there is then the possibility for day trips to other groups to celebrate festivals at their rambling houses, to join their walks and to learn about their history and culture. When an established network of these communities exists in several counties then there is a base that can be leveraged for mass cultural events. It should be the aim of all groups to reclaim the historic landscapes that Leo Varadkar, Simon Harris, Micheal Martin and others have abused for their open borders and globalist messaging. Summer camps that include concerts, lectures, keynotes by non-establishment thinkers billed as monster meetings at Tara, Béal na Bláth, the National Famine Museum, would mark a profound reclamation of Irish history by and for the people of Ireland. Not only would it mark ownership of and commitment to Ireland's past and future, it would be irresistible. And not only to natives. AUR and Filesz owe a great deal of their success to their diasporas. While the Irish diaspora cannot vote in Irish elections, they will—as proven with funding for Sinn Féin in the 1970s and 1980s—provide financial, media and networking backing to an overtly pro-Irish movement. It is essential that a cultural revival remains as 'do-it-yourself' as possible based on grassroots cooperation. However, when the cultural movement evolves into a political movement it would prove highly beneficial to have outside backing both in terms of influence and financing. This cultural revival stage of the movement must be heavily promoted on social media so as to attract maximum attention, excitement and membership. It should be heavily marketed at the Irish diaspora to make them feel included and, in an ideal situation, this phase would see a private fundraising initiative to grow a new media ecosystem alongside the movement. Because the establishment parties can count on the ready support of the national media to push their messaging, it is crucial that this new movement is accompanied by its own professional, and well-funded media wing. Even if said efforts can't break through the news media firewall in Ireland, with the Irish-American diaspora onside, they can get coverage internationally which will force the Irish national press to take note. This media wing will need to develop into a broadcast, radio, news and podcast network capable of influencing national political conversations by the time the movement shifts to politics.

Having established an energetic grassroots base and laid the cultural groundwork, then the movement can show its political face. There is now no need for the party to explicitly call itself nationalist, conservative or anything else because it will be implicitly understood that it is a party for people who love Ireland, who love Irish culture, history and identity—not in a stage-Irish way but in a traditional manner that is rooted in the landscape, customs and traditions of the Irish people. If an emerging party felt the need to define that element of the party then smart branding is advised and wording that is impossible for the national media and political enemies to corner in the minds of low information voters and national TV and newspaper consumers. Less is more. What will need to be defined is practical policy; and that needs to mark a radical alternative to the status quo, particularly in economic matters. That must be a laissez-faire model that works in the financial interests of the nation.

The cultural wing of the movement, a do-it-yourself ethos, rejecting Fianna Fáil and Fine Gael attempts to buy-in, renovating the rambling house with the sweat, funding and time of the community is a crucial step to breaking the handout mentality that has enslaved Irish people since the de Valera economy. Driving the cultural movement to the monster meeting level is an act of self-confidence building that will become the central focus of the economic vision of the party. A laissez-faire economic model supposes a grassroots approach to economic planning that places individuals, their economic needs and freedom to choose who to engage in contractual interaction at the heart of policymaking. A laissez-faire approach to government is dependent on minimal government intervention and shrinking the state in all possible directions. To give a sense of how different this would be to the current economic model supported by all Irish political parties to greater and lesser degrees, let's look at the example of Lisdoonvarna, Co. Clare.

An economically independent Ireland

In 2018, upon hearing that local hotelier James White, the owner of the King Thomond Hotel, planned to enter a deal with the government to house 115 asylum seekers in the village of 300 people, the villagers held a vote on the proposal. Lisdoonvarna is overwhelmingly dependent on tourism for its economic survival. The chairman of a local tourist board, Lisdoonvarna Fáilte, Paddy Dunne, offered to hold a secret ballot vote of villagers to assess the support for Mr White's plan. 197 people voted 'no' to the proposed IPAS centre with only 15 voting 'yes'. The decision was overwhelming. 93% of those eligible to vote did not want the centre.[17] Despite the outcome, after initially agreeing to abide by the result, Mr White took the massive taxpayer-funded pay cheque on offer from the state and singlehandedly destroyed the livelihoods of those people in the village and wider area dependent on the tourist trade. Without government intervention—the offer of a massive bribe to Mr White—he could not have rammed this IPAS centre into Lisdoonvarna against the will of the village. But with the government against them, the people of Lisdoonvarna knew that if they gathered at the gates of the hotel to stop the transfer of illegal immigrants, they would be faced with violence from the state via Garda special units. The state, based far away in Dublin, imposed its will on the people of Lisdoonvarna and in doing so destroyed the local economy, forcing tour groups, hospitality providers and other related private enterprises to scale back or shut down. It further changed the demographic and cultural future of the village forever. Further, Mr White and the government could rely on a financially dependent national media and NGO sector to gin up support for their position.

A laissez-faire approach to economics removes the state from a position of being able to offer absurd and above-market taxpayer-funded bribes to private businesses in order to carry out its political bidding. It can never be the role of the state to make overnight millionaires out of politically compliant individuals. A laissez-faire approach would have kept the state out of the matter and if there was a private offer to Mr White, that would have been a matter for Mr White and his neighbours to sort out. A political party with an economically laissez-faire and socially conservative outlook would not have involved itself, would have trusted the community to come to a reasonable solution and, when the people admirably chose to take a vote on the matter, would have supported the democratic will of the people—not steamrolled it. A laissez-faire economic model places an emphasis on the interactions of people at a grassroots level so when the overwhelming majority democratically voted 'no' to Mr White's frankly economically suicidal proposal for the village, they proved that people are, at the grassroots level, Libertarian in outlook. This brings up an important flaw in the current political model in Ireland. The heavy and authoritarian hand of the state can reach out from Dublin at any moment and turn ancient and peaceful villages upside down overnight without recourse for locals. The local government system is woefully inadequate in preventing this top-down enforcement of policy. A socially conservative but economically laissez-faire model that empowers people at the grassroots level shifts power to local communities and to local and County Councils, making them the primary decision-making points for communities rather than the Dublin-centric Dáil. When all ideas and policies come from Dublin and are enforced throughout the country, it kills individuality and regional distinctions and narrows creativity in public policy formation. More importantly, when the state has fostered the dependency of the media who act more as a Public Relations wing than a critic, and has inserted an NGO wedge between the electorate and the government, then highly progressive legislation coming out of Dublin and forced on small communities far away is oppressive. A laissez-faire model would make it a central policy to cut all unnecessary public funding to outside bodies and let the market —and the market simply means the people—decide which should survive. NGOs, especially those which are lobbyist groups propped up by the government for consensus-forming reasons, would quickly melt away. Only those actually respected and demanded by the public would survive through private funding and donations. The shrinking of the taxpayer-inflated NGO industrial complex would be broken overnight and universities, left with no demand for 'CRT and Black Studies' graduates to said NGOs, would be forced to offer degrees that are valuable to the open market. By simply closing the public purse, a socially conservative and economically laissez-faire government would end the NGO industrial complex overnight and with it, the corrosive influence of Social Justice Theory on society.

Similarly, by closing the public purse to the national media, forcing them to face the free market, there would be a strong initial correction of that market that would result in a number of major casualties. Bauer, Mediahuis and The Irish Times in particular have over-leveraged their market share and have been artificially propped up by the government for some time. They need to be allowed to fail. Doing so shrinks the number of news outlets and broadcasters in circulation but would actually lead to greater diversity of thought and economic stability for those who do survive. Outlets no longer dependent on the government for wages can return to fulfilling their obligations of holding the government to account and performing investigative journalism on political matters.

The most important influence a socially conservative but economically laissez-faire government or major party could have on economic matters is in offering a radical alternative to the FDI economy. Such a party grown out of a cultural movement that places a love of Ireland to the fore prioritises trade that benefits the nation. Since the late 1990s, the FDI economy has stopped working for native Irish interests and has, instead, become a vehicle for Fianna Fáil and Fine Gael politicians to polish their CVs, for their cronies to get rich and for American multinationals to make maximum profits while importing stunning numbers of immigrants to fill positions. Just as the people of Lisdoonvarna never gave the government permission to utterly transform their village overnight, neither has the broader Irish public ever given the government a mandate to utterly transform the nation. In fact, poll after poll has indicated the exact opposite, that people want an end to mass immigration. The FDI economy is not in and of itself a bad thing. If American multinationals want to come to Ireland to do business and provide a benefit to the nation then that is desirable. The FDI economy worked to Ireland's benefit until the mid-1990s because it provided high-status jobs to Irish people without exceeding the reach of the native workforce. Not only did this mean that the type of multinationals that were attracted— chief among them pharmaceutical and manufacture-led tech jobs— provided a useful mix of skilled and semi-skilled labour that aligned with the Irish workforce, but it also placed the native worker at the heart of the economy. This changed radically over the course of the Celtic Tiger and into the present.

As already noted, if any American big tech multinational were to look for a nation in which to open a major operating hub based on the skillsets of the native population, Ireland would be at the very bottom of the list. Ireland simply does not, never has and—based on current computing degree enrolment and dropout rates—never will be a nation that produces an abundance of big tech workers. Yet, despite this, successive governments have continued to lure big tech companies to Ireland with the 12.5% corporation tax break and worldwide tax avoidance loopholes. Successive governments have decided that the tax receipts are worth the housing crisis that has ensued as well as the breakdown in social cohesion that are side effects of mass non-EU hiring by big tech. They have sent a brutally authoritarian message to the native Irish population—if you are unwilling to do what we demand of you to fulfil our vision for the economy, you will be replaced in the workforce and in access to housing, upper-middle-class status and eventually access to the levers of power. It would not be necessary to strip out the current model that has made Ireland wealthy, it simply needs to be reoriented from a top-down model to a grassroots-up model. Rather than providing favourable conditions to multinational companies that squat in Ireland for economic benefits while recruiting from outside, all companies should be invited on the basis that they fit the current worker profile of the nation. Whereas the current authoritarian model demands that universities shape courses and graduates to service the needs of multinationals, the government should only encourage multinationals that fit the graduate profile of Irish universities. This would create a fundamental economic, social and psychological shift in the nation. Multinationals serve the Irish, not the other way around. This has a two-fold effect. When Irish degrees are simply churned out to fill multinational factory floors or else you get tossed on the scrapheap as someone else is imported to do the job, there is no incentive for entrepreneurship or pride in one's work. The fear of missing out on a steady if uninspiring job is powerful if ultimately motivationally castrating. However, when the relationship shifts to one where the worker and graduate are prioritised and made to feel that their skills are valuable, then not only does he feel happier and more motivated in his work but should he stay with that multinational and prove his industriousness, he can feel confident of a promotion or at least that his work is meaningful. More importantly, this prestige allows graduates to feel like they themselves can thrive as entrepreneurs outside of the FDI economy. By de facto appointing universities to be the true talisman in directing the FDI economy, a socially conservative, economically laissez-faire government also unleashes the power of said universities to become innovation hubs. Because those universities are, obviously, based in Ireland, unlike the Headquarters of a multinational in Boston or New York, and have the ability to mould and shape talent, they are uniquely placed to forge the economic future of the nation and spur native industry.

Having pruned the FDI economy to suit the needs of the native workforce and no more, then the proposed party will have secured a baseline of financial stability and employment. However, population growth and contraction are dynamic. The current FDI model, backed by all Irish parties, is based on infinite GDP growth propped up by unlimited legal immigration. This means perpetual growth and with it, the disappearance of Ireland, its culture and homogeneity—all gas no breaks, so to speak. A laissez-faire model on the other hand, directed at unleashing long-abandoned domestic industry, would allow dynamic expansion and contraction alongside the stability of the restructured FDI economy. By reducing social welfare benefits, by dismantling the multi-billion Euro IPAS industry, by reigning in government waste, by dismantling the NGO industrial complex and its Social Justice Theory conveyor belt in Irish universities, and by offloading payouts to the national press, the government would find itself, despite a reduction in FDI corporation tax receipts, in a position to take their boot off of the neck of domestic industry. For example, based on estimates extrapolated from pre-COVID returns when a VAT of 13.5% was last imposed on the hospitality industry, it is believed that this tax will have added between €1.3 and €1.6 billion to the exchequer when 2024 figures are announced. The cost of running IPAS centres for overwhelmingly fake asylum seekers in 2024 was just over €1 billion. Just by eliminating false asylum claims, Ireland could eliminate VAT on hospitality which employs between 180,000 and 200,000 people in Ireland, providing extra stability and tax incentives for further growth of the sector.

It would be a mistake for a socially conservative, economically laissez-faire government to fall back on the old reliables of farming and tourism alone. These are indigenous industries that should be cherished for their cultural significance, promoted, allowed to flourish and seen as essential contributors to the Irish economy. But unless the proposed party can disentangle Ireland from the EU and negotiate its own trade deals on agricultural produce, the room for growth is limited. A wiser near-term option would be to focus on exploiting new industries that can be domestically manned but have the potential to generate massive trade revenues. In a restructured FDI economy in which universities are innovation hubs, they will not simply produce worker bees for American multinationals, they must aim to replace those multinationals with Irish innovation in pharmaceuticals, medical instruments, niche tech, etc. Universities must produce innovators who can be turned out into a low-tax domestic industrial environment where they can thrive. Further to the old reliables of farming, tourism and hospitality, Ireland must aggressively assert its Atlantic fishing rights and harvest its large untapped oil and gas reserves in its waters. Extending into energy with renewed vigour opens up exciting domestic industries for Irish universities to produce graduates for. Establishing a university or technical college specialising in harvesting and processing of fossil and renewable energy in the Atlantic would send a stirring message of rugged independence across the nation. Indeed, in launching its economic vision for Ireland 2.0, this new party should echo what was and what could have been when Cumann na nGaedheal's W.T. Cosgrave electrified rural Ireland in 1929 when he opened Ardnacrusha hydro-electric power station.

Ireland 2.0 is the fulfilment of Cosgrave's vision of a laissez-faire economy, an Ireland of proud Irishmen and women who are given freedom from an economic dependency mindset to shape their future without the boot of the state, native or invader, on their neck for the first time in 800 years.

NOTES

Preface

1. Clare County Library. *The Burren: Introduction.* https://wfblink.net/a4b2vD
2. Lenihan, Eoin. "The Landscape Speaks: A Study of Ringfort Settlement and Dwelling in the Inchiquin Area, Co. Clare" M.A. thesis, National University of Ireland, Galway, 2004.

1. A Nation on Fire

1. Killaguile House | Galway: Landed Estates. University of Galway. https://wfblink.net/WT4Adb
2. "International Protection Accommodation Services (IPAS)." *gov.ie*, https://wfblink.net/lZ73SD
3. Micheál Martin. [@MichealMartinTD]. "I utterly condemn the criminal destruction at Ross Lake House Hotel in Galway. There is never any excuse or place for violence, hatred or intimidation. Those responsible for this criminal act do not speak for their community or this country." *X,* 17 Dec. 2023, 6.27 p.m., https://wfblink.net/lQLNKn
4. GBFM News. "Taoiseach Leo Varadkar 'Deeply Concerned' Over Fire at Ross Lake House in Roscahill." *GalwayBayFM,* 18 Dec. 2023, https://wfblink.net/HIrVj8
5. Dooley, Terence. *Burning the Big House: The Story of the Irish Country House in a Time of War and Revolution*, New Haven: Yale University Press, 2022. (Pp. 280-281)
6. Ibid. 137
7. McCarron, Jack. "Mapped: The Fires Linked to Accommodation for Migrants." *RTE.ie,* 26 July 2024, https://wfblink.net/CBqpW1
8. Fox, Kenneth. "Rate of Ukrainians Arriving in Ireland 10 Times the EU Average." *BreakingNews.ie,* 19 Nov. 2023, https://wfblink.net/jo4qiK
9. "Temporary Protection." *Migration and Home Affairs,* https://wfblink.net/VL4lwg
10. "Minister McEntee Announces Immediate Lifting of Visa Requirements Between Ukraine and Ireland." *gov.ie,* https://wfblink.net/lEhShY
11. Bray, Jennifer. "No Plan to Cap Refugee Numbers, as Taoiseach Says Co Clare Blockade 'Not Necessary.'" *The Irish Times,* 16 May 2023, https://wfblink.net/ZCp9Gs
12. Brennan, Michael. "Leo Varadkar and Cabinet Sub-committee Discussed Cutting Ukrainian Refugee Benefits." *Business Post,* https://wfblink.net/r6PRGU
13. Irish Tourism Industry Confederation. *Irish Tourism Industry Confederation PRESS RELEASE.* 2022, https://wfblink.net/aHpp5h
14. O'Donoghue, Patrick. "Lisdoonvarna: The Home of Matchmaking Where Refugees Now Outnumber Locals." *The Sunday Times,* 12 Aug. 2023, https://wfblink.net/qvphxS

15. McMahon, Páraic. "Hotel Operators Made Millionaires for Accommodating International Protection Applicants Says Clare TD." *Clare Echo*, 26 Mar. 2024, https://wfblink.net/ddvX6k

16. "Purchase Orders for €20,000 or above Quarter 1 2024 Department of Children, Equality, Disability, Integration and Youth." *gov.ie*, https://wfblink.net/FieGbP

17. "Purchase Orders for €20,000 or above Quarter 4 2023 Department of Children, Equality, Disability, Integration and Youth." *gov.ie*, https://wfblink.net/rUXiNH

18. "Lisdoonvarna Direct Provision Centres Receives €2.35m in State Fees in 2020." *Clare FM*, 22 Sept. 2024, https://wfblink.net/jWQzmI

19. McMahon, Páraic. "The Electoral Chair: A Sitting Councillor May Fall in North Clare & Fine Gael Factions." *Clare Echo*, 18 Apr. 2024, https://wfblink.net/ylliUE

20. Fáilte Ireland. *National Tourism Development Authority.* https://wfblink.net/SFOlVO

21. McDermott, Stephen. "Hotels, State Bodies and Direct Provision: The Companies Behind Ireland's Refugee Housing Sector." *TheJournal.ie*, 12 Apr. 2024, https://wfblink.net/bwN8hL

22. Horgan-Jones, Jack, and Cormac McQuinn. "Up To 10,000 Tourism Jobs Displaced Due to Hotel Bed Shortages, Ministers Told." *The Irish Times*, 9 May 2023, https://wfblink.net/sGhLVu

23. Doherty, Tomas. "Charts and Maps Show Which Areas House the Most Ukrainian Refugees." *BreakingNews.ie*, 20 Feb. 2024, https://wfblink.net/23Acfb

24. McNally, Seán McCárthaigh and Tadgh. "More Than 10% of Tourist Beds Being Used to House Refugees." *Irish Examiner*, 15 Dec. 2023, https://wfblink.net/qxCYti

25. Oireachtas. *Dáil Éireann Debate—Wednesday, 17 May 2023.* 17 May 2023, https://wfblink.net/JHrsGo

26. Gleeson, Colin. "About 60 Asylum Seekers Moved Into Santry Complex." *The Irish Times*, 27 May 2023, https://wfblink.net/A3v6so

27. Treacy, Matt. "Who Are the Companies who Regard Ballsbridge and Other Asylum Centres as Prime Investments?" *Gript*, 11 Jan. 2024, https://wfblink.net/4TNEyi

28. Clifford, Mick. "Hotel Housed Staff in Rooms Paid for by State for Asylum Seekers Use." *Irish Examiner*, 18 Sept. 2023, https://wfblink.net/ohMn3x

29. Gleeson, C. "About 60 Asylum Seekers Moved Into Santry Complex." *The Irish Times*, 27 May 2023, https://wfblink.net/a7qwUW

30. Gunning, Fatima. "Santry Residents 'Scared' Over Arrival of 'Hundreds of Unvetted Male' Asylum Seekers." *Gript*, 16 May 2023, https://wfblink.net/tWdi35

31. Ibid.

32. Uí Bhriain, Niamh. "Buncrana: Locals Block Migrant Bus, Say They Won't Accept Centre." *Gript*, 19 Oct. 2023, https://wfblink.net/fzDVip

33. Holland, Kitty, and Jack Power. "Dozens of People Take Part in Anti-asylum Seeker Protests in South Dublin." *The Irish Times*, 19 July 2023, https://wfblink.net/NhR2xk

34. Burne, Louise. "Leo Varadkar Slams Claims That Asylum Seekers Are 'unvetted Migrants.'" *Dublin Live*, 19 Dec. 2023, https://wfblink.net/GckBX9

35. Oireachtas. *International Protection.* 15 Apr. 2025, https://wfblink.net/zzuRTp

36. Uí Bhriain, Niamh. "REVEALED: Asylum Seekers' Fingerprints NOT Checked Against Criminal Databases." *Gript*, 19 Jan. 2024, https://wfblink.net/izsIJ4

37. Oireachtas. *Immigration Policy.* 15 Apr. 2025, https://wfblink.net/8PY51Y

38. Oireachtas. *Immigration Policy.* 21 Jan. 2025, https://wfblink.net/FhCFfY

39. Oireachtas. *Joint Committee on Justice Debate—Tuesday, 23 Apr 2024.* 23 Apr. 2024, https://wfblink.net/iY50pX

40. Oireachtas. *Dáil Éireann Debate—Thursday, 18 Jan 2024.* 18 Jan. 2024, https://wfblink.net/BajHe8

41. Whyte, Barry. "85% of Asylum Seekers Arrive at Dublin Airport Without Identity Documents." *Newstalk,* 29 Feb. 2024, https://wfblink.net/THbVtN

42. IPO. "Monthly Statistical Report on Applications for International Protection in December 2023." *ipo.gov.ie,* https://wfblink.net/LwHhsy

43. Oireachtas. *International Protection.* 15 Apr. 2025, https://wfblink.net/oYtvkm

44. "White Paper on Ending Direct Provision." *gov.ie,* https://wfblink.net/GhCXfD

45. "White Paper on Ending Direct Provision | Executive Summary in Various Languages." *gov.ie,* https://wfblink.net/EBHbQi

46. "Statistics". ipo.gov.ie, https://wfblink.net/6dWa8d

47. Oireachtas. *Asylum Seekers.* 16 Sept. 2024, https://wfblink.net/nusFio

48. "Designated Accommodation Centres." *gov.ie,* https://wfblink.net/cycıuP

49. McKeon, John and Department of Social Protection. Introduction By Mr John McKeon, Secretary General Department Of Social Protection, To The Committee Of Public Accounts. By Committee of Public Accounts, 18 Jan. 2024, https://wfblink.net/uZgthG

50. Bowers, Shauna. "More Than 200 Asylum Seekers Left Without Accommodation." *The Irish Times,* 15 Dec. 2023, https://wfblink.net/aE4ZMt

51. Government of the United Kingdom of Great Britain and Northern Ireland and Government of the Republic of Rwanda. Agreement Between The Government Of The United Kingdom Of Great Britain And Northern Ireland And The Government Of The Republic Of Rwanda For The Provision Of An Asylum Partnership To Strengthen Shared International Commitments On The Protection Of Refugees And Migrants. 2021, https://wfblink.net/ejFPbF

52. Oireachtas. *Joint Committee on Justice Debate—Tuesday, 23 Apr 2024.* 23 Apr. 2024, https://wfblink.net/5c94wF

53. Nolan, Darragh. "Photos Show Conditions Faced by Asylum Seekers Sleeping in Mount Street 'Tent City.'" *Irish Independent,* 30 Apr. 2024, https://wfblink.net/9foKNi

54. Oireachtas. *International Protection.* 16 Apr. 2025, https://wfblink.net/jqZ5vZ

55. Harris, Simon. "Speech of the Leader of Fine Gael, Simon Harris T.D.," *Fine Gael,* 6 Apr. 2024, https://wfblink.net/ssCLNM

56. Pollak, Sorcha. "Citywest Hotel in Dublin Was Paid €53.6m to Accommodate Asylum Seekers and Ukrainian Refugees in 2023." *The Irish Times,* 4 Apr. 2024, https://wfblink.net/NuuQ65

57. Carroll, Rory. "'This Is Cleansing': Dublin Sends in Police and Buses to Dismantle Tent City." *The Guardian,* 2 May 2024, https://wfblink.net/9Ibgbj

58. Holland, Kitty, and Vivienne Clarke. "Grand Canal Asylum Seeker Camp 'Dismantled' With Over 160 People Taken to 'Robust' Tented Accommodation." *The Irish Times,* 9 May 2024, https://wfblink.net/2IZNPo

59. Holland, Kitty, and Jack Power. "Around 40 Tents Pitched on Grand Canal in Dublin Hours After Clearance Operation." *The Irish Times,* 21 May 2024, https://wfblink.net/q6UbSz

60. Holland, Kitty, et al. "Grand Canal: Asylum Seekers' Tents Cleared in Latest Operation." *The Irish Times*, 30 May 2024, https://wfblink.net/MzRCpL

61. O'Brien, Fergal. "Asylum Seekers Pitch Around 30 Tents Along Grand Canal." *RTE.ie*, 20 Aug. 2024, https://wfblink.net/c5krRU

62. The High Court. "Between The Irish Human Rights And Equality Commission Applicant - and the Minister For Children, Equality, Disability, Integration And Youth, Ireland and The Attorney General Respondents", *courts.ie*, https://wfblink.net/PCkZQF

63. Horgan-Jones, Jack, and Seamus Enright. "Ireland Will Not 'Provide Loophole' for Any Other Country's Migration Challenges, Says Harris." *The Irish Times*, 28 Apr. 2024, https://wfblink.net/BJ7mzF

64. Oireachtas. *Dáil Éireann Debate—Tuesday, 30 Jan 2024*. 30 Jan. 2024, https://wfblink.net/B2R8f9

65. Libreri, Samantha. "Protest Over Tented Accommodation Plan in Wicklow." *RTE.ie*, 23 Mar. 2024, https://wfblink.net/HQ6SNC

66. Paul [Pseudonym]. "Trouble at Trudder's River Lodge." *The Greystones Guide*, 15 Mar. 2024, https://wfblink.net/X2mDN3

67. RTÉ News. "Investigation After Fire at Site Earmarked for IPAs." *RTE.ie*, 15 Apr. 2024, https://wfblink.net/gf4YWZ

68. Gript. "Gript Journalist Pepper-sprayed by Gardaí." *Gript*, 25 Apr. 2024, https://wfblink.net/72GqeP

69. Oireachtas. *Dáil Éireann Debate—Tuesday, 30 Apr 2024*. 30 Apr. 2024, https://wfblink.net/X74qMc

70. MacNamee, Garreth. "Violent Chaos at Centre for Asylum Seekers as Man Taken to Hospital." *Extra.ie*, 17 May 2024, https://wfblink.net/8UXtuB

71. Gallagher, Fiachra. "More Than 1,000 Protest Against Housing of Asylum Seekers at Coolock Factory." *The Irish Times*, 24 Mar. 2024, https://wfblink.net/GsgXsC

72. CYPSC. "Socio-Demographic Profile, Dublin City North, 2018" *cypsc.ie*, https://wfblink.net/JzbwJD

73. Mohan, Sathishaa. "Timeline of Trouble in Coolock on Monday 15th July 2024." *Irish Independent*, 21 July 2024, https://wfblink.net/FG7cGo

74. Helen McEntee. [@HMcEntee]. "I am appalled at the violent scenes in Coolock today. This is thuggish criminal behaviour and has no place in our society. The Garda Commissioner has kept me updated throughout the day and he has assured me that everything will be done to bring those responsible to justice." *X*, 15 Jul. 2024, 10.19 p.m., https://wfblink.net/zlDVin

75. Pepper, Diarmuid. "Taoiseach Simon Harris Condemns 'Reprehensible' and 'Criminal' Actions in Coolock." *TheJournal.ie*, 15 July 2024, https://wfblink.net/NYgvj6

76. Gorman, Alison O'Reilly and Sally. "Fifth Fire in a Week Breaks Out at Former Crown Paints Warehouse in Coolock." *Irish Examiner*, 22 July 2024, https://wfblink.net/aFT6mv

77. RTÉ News. "Coolock Site Will Be Used to Accommodate IPAs—O'Gorman." *RTE.ie*, 17 July 2024, https://wfblink.net/HGRgRP

78. Curry, Fran. "Tipp Today Podcast 04/06/24" Tipp Today Podcast, Tipp FM, 4 Jun. 2024, https://wfblink.net/AjSlml

79. McGuirk, Colm et al. "Almost Half of Best-paid Asylum Firms Are Offshore and Often Based in Tax Havens." *Business Plus*, 12 Feb. 2024, https://wfblink.net/PLXigF

80. Leahy, Pat. "Irish Times Poll: Public Mood on Immigration Hardening as Local and European Elections Approach." *The Irish Times*, 17 May 2024, https://wfblink.net/EjV2Gh

81. De Barra, Máirín. "New Poll: 22% of Voters Believe Irish People Being Replaced With Migrants." *Gript*, 2 Aug. 2024, https://wfblink.net/h3MGoI

2. A Crippled Democracy

1. Oireachtas. *Dáil Éireann Debate—Monday, 9 Jan 1922*. 9 Jan. 1922, https://wfblink.net/QjPKv3

2. Oireachtas. *Dáil Éireann Debate—Wednesday, 3 May 1933*. 3 May 1933, https://wfblink.net/dLoeqz

3. Oireachtas. Executive Authority (External Relations) Act, 1936. 12 Dec. 1936, https://wfblink.net/cAnxKI

4. Oireachtas. *Dáil Éireann Debate—Wednesday, 27 Apr 1938*. 27 Apr. 1938, https://wfblink.net/ueWXlX

5. Oireachtas. "The Republic of Ireland Bill, 1948." The Republic of Ireland Bill, 1948, Stationery Office, 15 Dec. 1948, https://wfblink.net/VJtqWS

6. Oireachtas. *Dáil Éireann Debate—Wednesday, 24 Nov 1948*. 24 Nov. 1948, https://wfblink.net/xslpLy

7. Oireachtas. *Dáil Éireann Debate—Monday, 19 Dec 1921*. 19 Dec. 1921, https://wfblink.net/psDs9z

8. Oireachtas. *Dáil Éireann Debate—Friday, 4 Jun 1937*. 4 June 1937, https://wfblink.net/KBoyjf

9. Senato della Repubblica. "Constitution of the Italian Republic." *Constitution of the Italian Republic*, 2019, https://wfblink.net/rKpAqB

10. Fahey, Tony. "Religion and Prosperity." *Studies: An Irish Quarterly Review*, vol. 90, no. 357, 2001, (Pp. 39–46).

11. O'Donoghue, T. A. "Catholicism and the Curriculum: The Irish Secondary School Experience, 1922-62". *Historical Studies in Education / Revue d'histoire De l'éducation*, Vol. 10, no. 1, May 1998, (Pp. 140-58).

12. Central Statistics Office. "Census 1936 Volume I—Population, Area and Valuation of each DED and each larger Unit of Area", *cso.ie*, https://wfblink.net/gLYXxy

13. Central Statistics Office. "Saorstát Éireann, Census of Population 1926, Vol. 10", cso.ie, https://wfblink.net/yFBejl

14. Barry, F. (2024). A reappraisal of Cumann na nGaedheal economic policy. *Irish Political Studies*, 39(2), (Pp.139–161).

15. Oireachtas. *Dáil Éireann Debate—Friday, 25 Apr 1924*. 25 Apr. 1924, https://wfblink.net/AFvyUx

16. Barry, F. (2024). A reappraisal of Cumann na nGaedheal economic policy. *Irish Political Studies*, 39(2), 139–161. https://wfblink.net/aHYotB

17. Oireachtas. *Electricity (Supply) Act 1927*. 28 May 1927, https://wfblink.net/Lniait

18. Oireachtas. *Dáil Éireann Debate—Tuesday, 5 May 1925*. 5 May 1925, https://wfblink.net/wAt2bd

19. O'Mahony, Canice and Andy Bielenberg. "The Shannon Scheme and the Electrification of the Irish Free State." (2002). https://wfblink.net/u2lh1S

20. Oireachtas. *Beet Sugar (Subsidy) Act, 1925.* 15 July 1925, https://wfblink.net/9hNd2J

21. Oireachtas. "Bille Siolruchain Eallach Stuic, 1925." Live Stock Breeding Bill, 1925, https://wfblink.net/rWeFln

22. Oireachtas. "Agricultural Credit Bill, 1927." Saorstat Eireann, 1927, https://wfblink.net/zXENQr

23. Barry, Frank. "A Reappraisal of Cumann Na nGaedheal Economic Policy." *Irish Political Studies*, vol. 39, no. 2, Apr. 2024, (Pp. 139–61).

24. Oireachtas. *Old Age Pensions Act, 1924.* 5 June 1924, https://wfblink.net/dW3lxD

25. Oireachtas. *Old Age Pensions Act, 1928.* 30 Mar. 1928, https://wfblink.net/mgMjr8

26. Oireachtas. *Dáil Éireann Debate—Wednesday, 29 Feb 1928.* 29 Feb. 1928, https://wfblink.net/fHy9vo

27. Oireachtas. *Land Act, 1923.* 9 Aug. 1923, https://wfblink.net/oTHgrm

28. Oireachtas. *Dáil Éireann Debate—Thursday, 17 Nov 1932.* 17 Nov. 1932, https://wfblink.net/u1fRWs

29. Oireachtas. *Seanad Éireann Díospóireacht—Saturday, 14 May 1927.* 14 May 1927, https://wfblink.net/6JP6pO

30. Oireachtas. *Dáil Éireann Debate—Friday, 15 Jul 1932.* 15 July 1932, https://wfblink.net/j7p9R1

31. Oireachtas. *Seanad Éireann Debate—Wednesday, 3 Aug 1932.* 3 Aug. 1932, https://wfblink.net/NQnzE9

32. Coogan, Tim Pat. Ireland in the Twentieth Century. London: Arrow, 2004. (Pp. 187)

33. Oireachtas. *Unemployment Assistance Act, 1933.* 16 Nov. 1933, https://wfblink.net/1jFN1b

34. Oireachtas. "Public Assistance (Acquisition of Land) Bill, 1934." saorstAt Eireann, 1934, https://wfblink.net/FfDgSG

35. Oireachtas. Industrial Credit Bill, *1933.* 1933, https://wfblink.net/NOz1ud

36. Oireachtas. "Control Of Manufactures Bill, 1932." Saorstat E1reann, 1932, https://wfblink.net/Fu9H5V

37. Press, J. P. "Protectionism And The Irish Footwear Industry, 1932-39." *Irish Economic and Social History*, vol. 13, 1986, pp. 74–89.

38. McCabe, Conor. *Sins of the Father: Tracing the Decisions That Shaped the Irish Economy.* The History Press, 2013, (p.24)

39. Oireachtas. Housing (Building Facilities) Bill, *1924.* 1924, https://wfblink.net/7rgdHU

40. Coogan, Tim Pat. Ireland in the Twentieth Century. London: Arrow, 2004. (p.188)

41. Oireachtas. *Dáil Éireann Debate—Wednesday, 25 Feb 1948.* 25 Feb. 1948, https://wfblink.net/2zoHvk

42. Flynn, Kevin Haddick. "The First Coalition: 60 Years On." *History Ireland*, vol. 16, no. 1, 2008, (Pp. 16–17).

43. CSO. *Population Changes Census of Population 2022—Summary Results—Central Statistics Office.* 20 Oct. 2023, https://wfblink.net/WSnP7I

44. Oireachtas. Industrial Development Authority Bill, *1949.* 1949, https://wfblink.net/fKpX6j

45. Oireachtas. Programme for Economic Expansion: Laid by the Government

before Each House of the Oireachtas, November, 1958, 1958, https://wfblink.net/T6vEt9

46. Oireachtas. "Industrial Development (Encouragement Of External Investment) Bill, 1957." *An Bille Um Fhorbairt Tionscail (Infheistiocht On gCjoigrich A Ghriosadh), 1957*, 1957, https://wfblink.net/kF1WFj

47. Oireachtas. *Imposition Of Duties (Confirmation Of Orders) Bill, 1963*. Stationery Office, 13 Nov. 1963, https://wfblink.net/LAZitG

48. Oireachtas. Exchange of Notes Between the Government of Ireland and the Government of the United Kingdom in Connection With Article Xii of the Free Trade Area Agreement Between the Two Governments Signed in London on 14th December, 1965. 1965, https://wfblink.net/UY2dWS

49. Perry, Patrick. "Development Programs in Ireland". *IMF Staff Papers* 1965.001 (1965)

50. Heinz, Wolfgang. "Economic Development and Interest Groups." *Politics and Society in Contemporary Ireland*, edited by Brian Girvin and Roland Sturm, Gower Publishing Company, 1986, (p.90)

51. Donnelly, Paul. "How Foreign Firms Transformed Ireland's Domestic Economy." *The Irish Times*, 13 Nov. 2013, https://wfblink.net/O3s4QM

52. Heinz, Wolfgang. "Economic Development and Interest Groups." *Politics and Society in Contemporary Ireland*, edited by Brian Girvin and Roland Sturm, Gower Publishing Company, 1986, (Pp. 91-92)

53. Keating, Paul, and Derry Desmond. Culture and Capitalism in Contemporary Ireland. Avebury, 1993. (Pp. 28-37)

54. "Trade Factsheets." *gov.ie*, https://wfblink.net/lT6XHf

55. Teagasc. *2020—CAP Provides Important Funds for Irish Farms—Teagasc | Agriculture and Food Development Authority*. https://wfblink.net/vX8CWP

56. Fogarty, M. P. and The Economic and Social Research Institute. "Irish Entrepreneurs Speak For Themselves." Broadsheet, The Economic and Social Research Institute, 1973, https://wfblink.net/20AAdK

57. Keating, Paul, and Derry Desmond. Culture and Capitalism in Contemporary Ireland. Avebury, 1993. (Pp.33-34)

58. CSO. *Migration Society Ireland and the EU at 50—Central Statistics Office*. 17 Oct. 2023, https://wfblink.net/cE8lHu

59. CSO. *Live Register Statement October 2000*, https://wfblink.net/dxjZqC

60. Oireachtas. *Finance Act, 1997*. 22, 1997, pp. 1–75. https://wfblink.net/s2Srsm

61. Everett, Mary and Bank's Statistics Department. "Foreign Direct Investment: An Analysis of Its Significance." *Quarterly Bulletin*, vol. 4, 2006, pp. 93–95. https://wfblink.net/Comkjm

62. Oireachtas. *Taxes Consolidation Act 1997*. 30 Nov. 1997, https://wfblink.net/KjdooQ

63. Oireachtas. Finance Act, *1998*. 1998, https://wfblink.net/79mofc

64. Phelan, Shane. "FitzPatrick 'misled Auditors on Loans up to €100m', Court Told." *Irish Independent*, 4 Nov. 2016, https://wfblink.net/L5VL46

65. O'Toole, Fintan. *Ship of Fools: How Stupidity and Corruption Sank the Celtic Tiger*. Faber, 2009, (p.198)

66. McCabe, Conor. *Sins of the Father: Tracing the Decisions That Shaped the Irish Economy*. The History Press, 2013, (p.55)

67. Oireachtas. Joint Committee of Inquiry into the Banking Crisis debate -Thursday, 23 Jul 2015, https://wfblink.net/8ADilG

68. Citizens Information. *Budget 2007*. https://wfblink.net/HWCojk

69. Duffy, Rónán. "Fine Gael Ministers Discussed US Corporations Paying 'Little or No Tax' Here in the 1980s." *TheJournal.ie*, 20 Dec. 2018, https://wfblink.net/EkG5Sj

70. Communications Directorate and Press and Information Unit. "Judgment of the Court in Case C-465/20 P | Commission V Ireland and Others." *Press Release*, press-release, 10 Sept. 2024, https://wfblink.net/WNqOKv

71. Oireachtas. *Dáil Éireann Debate—Wednesday, 7 Sep 2016*. 7 Sept. 2016, https://wfblink.net/gHnpfq

72. Department of Enterprise, Trade and Employment. *Annual Employment Survey 2020*. 2020, https://wfblink.net/c8k1Lw

73. McCarthy, Larry, et al. *Corporation Tax – 2020 Payments and 2019 Returns*. Apr. 2021, pp. 2–28. https://wfblink.net/TLk34v

74. IDA Ireland, et al. *Annual Employment Survey 2022*. Report, 2022, https://wfblink.net/ogF4FT

75. McCarthy, Larry. *Corporation Tax – 2022 Payments and 2021 Returns*. Report, May 2023, pp. 1–34. https://wfblink.net/Ov8bNR

76. O'Sullivan, Kevin. "Global Leaders Must Respond to Climate Alarm That Has Never Rung so Loudly, Taoiseach Tells Cop28." *The Irish Times*, 2 Dec. 2023, https://wfblink.net/OPCTLl

77. UNFCCC. *Fund for Responding to Loss and Damage*. https://wfblink.net/JO5s1Q

78. Ventura, Luca. "Richest Countries in the World 2024." *Global Finance Magazine*, 16 Apr. 2025, https://wfblink.net/ePCmoq

79. Webber, Jude. "Ireland's Luxury Problem: What to Do With Its €8.6bn Surplus." *Financial Times*, 2 Sept. 2024, https://wfblink.net/1u6Pid

80. Helliwell, John F., et al. "World Happiness Report 2015." *The World Happiness Report*, 23 Apr. 2015, https://wfblink.net/qm5ZHZ

81. Helliwell, John F., et al. "Happiness of the Younger, the Older, and Those in Between | the World Happiness Report.", 2024, https://wfblink.net/XJ3OjL

82. Eurofound. *Becoming Adults: Young People in a Post-pandemic World | European Foundation for the Improvement of Living and Working Conditions*. https://wfblink.net/8gY9fj

83. Central Bank of Ireland. "Quarterly Bulletin." *Quarterly Bulletin*, vol. 01, Mar. 2024, https://wfblink.net/U5t8oX

84. CSO. *Home Ownership and Rent Census of Population 2022 Profile 2—Housing in Ireland—Central Statistics Office*. 20 Oct. 2023, https://wfblink.net/9GcRCP

85. *Daft.ie Rental Price Report: Q2 2024 Infographic*. https://wfblink.net/r1NPWS

86. Ibid.

87. CSO. *Earnings and Labour Costs Q4 2023 (Final) Q1 2024 (Preliminary Estimates)—Central Statistics Office*. 29 May 2024, https://wfblink.net/ShVrmG

88. Leahy, Pat. "Housing Commission Report Suggests Underlying Housing Deficit of up to 256,000 Homes." *The Irish Times*, 21 May 2024, https://wfblink.net/enSl6v

89. CSO. *New Dwelling Completions Q4 2023—Central Statistics Office*. 25 Jan. 2024, https://wfblink.net/8d1TBp

90. "DNG New Homes Transactional Analysis." *DNG Estate Agents*, https://wfblink.net/fSAYuu

91. CSO. *Key Findings Population and Migration Estimates, April 2024—Central Statistics Office*. 27 Aug. 2024, https://wfblink.net/LZdxoi

92. Treacy, Matt. "22% of Population of Ireland Born Overseas, New Figures Show." *Gript*, 30 Mar. 2024, https://wfblink.net/v6ZjAo

93. CSO. *Population and Migration Estimates*, Central Statistics Office, Ireland, 10 Nov. 2003, https://wfblink.net/08inis

94. CSO. *Key Findings Population and Migration Estimates, April 2023—Central Statistics Office.* 26 Sept. 2023, https://wfblink.net/horpcP

95. CSO. *National Income and Expenditure Annual Results 2015—CSO—Central Statistics Office.* 6 Oct. 2016, https://wfblink.net/UyUJwl

96. Burke-Kennedy, Eoin. "The State's Top 10 Corporate Taxpayers: Who Are They?" *The Irish Times*, 30 Dec. 2021, https://wfblink.net/JUpOc2

97. O'Toole, Fintan. *Ship of Fools: How Stupidity and Corruption Sank the Celtic Tiger.* Faber, 2009, (p.162)

98. O'Brien, Carl. "Computer Science Graduates Earn More Than Other Graduates." *The Irish Times*, 7 Dec. 2018, https://wfblink.net/lD2zbE

99. Treacy, Matt. "More Than 70% of Google Jobs Don't Go to Irish People. Yet They're Crowding Dubs Out of the City." *Gript*, 1 Aug. 2021, https://wfblink.net/9ZIbXj

100. Treacy, Matt. "State Loses Bid to Refuse €13billion Apple Windfall." *Gript*, 10 Sept. 2024, https://wfblink.net/KWo37I

101. Treacy, Matt. "Amazon Recruits Almost All of Its Staff Here From Outside of the EU." *Gript*, 12 Sept. 2024, https://wfblink.net/w1A978

102. Gataveckaite, Gabija. "Sinn Féin Wanted to Extend Hate Speech Bill to Give Undocumented Migrants Special Protection." *Irish Independent*, 5 Apr. 2024, https://wfblink.net/P1JY63

103. Oireachtas. *Marriage Act 2015.* 29 Oct. 2015, https://wfblink.net/5ZpCLZ

104. Oireachtas. *Health (Regulation of Termination of Pregnancy) Act 2018.* 20 Dec. 2018, https://wfblink.net/8RNtBR

105. Oireachtas. *Health (Assisted Human Reproduction) Act 2024.* 2 July 2024, https://wfblink.net/2OZaBg

106. Horgan-Jones, Jack. "Sinn Féin Promises to Re-run Referendums on Care and Family if They Fail, Should It Be Returned to Government." *The Irish Times*, 20 Feb. 2024, https://wfblink.net/4Cedfp

107. Sinn Féin. *International Protection: A Fair System That Works.* https://wfblink.net/Pxgs1g

108. "Sinn Féin Backs 12.5% Corporation Tax Rate." *Business Post*, https://wfblink.net/noSukp

109. 192 Sinn Féin European Parliament Manifesto 2024. *Sinn Féin European Parliament Manifesto 2024*, https://wfblink.net/02IlgC

110. Fianna Fáil. "Europe Matters—Manifesto 2024." *Europe Matters*, 2024, https://wfblink.net/JDBxcC

111. Fine Gael. "European Election 2024 Manifesto." *European Election 2024 Manifesto*, pp. 4–8. https://wfblink.net/oUm5UW

112. Libreri, Samantha. "10 Key Points From Sinn Féin's Election Manifesto." *RTE.ie*, 28 Jan. 2020, https://wfblink.net/drp8X3

113. "Sinn Féin Costing Budget, 2019" *gov.ie,* https://wfblink.net/eZwCp8

114. Kelly, Fiach. "Election 2020: What Are the Differences Between FF and FG Promises?" *The Irish Times*, 24 Jan. 2020, https://wfblink.net/i2RSoz

115. Ibid.

116. Libreri, Samantha. "10 Key Points From Sinn Féin's Election Manifesto." *RTE.ie*, 28 Jan. 2020, https://wfblink.net/1kAmU3

117. Kelly, Fiach. "Election 2020: What Are the Differences Between FF and FG Promises?" *The Irish Times*, 24 Jan. 2020, https://wfblink.net/5duowU

118. Libreri, Samantha. "10 Key Points From Sinn Féin's Election Manifesto." *RTE.ie*, 28 Jan. 2020, https://wfblink.net/uosGMI

3. An Empty Vessel

1. Hand, G. J. "The Forgotten Statutes of Kilkenny: A Brief Survey." *Irish Jurist (1966-)*, vol. 1, no. 2, 1966, (Pp.299–312)

2. Ó'Siochrú, Micheál. *God's Executioner: Oliver Cromwell and the Conquest of Ireland*. Farber, 2008, (Pp. 237-238)

3. Killeen, Richard. *Ireland: Land, People, History*. Constable & Robinson, 2012, (Pp.105)

4. Cronin, Mike and O'Callaghan, Liam. *A History of Ireland (2nd Edition)*. Palgrave Macmillan, 2015, (p.74)

5. Arkins, T. "The Penal Laws and Irish Land." *Studies: An Irish Quarterly Review*, vol. 1, no. 3, 1912, (Pp. 514–23)

6. Simms, J. G. "The Bishops' Banishment Act of 1697 (9 Will. III, c. 1)." *Irish Historical Studies*, vol. 17, no. 66, 1970, (Pp.185–99)

7. Corcoran, T. "Enforcing the Penal Code on Education." *The Irish Monthly*, vol. 59, no. 693, 1931, (Pp.149–54)

8. Johnston, John I. D. "Hedge Schools of Tyrone and Monaghan." *Clogher Record*, vol. 7, no. 1, 1969, (Pp. 34–55)

9. O'Sullivan, Muiris, and Liam Downey. "Mass Rocks And Related Sites." *Archaeology Ireland*, vol. 28, no. 1, 2014, (Pp. 26–29)

10. Lyons, Tony. "'Inciting the Lawless and Profligate Adventure'— The Hedge Schools Of Ireland." *History Ireland*, vol. 24, no. 6, 2016, (Pp. 28–31)

11. Clare County Library. *Statistical Survey of the County of Clare 1808—Chapter V.10*. https://wfblink.net/N9bYLh

12. Lyons, Tony. "'Inciting the Lawless and Profligate Adventure'—The Hedge Schools Of Ireland." *History Ireland*, vol. 24, no. 6, 2016, (Pp. 28–31)

13. de Tocqueville, Alexis. *Journeys to England and Ireland*. Read Books, 2011, (Pp.121-122)

14. Ibid., 129-130

15. Ibid., 158

16. Ibid., 160

17. Ibid., 161

18. Ibid., 168

19. Kelly, John. *The Graves Are Walking*. Faber, 2012, (P.2).

20. Hatton, Timothy J., and Jeffrey G. Williamson. "After the Famine: Emigration from Ireland, 1850-1913." *The Journal of Economic History*, vol. 53, no. 3, 1993, (Pp.575–600).

21. Scally, Robert James. *The End of Hidden Ireland*. Oxford University Press, 1995, (Pp.23)

22. Reilly, Ciarán. "Wreckers and Levellers: Evicting Ireland's Poor During the Famine." *RTE.ie*, 14 Aug. 2024, https://wfblink.net/2QvHN7

23. Irish Examiner. "Brutality of Cork's Famine Years: 'I Saw Hovels Crowded With the Sick and the Dying in Every Doorway.'" *Irish Examiner*, 24 May 2020, https://wfblink.net/2kQphX

24. Kelly, John. *The Graves Are Walking*. Faber, 2012, (Pp.1)

25. O'Cathaoir, Brendan. "Grim Start to New Year of Hunger." *The Irish Times*, 4 Jan. 1997, https://wfblink.net/Jia6mq

26. Clare County Library. "Clare Genealogy: Family Histories—Donated Material: Vandeleurs of Kilrush County Clare by Senan Scanlan." *Clare County Library*, https://wfblink.net/U3ghUs

27. Moran, Gerard. "Lost Generation: Children and the Workhouse During the Famine." *RTE.ie*, 25 Feb. 2021, https://wfblink.net/zKTZuT

28. Falc'her-Poyroux, Erick. "The Great Famine in Ireland: a Linguistic and Cultural Disruption." Yann Bévant. La Grande Famine en Irlande 1845-1850, PUR, 2014, (p.2)

29. Killeen, Richard. *Ireland: Land, People, History*. Constable & Robinson, 2012, (Pp. 181)

30. Walsh, T. (2016). The National System of Education, 1831–2000. In: Walsh, B. (Ed.) *Essays in the History of Irish Education*. Palgrave Macmillan, London. (Pp.11)

31. Delay, Cara. "'The Gates Were Shut': Catholics, Chapels, and Power in Late Nineteenth-Century Ireland." *New Hibernia Review / Iris Éireannach Nua*, vol. 14, no. 1, 2010, pp. 14–35.

32. Hyde, Douglas. "The Necessity for De-Anglicising Ireland" *The Future*, 1892, https://wfblink.net/fFhUkQ

33. Walsh, T. (2016). The National System of Education, 1831–2000. In: Walsh, B. (Ed.) *Essays in the History of Irish Education*. Palgrave Macmillan, London.

34. O'Kelly, S. *The Weaver's Grave*. O'Brien Press, 1989, (p.10)

35. Silver, Carole. "On the Origin of Fairies: Victorians, Romantics, and Folk Belief." *Browning Institute Studies*, vol. 14, 1986, (Pp.141–56).

36. Moynihan, Maurice (Ed.) *Speeches and Statements by Eamon De Valera: 1917–73*. Gill & Macmillan, 1980, (p.466)

37. de Tocqueville, Alexis. *Journeys to England and Ireland*. Read Books, 2011, (Pp.172)

38. Oireachtas. *Health (Family Planning) Act, 1979*. 23 July 1979, https://wfblink.net/ysiwLp

39. Oireachtas. *Health (Family Planning) (Amendment) Act, 1985*. 12 Mar. 1985, https://wfblink.net/bBEqkU

40. Oireachtas. *Family Law (Divorce) Act, 1996*. 27 Nov. 1996, https://wfblink.net/ZyKoLL

41. One in Four. "Public Report 4: Murphy Report." *One in Four*, 12 Feb. 2025, https://wfblink.net/zXSxCR

42. World Inequality Lab, et al. "Historical Political Cleavages and Post-Crisis Transformations in Italy, Spain, Portugal and Ireland, 1953-2020." *World Inequality Lab – Working Paper*, 2021, https://wfblink.net/pSK6Yu

43. Oireachtas. *Seanad Éireann Debate—Wednesday, 5 Apr 2006*. 5 Apr. 2006, https://wfblink.net/956X56

44. Sayers, Peig, et al. *Peig: The Autobiography of Peig Sayers of the Great Blasket Island*. Talbot Press, 1973 (Pp. 13)

45. O'Sullivan, Maurice, et al. *Twenty Years A-Growing*. Oxford University Press, 2000, (Pp. 1)
46. Ibid., 90
47. Arensberg, Conrad Maynadier. The Irish Countryman: An Anthropological Study. Waveland Press, 1988, (Pp. 166)
48. Ibid., 172
49. Lenihan, Eddie and Green, Caroline. Eve. *Meeting the Other Crowd, The Fairy Stories of Hidden Ireland* 2004, Penguin, (Pp.115-118)
50. Clarity, James F. "Latoon Journal; if You Believe in Fairies, Don't Bulldoze Their Lair." *The New York Times*, 15 June 1999, https://wfblink.net/J4Wl7w
51. Millman, Lawrence. *Our like will not be there again; notes from the west of Ireland*. Ruminator Books, 1977 (Pp.7)
52. Housing Ireland Magazine. "Ireland's Exploding Housing Emergency." *Housing Ireland Magazine*, 24 July 2017, https://wfblink.net/496Kw2
53. Bohan, Harry. & Shouldice, Frank. *Community and the Soul of Ireland, The Need for Values-Based Change*. Liffey Press, 2002, (Pp. 36)
54. The Heritage Council. *Archaeology 2020. Repositioning Irish Archaeology in the Knowledge Society*. By University College Dublin and The Heritage Council, University College Dublin, 2006, https://wfblink.net/2rTio6
55. Chrisafis, Angelique. "Decision Due on Hill of Tara Motorway." *The Guardian*, 11 Nov. 2004, https://wfblink.net/PFTpGI
56. Heritage Ireland. *Hill of Tara. Heritage Ireland*, https://wfblink.net/3VA8Rj
57. CSO. *Census 2006—Non-Irish Nationals Living in Ireland—CSO—Central Statistics Office*. 1 Oct. 2012, https://wfblink.net/ii1WEd
58. CSO. *Population and Migration Estimates*, report, Central Statistics Office, Ireland, 14 Sept. 2005, https://wfblink.net/WUCeTB

4. Making the Irish "White"

1. Finn, Christina. "Taoiseach: 'St Patrick Was a Migrant to Ireland—a Single, Male, Undocumented One.'" *TheJournal.ie*, 13 Mar. 2024, https://wfblink.net/sBvBXV
2. "News." *gov.ie*, https://wfblink.net/KqdmSb
3. Neeson, Anthony. "Great Hunger Still Haunts: Martin." *Irish Echo Newspaper*, https://wfblink.net/r9hlQA
4. Fine Gael. "Speech of an Taoiseach Simon Harris T.D., Béal Na Bláth Commemoration." *Fine Gael*, 25 Aug. 2024, https://wfblink.net/QBrlG4
5. O'Callaghan, Sean. *To Hell or Barbados*. Brandon Books, 2001, (Pp. 43-44)
6. McGreevy, Ronan. "Remains of Irish Hero Patrick Sarsfield Located After More Than 300 Years." *The Irish Times*, 11 Feb. 2023, https://wfblink.net/WRU6EQ
7. Mahoney, Michael. "Irish Indentured Labour in the Caribbean—the National Archives Blog." *The National Archives Blog*, 14 Feb. 2022, https://wfblink.net/MxJK6Y
8. National Archives Ireland. *Ireland – Australia Transportation Records*. National Archives Ireland. https://wfblink.net/kT6xpn
9. Coogan, Tim. *Wherever the Green is Worn, The Story of the Irish Diaspora*. Arrow, 2002, (Pp.422,437)

10. Ó Cathaoir, Brendan. "Mitchel Politicised the Famine." Seanchas Ardmhacha: Journal of the Armagh Diocesan Historical Society, vol. 20, no. 2, 2005, (Pp.155–62)

11. Miller, Kerby. *Emigrants and Exiles, Ireland and the Irish Exodus to North America*. Oxford University Press, 1985, (Pp.286)

12. Mitchel, John. *The Last Conquest of Ireland (perhaps)*. Irishman Office, 1861. (Pp.187)

13. Coogan, Tim. *The Famine Plot*. St. Martin's Griffin, 2012, (p.229)

14. Coogan, Tim. *Wherever the Green is Worn, The Story of the Irish Diaspora*. Arrow, 2002, (p.458)

15. Quinnell, Sylvia. "Where Irish Settled in Australia." *Hotham History Project*, https://wfblink.net/fSIVJk

16. O'Neill, Siobhan. "Remembering the 4,000 Irish Famine Orphans Shipped to Australia." *The Irish Times*, 25 Oct. 2018, https://wfblink.net/fcsHTc

17. Huntsman, Leone. "Bounty Emigrants to Australia." *Clogher Record*, vol. 17, no. 3, 2002, (Pp.801–12)

18. Miller, Kerby. *Emigrants and Exiles, Ireland and the Irish Exodus to North America*. Oxford University Press, 1985, (Pp. 137)

19. Ibid., 140

20. Ibid.,193, 194, 196

21. Ibid., 212

22. Coogan, Tim. *Wherever the Green is Worn, The Story of the Irish Diaspora*. Arrow, 2002 (p.376)

23. Miller, Kerby. *Emigrants and Exiles, Ireland and the Irish Exodus to North America*. Oxford University Press, 1985, (Pp. 319)

24. McCaffrey, Lawrence J. "Irish America." *The Wilson Quarterly (1976-)*, vol. 9, no. 2, 1985, (Pp.78–93)

25. Shiels, Damian. *The Irish in the American Civil War*. The History Press, 2013, (Pp.27-30)

26. O'Riordan, Sean. "'I Am Very Uneasy to Know if My Husband Is Alive or Dead': Memorial Highlights Irish in US Civil War." *Irish Examiner*, 26 Nov. 2023, https://wfblink.net/6dhzRN

27. Shiels, Damian. *The Irish in the American Civil War*. The History Press, 2013, (p.70)

28. Ibid. 86

29. Cronin, Mike and O'Callaghan, Liam. *A History of Ireland (2nd Edition)*. Palgrave Macmillan, 2015, (p.4)

30. Killeen, Richard. *Ireland: Land, People, History*. Constable & Robinson, 2012, (p.18)

31. O'Sullivan, Niamh. "Scary Tales of New York: Life in the Irish Slums." *The Irish Times*, 23 Mar. 2013, https://wfblink.net/fXQDnE

32. White, Jack. "CSO Records 'Strong Outward Flow' to Australia With 10,600 People Moving There From Ireland." *The Irish Times*, 27 Aug. 2024, https://wfblink.net/hGa5kk

33. Hogan, J. Economic Crises and Policy Change in the Early 1980s: a Four Country Comparison. Journal of Australian Political Economy, No. 65, Winter 2010, (Pp.106-137)

34. The Irish Times. "Net Emigration at Highest Since 1989." *The Irish Times*, 21 Sept. 2010, https://wfblink.net/n1ZPv5

35. "Emigration Today, University College Cork." *University College Cork*, https://wfblink.net/5RBNRJ

36. Bohan, Harry. & Shouldice, Frank. *Community and the Soul of Ireland, The Need for Values-Based Change.* Liffey Press, 2002, (p.6)

37. Dwyer, Ryle. "With Reen at the Helm, We Can Look Ahead With a Sense of Confidence." *Irish Examiner*, 29 May 2020, https://wfblink.net/ToY2U5

38. Oireachtas. *Dáil Éireann Debate—Thursday, 30 Sep 2010.* 30 Sept. 2010, https://wfblink.net/T1elks

39. Scally, Derek, and Burke-Kennedy, Eoin. "Taoiseach Blames Crash on 'mad Borrowing' Frenzy." *The Irish Times*, 26 Jan. 2012, https://wfblink.net/h4FFmZ

40. Oireachtas. *Dáil Éireann Debate—Thursday, 4 Jun 2020.* 4 June 2020, https://wfblink.net/goI4Tf

41. Oireachtas. *Dáil Éireann Debate—Wednesday, 17 Jun 2020.* 17 June 2020, https://wfblink.net/qyZJTx

42. Colette Finn. [@ColetteFinnCork]. "White people in Ireland need to understand that we have an unearned privilege simply being white. Let's examine our own biases on International Migrant's Day." *X*, 18 Dec. 2023, 10.22 a.m., https://wfblink.net/bsEAVi

43. McIntosh, Peggy. "White Privilege: Unpacking the Invisible Knapsack." *Some Notes for Facilitators*, 2010, https://wfblink.net/KD0Rwb

44. Ray, William. "Unpacking Peggy McIntosh's Knapsack." *Quillette*, 20 June 2024, https://wfblink.net/9PfPtG

45. Kendi, Ibram. *How to Be an Antiracist.* Bodley Head, 2023, (p.24)

46. Ibid. 20

47. Owen, David. *Whiteness in Du Bois's The Souls of Black Folk.* Philosophia Africana 10(2), 2007, (Pp.107-126)

48. Race Traitor. *Wayback Machine.* https://wfblink.net/JghHdL

49. Ignatiev, N. "Abolish the White Race." *Harvard Magazine*, September-October, 2002, https://wfblink.net/WS2C7d

50. Ignatiev, Noel. *How the Irish Became White.* Routledge, 1995, (p.2)

51. O'Connell, Daniel. *Address from the People of Ireland To Their Countrymen and Countrywomen in America*, The Liberator, March 25, 1842.

52. Du Bois, W.E.B. "The Philadelphia Negro." Du Bois, W. E. B., and Isabel Eaton. The Philadelphia Negro: a social study. Philadelphia: Published for the University, 1899.

53. Hoeber, Francis W. "Drama in the Courtroom, Theater in the Streets: Philadelphia's Irish Riot of 1831." The Pennsylvania Magazine of History and Biography, vol. 125, no. 3, 2001, pp. 191–232. JSTOR, https://wfblink.net/qojVlP

54. Riach, Douglas. "Ireland and the campaign against American slavery 1830-1860." Ph.D. Thesis, University of Edinburgh, 1975, (p.156)

55. Ignatiev, Noel. *How the Irish Became White.* Routledge, 1995, (p.16)

56. Quinn, John. "The Rise and Fall of Repeal: Slavery and Irish Nationalism in Antebellum Philadelphia." *The Pennsylvania Magazine of History and Biography*, vol. 130, no. 1, 2006, pp. 45–78.

57. Geffen, Elizabeth. "Violence in Philadelphia in the 1840's and 1850's." Pennsylvania History 36, 1969, (Pp. 381-410)

58. Ignatiev, Noel. *How the Irish Became White.* Routledge, 1995, (p.45)

59. Ibid., 47

60. Miller, Kerby. *Emigrants and Exiles, Ireland and the Irish Exodus to North America.* Oxford University Press, 1985, (p.276)

61. Ibid., 258

62. Ibid., 260

63. Ignatiev, Noel. *How the Irish Became White.* Routledge, 1995, (p.81)

64. Ibid., 104

65. Gatewood, Willard B. "Aristocrats of Color: South and North The Black Elite, 1880-1920." *The Journal of Southern History*, vol. 54, no. 1, 1988, pp. 3–20.

5. The Social Justice Industrial Complex

1. Pluckrose, Helen, and Lindsay, James. *Cynical Theories.* Swift Press, 2021, (Pp.59-60)

2. Poulos, C. *Essentials of Autoethnography*, American Psychological Association, 2021, https://wfblink.net/MNVRQ3

3. Goldhill, Olivia. "A Hoax That Targeted Feminist Scholarship Accidentally Revealed a Bigger Problem With Academia." *Quartz*, 20 July 2022, https://wfblink.net/FqH6pu

4. Black Studies—Trinity Electives—Trinity College Dublin. https://wfblink.net/2Htjrs

5. Black Studies and CRT—UCD Module—*EDUC10210*. https://wfblink.net/1yOyJC

6. Malekmian, Shamim. "Dr Ebun Joseph: Why Black Studies Matter in Ireland and Responding to the Murder of George Floyd." *Hotpress*, 8 June 2020, https://wfblink.net/jDKlrg

7. Joseph, Ebun. "Making sense of race in global justice education." *Challenging Perceptions of Africa in Schools, Critical Approaches to Global Justice Education,* (Eds.) O'Toole, Barbara et al., Routledge, 2019, (Pp.162)

8. McGinnity, Francis et al. "Ethnicity and Nationality in the Irish Labour Market." Dublin: *ESRI and The Irish Human Rights and Equality Commission (IHREC)*, 2018, https://wfblink.net/8xiVYq

9. McGinnity, Frances and Kingston, Gillian. An Irish Welcome? Changing Irish Attitudes to Immigrants and Immigration: The Role of Recession and Immigration. *The Economic and Social Review.* Vol 48., 2017, (Pp.281-304)

10. Bidwell, Posy et al. "The national and international implications of a decade of doctor migration in the Irish context." *Health policy (Amsterdam, Netherlands)* vol. 110,(1),2013, (Pp.29-38)

11. Office of the Attorney General. "Twenty-Seventh Amendment of the Constitution Act, 2004, Schedule." *(C) Houses of the Oireachtas Service*, https://wfblink.net/BIohCY

12. O'Donoghue, Patrick. "Nigeria Is a Safe Country, Says Ambassador Amid Rise in Asylum Claims." *The Sunday Times*, 16 Nov. 2024, https://wfblink.net/ioy8J8

13. The Irish Times. "Nigerians Who Pose as Refugees Are Doing a Disservice to Themselves and Their Country." *The Irish Times*, 14 Aug. 2000, https://wfblink.net/1TYRQy

14. Hilliard, Mark. "Direct Provision in Ireland: How and Why the System Was Introduced." *The Irish Times*, 19 Nov. 2019, https://wfblink.net/zVI6p3

15. Mahon, Brian. "Taoiseach Admits Majority of Asylum Seekers Are Economic Migrants." *Extra.ie*, 5 Mar. 2025, https://wfblink.net/Nhq51Y

16. Joseph, Ebun. "Making sense of race in global justice education." *Challenging Perceptions of Africa in Schools, Critical Approaches to Global Justice Education*, (Eds.) O'Toole, Barbara et al., Routledge, 2019, (Pp.162-163)

17. Oireachtas. *Criminal Justice (Hate Offences) Act 2024*. 2024, https://wfblink.net/Vl6dZV

18. Parents in Uproar Following SPHE Portrayal of an 'Irish Family.' – Carol Nolan TD. https://wfblink.net/YCPSAZ

19. Ibid.

20. National Council for Curriculum and Assessment. *Social, Personal and Health Education (SPHE) Specification for Junior Cycle*. Feb. 2023, https://wfblink.net/b8jNsN

21. De Barra, Máirín. "'Don't Buy Them': New SPHE Book Contains 'Misleading' and 'Unscientific' Trans Content Say Parents." *Gript*, 5 Sept. 2024, https://wfblink.net/GeZP7I

22. Kempny, Marta, et al. Anti-racism Principles For Irish Higher Education Institutions. 2023, https://wfblink.net/Kzz4O9

23. Gender, Sexuality and Culture.—UCD—https://wfblink.net/9hmBgp

24. Race, Ethnicity, Conflict *(M.Phil.)*—Trinity College Dublin—*Courses, Trinity College Dublin*. https://wfblink.net/X3HO1X

25. Rights and Social Policy—Maynooth—"MSOCSC Social Science (Rights And Social Policy)." *Maynooth University*, https://wfblink.net/RtwsPd

26. Benefacts. *Nonprofit Sector Analysis 2021*. 2021, https://wfblink.net/UrbowG

27. Ibid.

28. Revenue. *Conditions for Retaining Charitable Tax Exemption*. https://wfblink.net/iYyWV3

29. Immigrant Council of Ireland. *Vision and Mission: Immigrant Council of Ireland*. https://wfblink.net/LoxaW2

30. Kavanagh, Gary. "An In-depth Look at the Funding of Ireland's Loudest NGO." *Gript*, 8 Feb. 2024, https://wfblink.net/dnV69W

31. Wilson, Jade. "Tributes Paid to Ashling Murphy at Vigils in Ireland, London and New York." *The Irish Times*, 15 Jan. 2022, https://wfblink.net/yk0Pww

32. Hogan, Caelainn. "Ashling Murphy's Killing Has Shocked Ireland – but Will It Change a Culture of Misogyny?" *The Guardian*, 18 Jan. 2022, https://wfblink.net/6Lrd4O

33. McCurry Cate and Ward James. "Thousands Gather Outside Leinster House for Emotional Vigil for Ashling Murphy." *BelfastTelegraph.co.uk*, 14 Jan. 2022, https://wfblink.net/2B9SUM

34. Martin, Micheál. "Dáil Statement by the Taoiseach, Micheál Martin on Violence Against Women." *gov.ie*, 19 Jan. 2022, https://wfblink.net/piJfTv

35. MacNamee, Garreth. "Puska Was a Convicted Sex Offender and 'Person of Interest' in Two Other Assaults on Women." *Extra.ie*, 11 Nov. 2023, https://wfblink.net/PdTHWx

36. "Directive 2004/38/EC Of The European Parliament And Of The Council", 29 Apr. 2004, *L_2004158EN.01007701.xml*. https://wfblink.net/GfwruF

37. Cotter, Eimear. "'I Sit at the Shrine I Made for Her in My Room Before Going to Bed Each Night" *Irish Independent*, 17 Nov. 2023, https://wfblink.net/OamEyv

38. McGuirk, John. "In Silencing Ryan Casey, the Media Abandons All Pretence." *Gript*, 20 Nov. 2023, https://wfblink.net/4jyLvy

39. https://www.youtube.com/watch?v=PnucUQTy-SA

40. Oireachtas. *Dáil Éireann Debate—Wednesday, 24 Jan 2024*. 24 Jan. 2024, https://wfblink.net/FioGH6

41. https://wfblink.net/ot2U2B

42. "Government Publishes Zero Tolerance Strategy to Tackle Domestic, Sexual and Gender-based Violence." *gov.ie*, https://wfblink.net/juFD9O

43. Lenihan, Eoin. "Irish Leftists Blame Violence Against Women on Misogyny to Hide the Real Cause: Open Borders." *The Federalist*, 28 Nov. 2023, https://wfblink.net/JuRswN

44. Dunphy, Liz. "One Year on From Ashling Murphy's Death Has Anything Really Changed?" *Irish Examiner*, 12 Jan. 2023, https://wfblink.net/oQgfdB

45. Charities Regulator. "Safe Ireland National Social Change Agency Company Limited by Guarantee". *Charities Regulator*, https://wfblink.net/o1AsXA

46. Department of Justice. "Zero Tolerance: Third National Strategy on Domestic, Sexual & Gender-Based Violence 2022-2026", https://wfblink.net/tKZHtC

47. Department of Children, Equality, Disability, Integration and Youth. "National Action Plan Against Racism", *gov.ie* https://wfblink.net/Bszb3H

48. Amnesty International. "Let's Talk About 'Yes': Consent Laws in Europe." *Amnesty International*, 18 Sept. 2024, https://wfblink.net/A4FB9g

49. Batha, Emma. "Rape Conviction Rates Rise 75% in Sweden After Change in the Law." *Reuters*, 22 June 2020, https://wfblink.net/EH6b3c

50. Department of Justice. "Monitoring the Implementation of Zero Tolerance: The Third National Strategy on Domestic, Sexual and Gender-Based Violence." *Zero Tolerance Third National Strategy on Domestic, Sexual & Gender-Based Violence 2022-2026*, 2022, p. 1. https://wfblink.net/A5TCvR

6. The National Media Firewall

1. RTE. "Opening Night President's Address." *RTÉ Archives*, 1 Dec. 2011, https://wfblink.net/yzpf6w

2. O'Connell, Hugh. "'Ireland's Watergate': How the Phone Tapping Scandal Would Lead to Haughey's Downfall... Eventually." *TheJournal.ie*, 27 Dec. 2013, https://wfblink.net/SfbsA1

3. Oireachtas. Interception of Postal Packets and Telecommunications Messages (Regulation) Act, 1993. 6 June 1993, https://wfblink.net/xRQ2Yd

4. Eidenmuller, Michael E. Online Speech Bank: Veronica Guerin -- International Press Freedom Award Acceptance Speech. https://wfblink.net/9gzCso

5. Office of the Attorney General. "Defamation Act 2009." *Houses of the Oireachtas Service*, https://wfblink.net/zk35R5

6. Carswell, Simon. "Self-help Guru Tony Robbins Sues Buzzfeed in Irish Courts." *The Irish Times*, 27 Nov. 2019, https://wfblink.net/TzHmgw

7. International Press Institute. "In Depth: Libel Damages Squeeze Ireland's Press." *ipi.media*, 11 Jan. 2017, https://wfblink.net/kWldpz

8. The Irish Times. "TV3 Ordered to Pay Half of €140,000 Award to Solicitor Pending Appeal." *The Irish Times*, 27 Nov. 2015, https://wfblink.net/yCFNAT

9. "Lappin V Mediahuis UK Ltd and Ors (Approved), [2023] IEHC 668 | High Court of Ireland, Judgment, Law, casemine.com." https://wfblink.net/qtz0Ut

10. Cox, James. "Sinn Féin Constituency Organiser's Defamation Claim Against Mediahuis and Reporter Dismissed." *BreakingNews.ie*, 29 Nov. 2023, https://wfblink.net/WHghke

11. Bell, Master, et al. "Neutral Citation No: [2024] NIMaster 1." *In The High Court Of Justice Of Northern Ireland—King's Bench Division*, by Mr McKenna and Miss Herdman, Jan. 2024, https://wfblink.net/BDfE3G

12. "Ireland: RSF and Its Partners Urge Sinn Féin to Stop Taking Intimidating Legal Action Against the Media and Journalists." *RSF*, https://wfblink.net/bf4AY5

13. Oireachtas. *Dáil Éireann Debate—Wednesday, 8 Nov 2023*. 8 Nov. 2023, https://wfblink.net/KB5Scq

14. Slattery, Laura. "Irish Times Group Returns to Profit as Revenues Climb 5%." *The Irish Times*, 8 Oct. 2024, https://wfblink.net/j8b5xL

15. Slattery, Laura. "The Irish Times Group Posts Operating Profit of €2.9m." *The Irish Times*, 24 Nov. 2022, https://wfblink.net/Q9ELTl

16. O'Donovan, Donal. "Profits up at Mediahuis Ireland's Newspaper Arm." *Irish Independent*, 22 Nov. 2024, https://wfblink.net/YXkaze

17. O'Donovan, Donal. "O'Brien's Communicorp Dialed up A Profit in 2019." *Irish Independent*, 23 Dec. 2020, https://wfblink.net/M8C9k1

18. Slattery, Laura. "News Publishers Welcome Zero VAT Rate as 'Tax on Information' Ends." *The Irish Times*, 27 Sept. 2022, https://wfblink.net/n3q04h

19. McDonald, Theo. "Almost 600 Hospitality Businesses Forced to Close Since Government's Hike in VAT Rate, Report Says." *Irish Independent*, 8 Aug. 2024, https://wfblink.net/izLwwK

20. Tóibín, Peadar. [@Toibin1]. "The winks, guffaws & grins from FF & FG TDs to the Press Gallery in #Budget23 as the Minister announced a zero VAT rate for newspapers, was more than a little uncomfortable." *X*, 27 Sept. 2022, 5.43 p.m., https://wfblink.net/yiFXyZ

21. O'Connell, Hugh. [@oconnellhugh]. "Cries of "hear, hear" from the press gallery as Paschal Donohoe announces the abolition of VAT on newspapers and digital publications" *X*, 27 Sept. 2022, 2.35 p.m., https://wfblink.net/ezBKXZ

22. O'Connell, Hugh. [@oconnellhugh]. "The politicians were pretty happy about it as well" *X*, 27 Sept. 2022, 2.35 p.m. https://wfblink.net/zl3RYA

23. Oireachtas. *Departmental Advertising*. 15 Apr. 2025, https://wfblink.net/byn8s6

24. RTE. *Annual Report and Group Financial Statements 2022*. 2022, https://wfblink.net/V2zRRX

25. *RTÉ Annual Report 2023*. Report, 2023, https://wfblink.net/ouMxV1

26. Cionnaith, Fiachra Ó. "€725m Funding Plan for RTÉ Not a 'Blank Cheque'—Martin." *RTE.ie*, 25 July 2024, https://wfblink.net/WjStjQ

27. Coimisiun na Mean. "Equality, Diversity & Inclusion—Coimisiún Na Meán." *Coimisiún Na Meán*, 13 Jan. 2025, https://wfblink.net/3Q1jwf

28. Broadcasting Authority of Ireland. "BAI Announces Funding of €7.2m Under Sound and Vision Scheme—Broadcasting Authority of Ireland." *Broadcasting Authority of Ireland*, 31 May 2021, https://wfblink.net/ZWo9bo

29. Broadcasting Authority of Ireland. "BAI Announces Funding of €5.9m Under Sound and Vision Scheme—Broadcasting Authority of Ireland." *Broadcasting Authority of Ireland*, 18 Nov. 2021, https://wfblink.net/GJsmoo

30. Broadcasting Authority of Ireland. "BAI Announces Funding of €6.4m Under Sound & Vision Scheme—Broadcasting Authority of Ireland." *Broadcasting Authority of Ireland*, 23 Mar. 2022, https://wfblink.net/3PURof

31. Broadcasting Authority of Ireland. "BAI Announces Funding of €6m Under Sound and Vision Scheme—Broadcasting Authority of Ireland." *Broadcasting Authority of Ireland*, 10 Aug. 2022, https://wfblink.net/wrYddi

32. Broadcasting Authority of Ireland. "BAI Announces Funding of €5m Under Sound and Vision Scheme—Broadcasting Authority of Ireland." *Broadcasting Authority of Ireland*, 19 Dec. 2022, https://wfblink.net/7zFklo

33. Broadcasting Authority of Ireland. "€4m Funding Awarded Under Our Latest Sound and Vision Round." *Coimisiún Na Meán*, 28 Jan. 2025, https://wfblink.net/6rGCO6

34. O'Rourke, Evelyn. "Coimisiún Na Meán Allocates €5.7 Million to News Outlets." *RTE.ie*, 6 Feb. 2025, https://wfblink.net/CukNwW

35. *Global Ireland—Ireland's Global Footprint to 2025 | Ireland.ie*. https://wfblink.net/tKioH5

36. Tighe, Mark. "News Media Applying for €1.8m State Grants Were Asked to Consider Focusing More on Climate Change and Rise of Populism" *Irish Independent*, 6 Oct. 2024, https://wfblink.net/UNvgmI

37. Ibid.

38. "Special Advisors to Ministers and Ministers of State of the 33rd Dáil." *gov.ie*, 17 Apr. 2025, https://wfblink.net/iDurxO

39. Cullen, Paul, and Ciarán D'Arcy. "New National Children's Hospital at St James's Granted Planning." *The Irish Times*, 28 Apr. 2016, https://wfblink.net/C64yaN

40. Cullen, Paul. "State Awards €1bn Children's Hospital Contract to BAM Ireland." *The Irish Times*, 4 Feb. 2017, https://wfblink.net/MeQBJe

41. Horgan-Jones, Jack, et al. "National Children's Hospital Cost Has Risen to More Than €2.2bn, Donnelly Confirms." *The Irish Times*, 13 Feb. 2024, https://wfblink.net/xQpbmX

42. O'Regan, Eilish. "Builders of New Children's Hospital Want Extra €853m." *Irish Independent*, 18 Feb. 2025, https://wfblink.net/7kZndg

43. Molony, Senan. "Micheál Martin Accuses Contractor of National Children's Hospital in Dáil of 'Delaying' Completion to 'Extract." *Irish Independent*, 30 May 2024, https://wfblink.net/xqTO5p

44. Burne, Louise. "Government Will 'robustly Push Back on' Further Bills for Children's Hospital." *Irish Mirror*, 18 Feb. 2025, https://wfblink.net/bALcPV

45. Ní Aodha, Gráinne. "Lessons Will Be Learned From 'Infamous' Leinster House Bike Shed, Dáil Told." *BreakingNews.ie*, 18 Sept. 2024, https://wfblink.net/odC9D7

46. Cionnaith, Fiachra Ó. "€1.4m Spend On Security Office 'Ridiculous'—Tánaiste." *RTE.ie*, 25 Sept. 2024, https://wfblink.net/Bs9021

47. Tóibín, Peadar. [@Toibin1]. "Long thread. I've completed a timeline of events relating to the bike shelter. A lot of people have been asking me if there were any political shenanigans at play. Here's the nuts and bolts of what I've uncovered." [Series of 12 Tweets] *X*, 26 Sept. 2024, 2.50 p.m., https://wfblink.net/EywihK

48. Murphy, Paul. "'We're Paying Too Much' – Value for Money and the OPW." *RTE.ie*, 1 Apr. 2021, https://wfblink.net/9rLqRB

49. Kelleher, Olivia. "Justice Minister Says 'No Facts' Back up Claim That Increased

Migration Leads to Rising Crime Rates." *Irish Examiner*, 17 Feb. 2024, https://wfblink.net/vojNg9

50. McShane, Ian, et al. "Thirty-sixth Amendment to the Constitution Exit Poll." *RTÉ & Behaviour & Attitudes Exit Poll*, report, 2018, https://wfblink.net/9WZqzT

51. Kenny, Aisling. "Govt Working on Plans for Influx of Ukrainian Refugees." *RTE.ie*, 2 Mar. 2022, https://wfblink.net/kNXPbY

52. The Irish Times. "Dublin Pensioner Opens Home to Traumatised Ukrainian Family." *The Irish Times*, 18 Mar. 2022, https://wfblink.net/1ZXcwd

53. Anderson, Nicola. "'We Can't Just Sit Around All Day, We Want the Dignity of Working,' Say Ukrainian Refugees Living in Sports Ha." *Irish Independent*, 16 Nov. 2022, https://wfblink.net/MJhHfC

54. McQuinn, Cormac. "More Than 7,100 Ukrainian Refugees Now in Employment in Ireland." *The Irish Times*, 22 Aug. 2022, https://wfblink.net/oRmWm7

55. McQuinn, Cormac. "17,000 Ukrainians Now in Full-time Employment in Ireland, TDs Told." *The Irish Times*, 18 Jan. 2024, https://wfblink.net/aITtzY

56. Pepper, Diarmuid. "President Says Israel Reducing Humanitarian Law 'To Tatters', Criticises EU Commission President." *TheJournal.ie*, 16 Oct. 2023, https://wfblink.net/RG0ob3

57. Finn, Christina. "Israeli Ambassador's Comments About President Michael D Higgins 'unhelpful', Says Coveney." *TheJournal.ie*, 23 Oct. 2023, https://wfblink.net/OjVaCo

58. McCormack, Jayne. Sinn Féin Call for Israeli Ambassador to Ireland to Be Expelled. 3 Nov. 2023, https://wfblink.net/TWmoXq

59. Correspondent, Paul Hosford Political. "EU's Response to War on Gaza Is 'Despicable', Says Holly Cairns." *Irish Examiner*, 15 Nov. 2023, https://wfblink.net/7WV7hc

60. Oireachtas. *Dáil Éireann Debate—Thursday, 7 Nov 2024*. 7 Nov. 2024, https://wfblink.net/Unf9mV

61. O'Cearbhaill, Muiris. "First Group of Children Arrive From Palestine to Receive Life-saving Healthcare in Ireland." *TheJournal.ie*, 20 Dec. 2024, https://wfblink.net/GiXynX

62. Kelly, Emma O. "Palestinian Family Sleeping in Car 'Feel Hopeless'" *RTE.ie*, 27 Feb. 2025, https://wfblink.net/pSzxQq

63. Pollak, Sorcha. "Number of Palestinians Seeking Asylum in Ireland Rises Eightfold." *The Irish Times*, 7 Feb. 2025, https://wfblink.net/pop1XF

64. Conneely, Ailbhe. "Murder of Ashling Murphy Was a 'Watershed Moment'" *RTE.ie*, 10 Nov. 2023, https://wfblink.net/3hzOi4

65. Conneely, Ailbhe. "Shortcomings in Govt Policy on Gender-based Violence." *RTE.ie*, 8 Dec. 2023, https://wfblink.net/Yo5ysz

66. McGee, Harry. "Charlie Flanagan: 'My Father Was a Controversial Figure . . . I Disagreed With Much of What He Stood For.'" *The Irish Times*, 30 Sept. 2023, https://wfblink.net/NwXST7

67. Maynes, Maria. "Mattie McGrath: I Was Locked Out of Meeting on Clonmel Modular Homes." *Gript*, 24 Apr. 2024, https://wfblink.net/rUkzMB

68. Ibid.

69. Kelleher, Eoin. "'Disquiet' in Tipperary Over Plans to House Ukrainians in 82 Modular Homes in Clonmel." *Irish Independent*, 19 Apr. 2024, https://wfblink.net/zm3PQa

70. RTÉ News. "Clonmel Assault Condemned as 'Intolerable'—Smyth." *RTE.ie*, 18 May 2024, https://wfblink.net/WK47p0

71. Dalton, Eoghan. "Protestors Have Disrupted Events and Threatened People—Simply for Supporting Those in Need." *TheJournal.ie*, 6 Oct. 2024, https://wfblink.net/cAL2oM

72. Buchanan, Myles. "Wicklow Screening of Anti-racism Film to Go Ahead After Three Venues Cancel." *Irish Independent*, 20 Sept. 2024, https://wfblink.net/FYATZH

73. Paul [Pseudonym]. "Speakers' Corner: Kellie McConnell." *The Greystones Guide*, 18 May 2024, https://wfblink.net/W6nmhT

74. Bernadette d'Arcy. [@Bernieadufe]. "#FreePalestine A brilliant show of solidarity with Palestine today in Dublin. Our government has to listen to the people on the street. #StopGenocideinGazaNow #FreePalestine" *X*, 31 Aug. 2024, 8.54 p.m., https://wfblink.net/GlArgP

75. Reuters Institute. "Interactive." *Reuters Institute for the Study of Journalism*, 2024, https://wfblink.net/5NG9U5

76. Murrell, Colleen, et al. Digital News Report Ireland 2024. *Digital News Report Ireland 2024*, https://wfblink.net/2gwfrE

77. O'Neill, Conor. "How Ireland Voted in Maps and Charts." *Sky News*, 1 Dec. 2024, https://wfblink.net/YEatK4

78. McHale, Michael. "Irish Over-65 Population Increases by More Than One-third in a Decade." *Irish Medical Times*, 17 Feb. 2025, https://wfblink.net/6gS1ps

7. Ireland 2.0

1. Aontú. "Housing Crisis—Aontú." *Aontú*, 7 Jan. 2025, https://wfblink.net/NtP95Q

2. Independent Ireland. *Housing and Planning*. https://wfblink.net/PBZd7z

3. Irish Freedom Party. *Political Programme and Constitution of the Irish Freedom Party*. https://wfblink.net/XUltq3

4. European Movement Ireland. "Press Release: Support for Ireland Remaining a Member of the EU Remains Stable and Overwhelmingly Positive." *European Movement Ireland*, 21 Dec. 2023, https://wfblink.net/2p7chG

5. McDermott, Stephen. "The Far-right Failed in the General Election—but Reports of Their Death Have Been Exaggerated." *TheJournal.ie*, 4 Dec. 2024, https://wfblink.net/EuJF2P

6. Gallagher, Conor. "The Mystery of the Far-right National Party's €400,000 Gold: Where Could It Have Come From?" *The Irish Times*, 28 July 2023, https://wfblink.net/oag0st

7. Sherry, Alan. "Justin Barrett Is a 'Tout' for Going to Gardai About Gold Bars, New Party Chief Claims." *SundayWorld.com*, 7 Oct. 2023, https://wfblink.net/HcZBW5

8. Logos Revealed. "Logos Academy Episode 38: Justin Barrett." *Rumble*, 21 Mar. 2001, https://wfblink.net/YdLG2P

9. Bensmann, Marcus. "Germany, the Far-right and 'The People.'" *Voxeurop*, 23 Feb. 2025, https://wfblink.net/sJHTw2

10. Salido-Medina, José. (2025) Extremism and Places of Worship: Analysis of Strategies and Ideological Motivations. *Peace Review* 37:1, 2025, (Pp.118-133)

11. Deutsche Welle (DW). "Germany: AfD Youth Group Can Be Classified as 'extremist.'" *dw.com*, 6 Feb. 2024, https://wfblink.net/Cd5A5P

12. Pfeifer, Hans. "Why Germany's Far-right AfD Youth Wing Faces a Ban." *dw.com*, 27 Feb. 2024, https://wfblink.net/Hx2Not

13. Table Media. "Alice Weidel Beendet Zusammenarbeit Mit Ihrem Referenten Roland Hartwig." *Table.Media*, 15 Jan. 2024, https://wfblink.net/1UjvUt

14. Woods, Keith. "Nationalism Doesn't Need National Socialism." *Keith Woods*, 5 Mar. 2025, https://wfblink.net/5li6jR

15. Woods, Keith. "Nationalism Vs. Neo-Nazism." *Keith Woods*, 23 Mar. 2025, https://wfblink.net/ir1tTG

16. Kosa, Andras, et al. "At Viktor Orban's Romanian Summer Camp, He Praises Trump and Says the Ukraine War Is Our 'Red Pill.'" *RadioFreeEurope/RadioLiberty*, 29 July 2024, https://wfblink.net/SpPgPr

17. Deegan, Gordon. "Lisdoonvarna Locals Reject Direct Provision Plan." *The Irish Times*, 2 Mar. 2018, https://wfblink.net/T5XAnc

BIBLIOGRAPHY

Amnesty International. "Let's Talk About 'Yes': Consent Laws in Europe." Amnesty International, 18 Sept. 2024, https://wfblink.net/pWVUoe.

Anderson, Nicola. "'We Can't Just Sit Around All Day, We Want the Dignity of Working,' Say Ukrainian Refugees Living in Sports Ha." Irish Independent, 16 Nov. 2022, https://wfblink.net/zLNpXs.

Arensberg, Conrad Maynadier. The Irish Countryman: An Anthropological Study. Waveland Press, 1988.

Arkins, T. "The Penal Laws and Irish Land." Studies: An Irish Quarterly Review, vol. 1, no. 3, 1912, (Pp. 514–23).

Barry, F. (2024). A reappraisal of Cumann na nGaedheal economic policy. Irish Political Studies, 39(2), (Pp.139–161).

Batha, Emma. "Rape Conviction Rates Rise 75% in Sweden After Change in the Law." Reuters, 22 June 2020, https://wfblink.net/MKvHaG.

Bell, Master, et al. "Neutral Citation No: [2024] NIMaster 1." IN THE HIGH COURT OF JUSTICE OF NORTHERN IRELAND—KING'S BENCH DIVISION, by Mr McKenna and Miss Herdman, Jan. 2024, https://wfblink.net/OSWW5D.

Benefacts. Nonprofit Sector Analysis 2021. 2021, benefactslegacy.ie/wp-content/uploads/2022/03/benefacts-nonprofit-sector-analysis-2021.pdf.

Bernadette d'Arcy. [@Bernieadufe]. "#FreePalestine A brilliant show of solidarity with Palestine today in Dublin. Our government has to listen to the people on the street. #StopGenocideinGazaNow #FreePalestine" X, 31 Aug. 2024, 8.54 p.m., https://wfblink.net/V7d3A6.

Bidwell, Posy et al. "The national and international implications of a decade of doctor migration in the Irish context." Health policy (Amsterdam, Netherlands) vol. 110,(1), 2013, (Pp.29-38).

Bohan, Harry. & Shouldice, Frank. Community and the Soul of Ireland, The Need for Values-Based Change. Liffey Press, 2002.

Broadcasting Authority of Ireland. "BAI Announces Funding of €7.2m Under Sound and Vision Scheme—Broadcasting Authority of Ireland." Broadcasting Authority of Ireland, 31 May 2021, https://wfblink.net/8DWSJj.

Broadcasting Authority of Ireland. "BAI Announces Funding of €5.9m Under Sound and Vision Scheme—Broadcasting Authority of Ireland." Broadcasting Authority of Ireland, 18 Nov. 2021, https://wfblink.net/xOfiZb.

Broadcasting Authority of Ireland. "BAI Announces Funding of €6.4m Under Sound & Vision Scheme—Broadcasting Authority of Ireland." Broadcasting Authority of Ireland, 23 Mar. 2022, https://wfblink.net/xFTjWt.

Broadcasting Authority of Ireland. "BAI Announces Funding of €6m Under Sound and

Vision Scheme—Broadcasting Authority of Ireland." Broadcasting Authority of Ireland, 10 Aug. 2022, https://wfblink.net/u5VRKS.

Broadcasting Authority of Ireland. "BAI Announces Funding of €5m Under Sound and Vision Scheme—Broadcasting Authority of Ireland." Broadcasting Authority of Ireland, 19 Dec. 2022, https://wfblink.net/lpazrH.

Bray, Jennifer. "No Plan to Cap Refugee Numbers, as Taoiseach Says Co Clare Blockade 'Not Necessary.'" The Irish Times, 16 May 2023, https://wfblink.net/ahwhRy.

Brennan, Michael. "Leo Varadkar and Cabinet Sub-committee Discussed Cutting Ukrainian Refugee Benefits." Business Post, https://wfblink.net/eK7HR4.

Buchanan, Myles. "Wicklow Screening of Anti-racism Film to Go Ahead After Three Venues Cancel." Irish Independent, 20 Sept. 2024, https://wfblink.net/7Jut2Z.

Burke-Kennedy, Eoin. "The State's Top 10 Corporate Taxpayers: Who Are They?" The Irish Times, 30 Dec. 2021, https://wfblink.net/wdafGO.

Burne, Louise. "Leo Varadkar Slams Claims That Asylum Seekers Are 'unvetted Migrants.'" Dublin Live, 19 Dec. 2023, https://wfblink.net/svUc5I.

Burne, Louise. "Government Will 'robustly Push Back on' Further Bills for Children's Hospital." Irish Mirror, 18 Feb. 2025, https://wfblink.net/zlvmrC.

Business Post. "Sinn Féin Backs 12.5% Corporation Tax Rate." Business Post, https://wfblink.net/gd1UiF.

Carswell, Simon. "Self-help Guru Tony Robbins Sues Buzzfeed in Irish Courts." The Irish Times, 27 Nov. 2019, https://wfblink.net/yczqLT.

Central Bank of Ireland. "Quarterly Bulletin." Quarterly Bulletin, vol. 01, Mar. 2024, https://wfblink.net/974ezh.

Central Statistics Office. "Saorstát Éireann, Census of Population 1926, Vol. 10", cso.ie, https://wfblink.net/iEbX9s.

Central Statistics Office. "Census 1936 Volume 1—Population, Area and Valuation of each DED and each larger Unit of Area", cso.ie, https://wfblink.net/h0hhzH.

Central Statistics Office. Live Register Statement October 2000. 2000, https://wfblink.net/gh8G3l.

Central Statistics Office. Population and Migration Estimates, Central Statistics Office, Ireland, 10 Nov. 2003, https://wfblink.net/LV4QCR.

Central Statistics Office. Population and Migration Estimates, report, Central Statistics Office, Ireland, 14 Sept. 2005, https://wfblink.net/PdHC7T.

Central Statistics Office. "Census 2006—Non-Irish Nationals Living in Ireland—CSO —Central Statistics Office." 1 Oct. 2012, https://wfblink.net/Jwn4i1.

Central Statistics Office. National Income and Expenditure Annual Results 2015—CSO —Central Statistics Office. 6 Oct. 2016, https://wfblink.net/sCBZsB.

Central Statistics Office. Population Changes Census of Population 2022—Summary Results—Central Statistics Office. 20 Oct. 2023, https://wfblink.net/i5k5zo.

Central Statistics Office. Home Ownership and Rent Census of Population 2022 Profile 2—Housing in Ireland—Central Statistics Office. 20 Oct. 2023, https://wfblink.net/KPoiwb.

Central Statistics Office. Earnings and Labour Costs Q4 2023 (Final) Q1 2024 (Preliminary Estimates)—Central Statistics Office. 29 May 2024, https://wfblink.net/P7GULU.

Central Statistics Office. Key Findings Population and Migration Estimates, April 2023—Central Statistics Office. 26 Sept. 2023, https://wfblink.net/7TkVaz.

Central Statistics Office. Migration Society Ireland and the EU at 50—Central Statistics Office. 17 Oct. 2023, https://wfblink.net/GMXC9t.

Central Statistics Office. New Dwelling Completions Q4 2023—Central Statistics Office. 25 Jan. 2024, https://wfblink.net/e8CdaF.

Central Statistics Office. Key Findings Population and Migration Estimates, April 2024—Central Statistics Office. 27 Aug. 2024, https://wfblink.net/lK9JgV.

Charities Regulator. "Safe Ireland National Social Change Agency Company Limited by Guarantee". Charities Regulator, https://wfblink.net/cqrYqy.

Chrisafis, Angelique. "Decision Due on Hill of Tara Motorway." The Guardian, 11 Nov. 2004, https://wfblink.net/J5VoHI.

Cionnaith, Fiachra Ó. "€725m Funding Plan for RTÉ Not a 'Blank Cheque'—Martin." RTE.ie, 25 July 2024, https://wfblink.net/FVeWdX.

Cionnaith, Fiachra Ó. "€1.4m Spend On Security Office 'Ridiculous'—Tánaiste." RTE.ie, 25 Sept. 2024, https://wfblink.net/dXhsFW.

Citizens Information. Budget 2007. https://wfblink.net/BJsXhG.

Clare County Library. The Burren: Introduction. https://wfblink.net/9CBIYn.

Clare County Library. Statistical Survey of the County of Clare 1808—Chapter V.10. https://wfblink.net/LsjhVE.

Clare FM. "Lisdoonvarna Direct Provision Centres Receives €2.35m in State Fees in 2020." Clare FM, 22 Sept. 2024, https://wfblink.net/QZ9qS8.

Clarity, James F. "Latoon Journal; if You Believe in Fairies, Don't Bulldoze Their Lair." The New York Times, 15 June 1999, https://wfblink.net/EnjX68.

Clifford, Mick. "Hotel Housed Staff in Rooms Paid for by State for Asylum Seekers Use." Irish Examiner, 18 Sept. 2023, https://wfblink.net/1DxHow.

Coimisiun na Mean. "Equality, Diversity & Inclusion—Coimisiún Na Meán." Coimisiún Na Meán, 13 Jan. 2025, https://wfblink.net/kORDMK.

Colette Finn. [@ColetteFinnCork]. "White people in Ireland need to understand that we have an unearned privilege simply being white. Let's examine our own biases on International Migrant's Day." X, 18 Dec. 2023, 10.22 a.m., https://wfblink.net/c9o8OS.

Communications Directorate and Press and Information Unit. "Judgment of the Court in Case C-465/20 P | Commission V Ireland and Others." Press Release, press-release, 10 Sept. 2024, https://wfblink.net/JZfMzX.

Conneely, Ailbhe. "Murder of Ashling Murphy Was a 'Watershed Moment'" RTE.ie, 10 Nov. 2023, https://wfblink.net/ZMUoMS.

Conneely, Ailbhe. "Shortcomings in Govt Policy on Gender-based Violence." RTE.ie, 8 Dec. 2023, https://wfblink.net/hgIjhF.

Coogan, Tim. Wherever the Green is Worn, The Story of the Irish Diaspora. Arrow, 2002.

Coogan, Tim. Ireland in the Twentieth Century. London: Arrow, 2004.

Coogan, Tim. The Famine Plot. St. Martin's Griffin, 2012.

Corcoran, T. "Enforcing the Penal Code on Education." The Irish Monthly, vol. 59, no. 693, 1931, (Pp.149–54).

Cotter, Eimear. "'I Sit at the Shrine I Made for Her in My Room Before Going to Bed Each Night" Irish Independent, 17 Nov. 2023, https://wfblink.net/3m3vYh.

Cox, James. "Sinn Féin Constituency Organiser's Defamation Claim Against Mediahuis and Reporter Dismissed." BreakingNews.ie, 29 Nov. 2023, https://wfblink.net/0As2EQ.

Cronin, Mike and O'Callaghan, Liam. A History of Ireland (2nd Edition). Palgrave Macmillan, 2015.

Cullen, Paul, and Ciarán D'Arcy. "New National Children's Hospital at St James's Granted Planning." The Irish Times, 28 Apr. 2016, https://wfblink.net/VMAQT2.

Cullen, Paul. "State Awards €1bn Children's Hospital Contract to BAM Ireland." The Irish Times, 4 Feb. 2017, https://wfblink.net/wsTZxE.

Curry, Fran. "Tipp Today Podcast 04/06/24" Tipp Today Podcast, Tipp FM, 4 Jun. 2024, https://wfblink.net/bNHZVw.

CYPSC. "Socio-Demographic Profile, Dublin City North, 2018" cypsc.ie, https://wfblink.net/nmbQ1A.

Daft. Rental Price Report: Q2 2024 Infographic. https://wfblink.net/burCtn.

Dalton, Eoghan. "'Protestors Have Disrupted Events and Threatened People—Simply for Supporting Those in Need.'" TheJournal.ie, 6 Oct. 2024, https://wfblink.net/svHkZw.

De Barra, Máirín. "New Poll: 22% of Voters Believe Irish People Being Replaced With Migrants." Gript, 2 Aug. 2024, https://wfblink.net/YMZfAz.

De Barra, Máirín. "'Don't Buy Them': New SPHE Book Contains 'Misleading' and 'Unscientific' Trans Content Say Parents." Gript, 5 Sept. 2024, https://wfblink.net/avhZDm.

Deegan, Gordon. "Lisdoonvarna Locals Reject Direct Provision Plan." The Irish Times, 2 Mar. 2018, https://wfblink.net/AldZhA.

Department of Children, Equality, Disability, Integration and Youth. "National Action Plan Against Racism", gov.ie https://wfblink.net/zSIbRq.

Department of Enterprise, Trade and Employment. Annual Employment Survey 2020. 2020, https://wfblink.net/U1a0Gd.

Department of Justice. "Monitoring the Implementation of Zero Tolerance: The Third National Strategy on Domestic, Sexual and Gender-Based Violence." Zero Tolerance Third National Strategy on Domestic, Sexual & Gender-Based Violence 2022-2026, 2022, p. 1. https://wfblink.net/Ds6oEI.

Department of Justice. "ZERO TOLERANCE: Third National Strategy on Domestic, Sexual & Gender-Based Violence 2022-2026", https://wfblink.net/W4jOiu.

Deutsche Welle (DW). "Germany: AfD Youth Group Can Be Classified as 'extremist.'" dw.com, 6 Feb. 2024, https://wfblink.net/QqUwND.

Die Presse. "Küssel: Schlüsselfigur Der Neonazi-Szene." Die Presse, 14 May 2012, https://wfblink.net/dOJtml.

DNG. "DNG New Homes Transactional Analysis." DNG Estate Agents, https://wfblink.net/KFBYVd.

Donnelly, Paul. "How Foreign Firms Transformed Ireland's Domestic Economy." The Irish Times, 13 Nov. 2013, https://wfblink.net/6OlFCZ.

Dooley, Terence. Burning the Big House: The Story of the Irish Country House in a Time of War and Revolution, New Haven: Yale University Press, 2022.

Du Bois, W.E.B. "The Philadelphia Negro." Du Bois, W. E. B., and Isabel Eaton. The Philadelphia Negro: a social study. University of Pennsylvania, 1899.

Duffy, Rónán. "Fine Gael Ministers Discussed US Corporations Paying 'Little or No Tax' Here in the 1980s." TheJournal.ie, 20 Dec. 2018, https://wfblink.net/Z30Izo.

Dunphy, Liz. "One Year on From Ashling Murphy's Death Has Anything Really Changed?" Irish Examiner, 12 Jan. 2023, https://wfblink.net/mQKl57.

Dwyer, Ryle. "With Reen at the Helm, We Can Look Ahead With a Sense of Confidence." Irish Examiner, 29 May 2020, https://wfblink.net/k3SyCO.

Eidenmuller, Michael E. Online Speech Bank: Veronica Guerin -- International Press Freedom Award Acceptance Speech. https://wfblink.net/j1Lxck.

Eur-Lex. "Directive 2004/38/ec Of The European Parliament And Of The Council", 29 Apr. 2004, L_2004158EN.01007701.xml. https://wfblink.net/UtqPwl.

Eurofound. Becoming Adults: Young People in a Post-pandemic World | European Foundation for the Improvement of Living and Working Conditions. https://wfblink.net/WgzVsf.

Europa-EU. "Temporary Protection." Migration and Home Affairs, https://wfblink.net/ot5Dr1.

European Movement Ireland. "Press Release: Support for Ireland Remaining a Member of the EU Remains Stable and Overwhelmingly Positive." European Movement Ireland, 21 Dec. 2023, https://wfblink.net/WHSRxG.

Everett, Mary and Bank's Statistics Department. "Foreign Direct Investment: An Analysis of Its Significance." Quarterly Bulletin, vol. 4, 2006, pp. 93–95. https://wfblink.net/QeyKxs.

Fahey, Tony. "Religion and Prosperity." Studies: An Irish Quarterly Review, vol. 90, no. 357, 2001, (Pp. 39–46).

Fáilte Ireland. Fáilte Ireland: National Tourism Development Authority. https://wfblink.net/RXM44t.

Fianna Fáil. "Europe Matters—Manifesto 2024." Europe Matters, 2024, https://wfblink.net/wsXc4i.

Fine Gael. "European Election 2024 Manifesto." European Election 2024 Manifesto, pp. 4–8. https://wfblink.net/P1Yzgr.

Fine Gael. "Speech of an Taoiseach Simon Harris T.D., Béal Na Bláth Commemoration." Fine Gael, 25 Aug. 2024, https://wfblink.net/isJvpo.

Finn, Christina. "Taoiseach: 'St Patrick Was a Migrant to Ireland—a Single, Male, Undocumented One.'" TheJournal.ie, 13 Mar. 2024, https://wfblink.net/VXqshG.

Finn, Christina. "Israeli Ambassador's Comments About President Michael D Higgins 'unhelpful', Says Coveney." TheJournal.ie, 23 Oct. 2023, https://wfblink.net/uXEGJ4.

Flynn, Kevin Haddick. "The First Coalition: 60 Years On." History Ireland, vol. 16, no. 1, 2008, (Pp. 16–17).

Fogarty, M. P. and The Economic and Social Research Institute. "Irish Entrepreneurs Speak For Themselves." Broadsheet, The Economic and Social Research Institute, 1973, https://wfblink.net/klp0z5.

Fox, Kenneth. "Rate of Ukrainians Arriving in Ireland 10 Times the EU Average." BreakingNews.ie, 19 Nov. 2023, https://wfblink.net/NaGdIc.

Gallagher, Conor. "The Mystery of the Far-right National Party's €400,000 Gold: Where Could It Have Come From?" The Irish Times, 28 July 2023, https://wfblink.net/QLG6pI.

Gallagher, Fiachra. "More Than 1,000 Protest Against Housing of Asylum Seekers at Coolock Factory." The Irish Times, 24 Mar. 2024, https://wfblink.net/YSdhBW.

Gatewood, Willard "Aristocrats of Color: South and North The Black Elite, 1880-1920." The Journal of Southern History, vol. 54, no. 1, 1988, (Pp. 3–20)

Gataveckaite, Gabija. "Sinn Féin Wanted to Extend Hate Speech Bill to Give Undocumented Migrants Special Protection." Irish Independent, 5 Apr. 2024, https://wfblink.net/ohaSYv.

GBFM News. "Taoiseach Leo Varadkar 'Deeply Concerned' Over Fire at Ross Lake House in Roscahill." GalwayBayFM, 18 Dec. 2023, https://wfblink.net/PvQNvq.

Geffen, Elizabeth. "Violence in Philadelphia in the 1840's and 1850's." Pennsylvania History 36, 1969, (Pp. 381-410).

Gleeson, Colin. "About 60 Asylum Seekers Moved Into Santry Complex." The Irish Times, 27 May 2023, https://wfblink.net/OWXzRl.

Global Ireland—Ireland's Global Footprint to 2025 | Ireland.ie. https://wfblink.net/xvJKiq.

Goldhill, Olivia. "A Hoax That Targeted Feminist Scholarship Accidentally Revealed a Bigger Problem With Academia." Quartz, 20 July 2022, https://wfblink.net/hgbERP.

Gov.ie. "Designated Accommodation Centres." gov.ie, https://wfblink.net/V90Ngm.

Gov.ie. "Trade Factsheets." gov.ie, https://wfblink.net/5vA38k.

Gov.ie. "Government Publishes Zero Tolerance Strategy to Tackle Domestic, Sexual and Gender-based Violence." gov.ie, https://wfblink.net/2SvLSm.

Gov.ie "International Protection Accommodation Services (IPAS)." gov.ie, https://wfblink.net/1JV2TR.

Gov.ie "Minister McEntee Announces Immediate Lifting of Visa Requirements Between Ukraine and Ireland." gov.ie, https://wfblink.net/dO1xL8.

Gov.ie. "White Paper on Ending Direct Provision." gov.ie, https://wfblink.net/EekkT4.

Gov.ie. "White Paper on Ending Direct Provision | Executive Summary in Various Languages." gov.ie, https://wfblink.net/XaPXP8.

Gov.ie. "Purchase Orders for €20,000 or above Quarter 1 2024 Department of Children, Equality, Disability, Integration and Youth." gov.ie, https://wfblink.net/yrtFkB.

Gov.ie. "Purchase Orders for €20,000 or above Quarter 4 2023 Department of Children, Equality, Disability, Integration and Youth." gov.ie, https://wfblink.net/ShYHh3.

Gov.uk. "Government of the United Kingdom of Great Britain and Northern Ireland and Government of the Republic of Rwanda." https://wfblink.net/dw3wDW.

Gript. "Gript Journalist Pepper-sprayed by Gardaí." Gript, 25 Apr. 2024, https://wfblink. net/MZ3NSA.

Gunning, Fatima. "Santry Residents 'Scared' Over Arrival of 'Hundreds of Unvetted Male' Asylum Seekers." Gript, 16 May 2023, https://wfblink.net/MqVVZN.

Hand, G. J. "The Forgotten Statutes of Kilkenny: A Brief Survey." Irish Jurist (1966-), vol. 1, no. 2, 1966, (Pp.299–312).

Harris, Simon. "Speech of the Leader of Fine Gael, Simon Harris T.D.," Fine Gael, 6 Apr. 2024, https://wfblink.net/Pp31ZY.

Helen McEntee. [@HMcEntee]. "I am appalled at the violent scenes in Coolock today. This is thuggish criminal behaviour and has no place in our society. The Garda Commissioner has kept me updated throughout the day and he has assured me that everything will be done to bring those responsible to justice." X, 15 Jul. 2024, 10.19 p.m., https://wfblink.net/UQrJTQ.

Helliwell, John F., et al. "World Happiness Report 2015." The World Happiness Report, 23 Apr. 2015, https://wfblink.net/FK8vHS.

Helliwell, John F., et al. "Happiness of the Younger, the Older, and Those in Between | the World Happiness Report.", 2024, https://wfblink.net/uwLlTK.

Heinz, Wolfgang. "Economic Development and Interest Groups." Politics and Society in Contemporary Ireland, edited by Brian Girvin and Roland Sturm, Gower Publishing Company, 1986, (Pp. 91-92).

Heritage Ireland. Hill of Tara. Heritage Ireland, https://wfblink.net/LbUyJB.

Hilliard, Mark. "Direct Provision in Ireland: How and Why the System Was Introduced." The Irish Times, 19 Nov. 2019, https://wfblink.net/ZjXOtG.

Hoeber, Francis W. "Drama in the Courtroom, Theater in the Streets: Philadelphia's Irish Riot of 1831." The Pennsylvania Magazine of History and Biography, vol. 125, no. 3, 2001, pp. 191–232.

Hogan, Caelainn. "Ashling Murphy's Killing Has Shocked Ireland – but Will It Change a Culture of Misogyny?" The Guardian, 18 Jan. 2022, https://wfblink.net/lNdx4X.

Hogan, J. Economic Crises and Policy Change in the Early 1980s: a Four Country Comparison. Journal of Australian Political Economy, No. 65, Winter 2010, (Pp.106-137).

Holland, Kitty, and Jack Power. "Dozens of People Take Part in Anti-asylum Seeker Protests in South Dublin." The Irish Times, 19 July 2023, https://wfblink.net/ KOIJd3.

Holland, Kitty, and Vivienne Clarke. "Grand Canal Asylum Seeker Camp 'Dismantled' With Over 160 People Taken to 'Robust' Tented Accommodation." The Irish Times, 9 May 2024, https://wfblink.net/GRMxm6.

Holland, Kitty, and Jack Power. "Around 40 Tents Pitched on Grand Canal in Dublin Hours After Clearance Operation." The Irish Times, 21 May 2024, https://wfblink. net/E65Xty.

Holland, Kitty, et al. "Grand Canal: Asylum Seekers' Tents Cleared in Latest Operation." The Irish Times, 30 May 2024, https://wfblink.net/iqhdvJ.

Horgan-Jones, Jack. "Sinn Féin Promises to Re-run Referendums on Care and Family if

They Fail, Should It Be Returned to Government." The Irish Times, 20 Feb. 2024, https://wfblink.net/Ba6rGq.

Horgan-Jones, Jack, and Cormac McQuinn. "Up To 10,000 Tourism Jobs Displaced Due to Hotel Bed Shortages, Ministers Told." The Irish Times, 9 May 2023, https://wfblink.net/OGyHFb.

Horgan-Jones, Jack, and Seamus Enright. "Ireland Will Not 'Provide Loophole' for Any Other Country's Migration Challenges, Says Harris." The Irish Times, 28 Apr. 2024, https://wfblink.net/b5e0NX.

Horgan-Jones, Jack, et al. "National Children's Hospital Cost Has Risen to More Than €2.2bn, Donnelly Confirms." The Irish Times, 13 Feb. 2024, https://wfblink.net/fPahVC.

Hosford, Paul. "EU's Response to War on Gaza Is 'Despicable', Says Holly Cairns." Irish Examiner, 15 Nov. 2023, https://wfblink.net/bXKB8b.

Housing Ireland Magazine. "Ireland's Exploding Housing Emergency." Housing Ireland Magazine, 24 July 2017, https://wfblink.net/wmgXZ3.

Huntsman, Leone. "Bounty Emigrants to Australia." Clogher Record, vol. 17, no. 3, 2002, (Pp.801–12).

IDA Ireland. Annual Employment Survey 2022. Report, 2022, https://wfblink.net/YFWnlx.

Ignatiev, Noel. How the Irish Became White. Routledge, 1995, (p.2).

Ignatiev, N. "Abolish the White Race." Harvard Magazine, September-October, 2002, https://wfblink.net/osXK74.

Immigrant Council of Ireland. Vision and Mission: Immigrant Council of Ireland. https://wfblink.net/JEuVOA.

International Press Institute. "In Depth: Libel Damages Squeeze Ireland's Press." ipi.-media, 11 Jan. 2017, https://wfblink.net/hx6its.

IPO. "Monthly Statistical Report on Applications for International Protection in December 2023." ipo.gov.ie, https://wfblink.net/Fc4uG1.

IPO. "Statistics". ipo.gov.ie, https://wfblink.net/KOwQUh.

Irish Freedom Party. Political Programme and Constitution of the Irish Freedom Party. https://wfblink.net/DQaXPe.

Irish Tourism Industry Confederation. Irish Tourism Industry Confederation PRESS RELEASE. 2022, https://wfblink.net/m5I04O.

Johnston, John I. D. "Hedge Schools of Tyrone and Monaghan." Clogher Record, vol. 7, no. 1, 1969, (Pp. 34–55).

Joseph, Ebun. "Making sense of race in global justice education." Challenging Perceptions of Africa in Schools, Critical Approaches to Global Justice Education, (Eds.) O'Toole, Barbara et al., Routledge, 2019, (Pp. 162).

Kavanagh, Gary. "An In-depth Look at the Funding of Ireland's Loudest NGO." Gript, 8 Feb. 2024, https://wfblink.net/noFRdo.

Keating, Paul and Desmond, Derry. Culture and Capitalism in Contemporary Ireland. Avebury, 1993.

Kelly, Fiach. "Election 2020: What Are the Differences Between FF and FG Promises?" The Irish Times, 24 Jan. 2020, https://wfblink.net/URabVk.

Kelleher, Eoin. "'Disquiet' in Tipperary Over Plans to House Ukrainians in 82 Modular Homes in Clonmel." Irish Independent, 19 Apr. 2024, https://wfblink.net/PrVzWC.

Kelleher, Olivia. "Justice Minister Says 'No Facts' Back up Claim That Increased Migration Leads to Rising Crime Rates." Irish Examiner, 17 Feb. 2024, https://wfblink.net/qpFcBx.

Kempny, Marta, et al. Anti-racism Principles For Irish Higher Education Institutions. 2023, https://wfblink.net/PRzwtS.

Kendi, Ibram. How to Be an Antiracist. Bodley Head, 2023.

Kenny, Aisling. "Govt Working on Plans for Influx of Ukrainian Refugees." RTE.ie, 2 Mar. 2022, https://wfblink.net/19tbga.

Killeen, Richard. Ireland: Land, People, History. Constable & Robinson, 2012.

Lappin V Mediahuis UK Ltd and Ors (Approved), [2023] IEHC 668 | High Court of Ireland, Judgment, Law, casemine.com. https://wfblink.net/xgPPMx.

Leahy, Pat. "Irish Times Poll: Public Mood on Immigration Hardening as Local and European Elections Approach." The Irish Times, 17 May 2024, https://wfblink.net/2beSAb.

Leahy, Pat. "Housing Commission Report Suggests Underlying Housing Deficit of up to 256,000 Homes." The Irish Times, 21 May 2024, https://wfblink.net/X7wAC5.

Lenihan, Eddie and Green, Caroline. Eve. Meeting the Other Crowd, The Fairy Stories of Hidden Ireland 2004, Penguin.

Lenihan, Eoin. "The Landscape Speaks: A Study of Ringfort Settlement and Dwelling in the Inchiquin Area, Co. Clare" M.A. thesis, National University of Ireland, Galway, 2004.

Lenihan, Eoin. "Irish Leftists Blame Violence Against Women on Misogyny to Hide the Real Cause: Open Borders." The Federalist, 28 Nov. 2023, https://wfblink.net/biOTCn.

Libreri, Samantha. "Protest Over Tented Accommodation Plan in Wicklow." RTE.ie, 23 Mar. 2024, https://wfblink.net/plcu7k.

Libreri, Samantha. "10 Key Points From Sinn Féin's Election Manifesto." RTE.ie, 28 Jan. 2020, https://wfblink.net/romDdz.

Logos Academy Episode 38: Justin Barrett. Rumble, 21 Mar. 2001, https://wfblink.net/EynyuA.

Lyons, Tony. "'Inciting the Lawless and Profligate Adventure'—The Hedge Schools Of Ireland." History Ireland, vol. 24, no. 6, 2016, (Pp. 28–31).

MacNamee, Garreth. "Puska Was a Convicted Sex Offender and 'Person of Interest' in Two Other Assaults on Women." Extra.ie, 11 Nov. 2023, https://wfblink.net/JmncqH.

MacNamee, Garreth. "Violent Chaos at Centre for Asylum Seekers as Man Taken to Hospital." Extra.ie, 17 May 2024, https://wfblink.net/tqAQLO.

Mahon, Brian. "Taoiseach Admits Majority of Asylum Seekers Are Economic Migrants." Extra.ie, 5 Mar. 2025, https://wfblink.net/wwVLMe.

Mahoney, Michael. "Irish Indentured Labour in the Caribbean—the National Archives Blog." The National Archives Blog, 14 Feb. 2022, https://wfblink.net/3sLbcA.

Malekmian, Shamim. "Dr Ebun Joseph: Why Black Studies Matter in Ireland and

Responding to the Murder of George Floyd." Hotpress, 8 June 2020, https://wfblink. net/ekOpMQ.

Martin, Micheál. "Dáil Statement by the Taoiseach, Micheál Martin on Violence Against Women." gov.ie, 19 Jan. 2022, https://wfblink.net/yLhLgb.

Maynes, Maria. "Mattie McGrath: I Was Locked Out of Meeting on Clonmel Modular Homes." Gript, 24 Apr. 2024, https://wfblink.net/NuliCC.

Maynooth University. Rights and Social Policy—Maynooth—"MSOCSC Social Science (Rights And Social Policy)." Maynooth University, https://wfblink.net/ BVP4cv.

McCabe, Conor. Sins of the Father: Tracing the Decisions That Shaped the Irish Economy. The History Press, 2013, (p.24).

McCarron, Jack. "Mapped: The Fires Linked to Accommodation for Migrants." RTE.ie, 26 July 2024, https://wfblink.net/WCcmIx.

McCarthy, Larry, et al. Corporation Tax – 2020 Payments and 2019 Returns. Apr. 2021, pp. 2–28. https://wfblink.net/xGwweZ.

McCarthy, Larry. Corporation Tax – 2022 Payments and 2021 Returns. Report, May 2023, pp. 1–34. https://wfblink.net/WNshoG.

McCormack, Jayne. Sinn Féin Call for Israeli Ambassador to Ireland to Be Expelled. 3 Nov. 2023, https://wfblink.net/jSn8JW.

McCurry Cate and Ward James. "Thousands Gather Outside Leinster House for Emotional Vigil for Ashling Murphy." BelfastTelegraph.co.uk, 14 Jan. 2022, https:// wfblink.net/WOjV7k.

McDermott, Stephen. "Hotels, State Bodies and Direct Provision: The Companies Behind Ireland's Refugee Housing Sector." TheJournal.ie, 12 Apr. 2024, https:// wfblink.net/pUtB3E.

McDermott, Stephen. "The Far-right Failed in the General Election—but Reports of Their Death Have Been Exaggerated." TheJournal.ie, 4 Dec. 2024, https://wfblink. net/W8icEo.

McDonald, Theo. "Almost 600 Hospitality Businesses Forced to Close Since Government's Hike in VAT Rate, Report Says." Irish Independent, 8 Aug. 2024, https:// wfblink.net/XX6wfs.

McGee, Harry. "Charlie Flanagan: 'My Father Was a Controversial Figure . . . I Disagreed With Much of What He Stood For.'" The Irish Times, 30 Sept. 2023, https://wfblink.net/SdA5A2.

McGinnity, Francis et al. "Ethnicity and Nationality in the Irish Labour Market." Dublin: ESRI and The Irish Human Rights and Equality Commission (IHREC), 2018, https://wfblink.net/CisOKg.

McGinnity, Frances and Kingston, Gillian. An Irish Welcome? Changing Irish Attitudes to Immigrants and Immigration: The Role of Recession and Immigration. The Economic and Social Review. Vol 48., 2017, (Pp.281-304).

McGreevy, Ronan. "Remains of Irish Hero Patrick Sarsfield Located After More Than 300 Years." The Irish Times, 11 Feb. 2023, https://wfblink.net/dSY3sK.

McGuirk, Colm et al. "Almost Half of Best-paid Asylum Firms Are Offshore and Often Based in Tax Havens." Business Plus, 12 Feb. 2024, https://wfblink.net/EnBhBj.

McGuirk, John. "In Silencing Ryan Casey, the Media Abandons All Pretence." Gript, 20 Nov. 2023, https://wfblink.net/blpHkn.

McHale, Michael. "Irish Over-65 Population Increases by More Than One-third in a Decade." Irish Medical Times, 17 Feb. 2025, https://wfblink.net/hRFLu1.

McIntosh, Peggy. "White Privilege: Unpacking the Invisible Knapsack." Some Notes for Facilitators, 2010, https://wfblink.net/H2B365.

McKeon, John and Department of Social Protection. Introduction By Mr John McKeon, Secretary General Department Of Social Protection, To The Committee Of Public Accounts. By Committee of Public Accounts, 18 Jan. 2024, https://wfblink.net/MTgGa9.

McMahon, Páraic. "Hotel Operators Made Millionaires for Accommodating International Protection Applicants Says Clare TD." Clare Echo, 26 Mar. 2024, https://wfblink.net/pJJV87.

McMahon, Páraic. "The Electoral Chair: A Sitting Councillor May Fall in North Clare & Fine Gael Factions." Clare Echo, 18 Apr. 2024, https://wfblink.net/2zOvPp.

McNally, Seán McCárthaigh and Tadgh. "More Than 10% of Tourist Beds Being Used to House Refugees." Irish Examiner, 15 Dec. 2023, https://wfblink.net/rIbIUZ.

McQuinn, Cormac. "More Than 7,100 Ukrainian Refugees Now in Employment in Ireland." The Irish Times, 22 Aug. 2022, https://wfblink.net/EV9Kb0.

McQuinn, Cormac. "17,000 Ukrainians Now in Full-time Employment in Ireland, TDs Told." The Irish Times, 18 Jan. 2024, https://wfblink.net/tSfQYf.

McShane, Ian, et al. "Thirty-sixth Amendment to the Constitution Exit Poll." RTÉ & Behaviour & Attitudes Exit Poll, report, 2018, https://wfblink.net/tEYxZV.

Meisel, By Simon Cox and Anna. Martin Sellner: The New Face of the Far Right in Europe. 19 Sept. 2018, https://wfblink.net/FB7oDG.

Micheál Martin. [@MichealMartinTD]. "I utterly condemn the criminal destruction at Ross Lake House Hotel in Galway. There is never any excuse or place for violence, hatred or intimidation. Those responsible for this criminal act do not speak for their community or this country." X, 17 Dec. 2023, 6.27 p.m., https://wfblink.net/lFCQ4u.

Miller, Kerby. Emigrants and Exiles, Ireland and the Irish Exodus to North America. Oxford University Press, 1985.

Millman, Lawrence. Our like will not be there again; notes from the west of Ireland. Ruminator Books, 1977.

Mitchel, John. The Last Conquest of Ireland (perhaps). Irishman Office, 1861.

Mohan, Sathishaa. "Timeline of Trouble in Coolock on Monday 15th July 2024." Irish Independent, 21 July 2024, https://wfblink.net/8mGTlY.

Molony, Senan. "Micheál Martin Accuses Contractor of National Children's Hospital in Dáil of 'Delaying' Completion to 'Extract." Irish Independent, 30 May 2024, https://wfblink.net/kqgZpS.

Murrell, Colleen, et al. Digital News Report Ireland 2024. Digital News Report Ireland 2024, https://wfblink.net/pPb4WS.

Murphy, Paul. "'We're Paying Too Much' – Value for Money and the OPW." RTE.ie, 1 Apr. 2021, https://wfblink.net/JpHXZq.

National Archives Ireland. Ireland – Australia Transportation Records. National Archives Ireland. https://wfblink.net/PLliEC.

National Council for Curriculum and Assessment. Social, Personal and Health Education (SPHE) Specification for Junior Cycle. Feb. 2023, https://wfblink.net/qJj1Ws.

Neeson, Anthony. "Great Hunger Still Haunts: Martin." Irish Echo Newspaper, https://wfblink.net/4DBeUq.

Ní Aodha, Gráinne. "Lessons Will Be Learned From 'Infamous' Leinster House Bike Shed, Dáil Told." BreakingNews.ie, 18 Sept. 2024, https://wfblink.net/rCfbBd.

Nolan, Carol. "Parents in Uproar Following SPHE Portrayal of an 'Irish Family.'" – Carol Nolan TD. https://wfblink.net/tneuPf.

Nolan, Darragh. "Photos Show Conditions Faced by Asylum Seekers Sleeping in Mount Street 'Tent City.'" Irish Independent, 30 Apr. 2024, https://wfblink.net/GfCcYB.

O'Brien, Carl. "Computer Science Graduates Earn More Than Other Graduates." The Irish Times, 7 Dec. 2018, https://wfblink.net/Zx8skx.

O'Brien, Fergal. "Asylum Seekers Pitch Around 30 Tents Along Grand Canal." RTE.ie, 20 Aug. 2024, https://wfblink.net/CvONHy.

O'Callaghan, Sean. To Hell or Barbados. Brandon Books, 2001.

O'Cearbhaill, Muiris. "First Group of Children Arrive From Palestine to Receive Lifesaving Healthcare in Ireland." TheJournal.ie, 20 Dec. 2024, https://wfblink.net/tl11pe.

O'Connell, Daniel. "Address from the People of Ireland To Their Countrymen and Countrywomen in America!", The Liberator, March 25, 1842.

O'Connell, Hugh. [@oconnellhugh]. "Cries of "hear, hear" from the press gallery as Paschal Donohoe announces the abolition of VAT on newspapers and digital publications" X, 27 Sept. 2022, 2.35 p.m., https://wfblink.net/wLxmkr.

O'Connell, Hugh. [@oconnellhugh]. "The politicians were pretty happy about it as well" X, 27 Sept. 2022, 2.35 p.m., https://wfblink.net/hai6IM.

O'Connell, Hugh. "'Ireland's Watergate': How the Phone Tapping Scandal Would Lead to Haughey's Downfall... Eventually." TheJournal.ie, 27 Dec. 2013, https://wfblink.net/keoM4j.

O'Donoghue, Patrick. "Lisdoonvarna: The Home of Matchmaking Where Refugees Now Outnumber Locals." The Sunday Times, 12 Aug. 2023, https://wfblink.net/xFKuVZ.

O'Donoghue, Patrick. "Nigeria Is a Safe Country, Says Ambassador Amid Rise in Asylum Claims." The Sunday Times, 16 Nov. 2024, https://wfblink.net/TrrVhU.

O'Donoghue, T. A. "Catholicism and the Curriculum: The Irish Secondary School Experience, 1922-62". Historical Studies in Education / Revue d'histoire De l'éducation, Vol. 10, no. 1, May 1998, (Pp. 140-58).

O'Donovan, Donal. "O'Brien's Communicorp Dialed up A Profit in 2019." Irish Independent, 23 Dec. 2020, https://wfblink.net/O8TKQJ.

O'Donovan, Donal. "Profits up at Mediahuis Ireland's Newspaper Arm." Irish Independent, 22 Nov. 2024, https://wfblink.net/v2bPwV.

O'Kelly, Emma. "Palestinian Family Sleeping in Car 'Feel Hopeless'" RTE.ie, 27 Feb. 2025, https://wfblink.net/xMgg1x.

O'Mahony, Canice and Andy Bielenberg. "The Shannon Scheme and the Electrification of the Irish Free State." (2002). https://wfblink.net/JUN9PZ.

O'Neill, Conor. "How Ireland Voted in Maps and Charts." Sky News, 1 Dec. 2024, https://wfblink.net/maZLjJ.

O'Neill, Siobhan. "Remembering the 4,000 Irish Famine Orphans Shipped to Australia." The Irish Times, 25 Oct. 2018, https://wfblink.net/5a4xso.

O'Regan, Eilish. "Builders of New Children's Hospital Want Extra €853m." Irish Independent, 18 Feb. 2025, https://wfblink.net/1gIUVq.

O'Reilly, Alison and Gorman, Sally. "Fifth Fire in a Week Breaks Out at Former Crown Paints Warehouse in Coolock." Irish Examiner, 22 July 2024, https://wfblink.net/Koif20.

O'Riordan, Sean. "'I Am Very Uneasy to Know if My Husband Is Alive or Dead': Memorial Highlights Irish in US Civil War." Irish Examiner, 26 Nov. 2023, https://wfblink.net/d9m50k.

O'Siochrú, Micheál. God's Executioner: Oliver Cromwell and the Conquest of Ireland. Farber, 2008.

O'Sullivan, Kevin. "Global Leaders Must Respond to Climate Alarm That Has Never Rung so Loudly, Taoiseach Tells Cop28." The Irish Times, 2 Dec. 2023, https://wfblink.net/tjzCuj.

O'Sullivan, Maurice, et al. Twenty Years A-Growing. Oxford University Press, 2000.

O'Sullivan, Niamh. "Scary Tales of New York: Life in the Irish Slums." The Irish Times, 23 Mar. 2013, https://wfblink.net/twKP6E.

O'Sullivan, Muiris, and Liam Downey. "Mass Rocks And Related Sites." Archaeology Ireland, vol. 28, no. 1, 2014, (Pp. 26–29).

O'Toole, Fintan. Ship of Fools: How Stupidity and Corruption Sank the Celtic Tiger. Faber, 2009.

Office of the Attorney General. "Twenty-Seventh Amendment of the Constitution Act, 2004, Schedule." (C) Houses of the Oireachtas Service, https://wfblink.net/stc9Fh.

Office of the Attorney General. "Defamation Act 2009." Houses of the Oireachtas Service, https://wfblink.net/PKL6Ed.

Oireachtas. Dáil Éireann Debate—Monday, 19 Dec 1921. 19 Dec. 1921, https://wfblink.net/wcQQiP.

Oireachtas. Dáil Éireann Debate—Monday, 9 Jan 1922. 9 Jan. 1922, https://wfblink.net/8V4mLs.

Oireachtas. Land Act, 1923. 9 Aug. 1923, https://wfblink.net/le0gdb.

Oireachtas. Dáil Éireann Debate—Friday, 25 Apr 1924. 25 Apr. 1924, https://wfblink.net/gN8irQ.

Oireachtas. Old Age Pensions Act, 1924. 5 June 1924, https://wfblink.net/n80w9v.

Oireachtas. Housing (Building Facilities) Bill, 1924. 1924, https://wfblink.net/vHYCoX.

Oireachtas. "Bille Siolruchain Eallach Stuic, 1925." Live Stock Breeding Bill, 1925, https://wfblink.net/aJyTDr.

Oireachtas. Beet Sugar (Subsidy) Act, 1925. 15 July 1925, https://wfblink.net/LR0oYL.

Oireachtas. Dáil Éireann Debate—Tuesday, 5 May 1925. 5 May 1925, https://wfblink.net/prp5qQ.

Oireachtas. Electricity (Supply) Act 1927. 28 May 1927, https://wfblink.net/MR8Xh9.

Oireachtas. "Agricultural Credit Bill, 1927." Saorstat Eireann, 1927, https://wfblink.net/oiTZNI.

Oireachtas. Seanad Éireann Díospóireacht—Saturday, 14 May 1927. 14 May 1927, https://wfblink.net/phEOAe.

Oireachtas. Dáil Éireann Debate—Wednesday, 29 Feb 1928. 29 Feb. 1928, https://wfblink.net/BfwSZ8.

Oireachtas. Old Age Pensions Act, 1928. 30 Mar. 1928, https://wfblink.net/z8apFg.

Oireachtas. "Control Of Manufactures Bill, 1932." Saorstat Eireann, 1932, https://wfblink.net/ApxWqN.

Oireachtas. Dáil Éireann Debate—Friday, 15 Jul 1932. 15 July 1932, https://wfblink.net/31pzVo.

Oireachtas. Seanad Éireann Debate—Wednesday, 3 Aug 1932. 3 Aug. 1932, https://wfblink.net/ObQRYw.

Oireachtas. Dáil Éireann Debate—Thursday, 17 Nov 1932. 17 Nov. 1932, https://wfblink.net/hGor3E.

Oireachtas. Industrial Credit Bill, 1933. 1933, https://wfblink.net/gTBnXV.

Oireachtas. Unemployment Assistance Act, 1933. 16 Nov. 1933, https://wfblink.net/3yMDr5.

Oireachtas. Dáil Éireann Debate—Wednesday, 3 May 1933. 3 May 1933, https://wfblink.net/CutVd3.

Oireachtas. "Public Assistance (Acquisition Of Land) Bill, 1934." saorstAt Eireann, 1934, https://wfblink.net/NeoO5D.

Oireachtas. Executive Authority (External Relations) Act, 1936. 12 Dec. 1936, https://wfblink.net/GgKkDF.

Oireachtas. Dáil Éireann Debate—Friday, 4 Jun 1937. 4 June 1937, https://wfblink.net/g3TCkp.

Oireachtas. Dáil Éireann Debate—Wednesday, 27 Apr 1938, https://wfblink.net/zDdn1o.

Oireachtas. Dáil Éireann Debate—Wednesday, 25 Feb 1948, https://wfblink.net/VbJoBc.

Oireachtas. Dáil Éireann Debate—Wednesday, 24 Nov 1948, https://wfblink.net/jo2cnZ.

Oireachtas. "The Republic of Ireland Bill, 1948." The Republic of Ireland Bill, 1948, Stationery Office, 15 Dec. 1948, https://wfblink.net/oTr1Ck.

Oireachtas. Industrial Development Authority Bill, 1949. https://wfblink.net/7Imb5X.

Oireachtas. "Industrial Development (Encouragement Of External Investment) Bill, 1957." An Bille Um Fhorbairt Tionscail (Infheistiocht On gCjoigrich a Ghriosadh), 1957, https://wfblink.net/HnpPD5.

Oireachtas. Programme for Economic Expansion: Laid by the Government before Each House of the Oireachtas, November, 1958, https://wfblink.net/oNwvT4.

Oireachtas. Imposition Of Duties (Confirmation Of Orders) Bill, 1963. Stationery Office, 13 Nov. 1963, https://wfblink.net/esBMVr.

Oireachtas. Exchange Of Notes Between The Government Of Ireland And The

Government Of The United Kingdom In Connection With Article Xii Of The Free Trade Area Agreement Between The Two Governments Signed In London On 14th December, 1965. 1965, https://wfblink.net/Cmwksa.

Oireachtas. Finance Act, 1997. 22, 1997, pp. 1–75. https://wfblink.net/3WkEg0.

Oireachtas. Taxes Consolidation Act 1997. 30 Nov. 1997, https://www.oireachtas.ie/en/bills/bill/1997/42.

Oireachtas. FINANCE ACT, 1998. https://wfblink.net/QEozyX.

Oireachtas. Interception of Postal Packets and Telecommunications Messages (Regulation) Act, 1993. 6 June 1993, https://wfblink.net/3zCXrW.

Oireachtas. Dáil Éireann Debate—Thursday, 30 Sep 2010, https://wfblink.net/h85EiR.

Oireachtas. Joint Committee of Inquiry into the Banking Crisis debate—Thursday, 23 Jul 2015, https://wfblink.net/s88mni.

Oireachtas. Dáil Éireann Debate—Wednesday, 7 Sep 2016. 7 Sept. 2016, https://wfblink.net/aedGl7.

Oireachtas. Marriage Act 2015. 29 Oct. 2015, https://wfblink.net/StudbV.

Oireachtas. Health (Regulation of Termination of Pregnancy) Act 2018. 20 Dec. 2018, https://wfblink.net/AidiK3.

Oireachtas. Health (Assisted Human Reproduction) Act 2024. 2 July 2024, https://wfblink.net/1aXmCp.

Oireachtas. Dáil Éireann Debate—Wednesday, 17 May 2023, https://wfblink.net/LENvXh.

Oireachtas. Dáil Éireann Debate—Wednesday, 8 Nov 2023, https://wfblink.net/R3k54y.

Oireachtas. Criminal Justice (Hate Offences) Act 2024. 2024, https://wfblink.net/Dggcdy.

Oireachtas. Dáil Éireann Debate—Thursday, 18 Jan 2024, https://wfblink.net/aut504.

Oireachtas. Dáil Éireann Debate—Wednesday, 24 Jan 2024, https://wfblink.net/X983qC.

Oireachtas. Dáil Éireann Debate—Tuesday, 30 Jan 2024, https://wfblink.net/gbeztY.

Oireachtas. Joint Committee on Justice Debate—Tuesday, 23 Apr 2024. 23 Apr. 2024, https://wfblink.net/lmGcGU.

Oireachtas. Dáil Éireann Debate—Tuesday, 30 Apr 2024. 30 Apr. 2024, https://wfblink.net/sv46iT.

Oireachtas. Criminal Justice (Hate Offences) Act 2024. 2024, https://wfblink.net/Dsiji3.

Oireachtas. Asylum Seekers. 16 Sept. 2024, https://wfblink.net/ACy21V.

Oireachtas. Dáil Éireann Debate—Thursday, 7 Nov 2024, https://wfblink.net/rIW3JV.

Oireachtas. International Protection. 15 Apr. 2025, https://wfblink.net/wzC945.

Oireachtas. Immigration Policy. 21 Jan. 2025, https://wfblink.net/KhVSse.

Oireachtas. Departmental Advertising. 15 Apr. 2025, https://wfblink.net/VfaCEZ.

Oireachtas. Immigration Policy. 15 Apr. 2025, https://wfblink.net/NeMCHA.

Oireachtas. International Protection. 16 Apr. 2025, https://wfblink.net/RJGX3V.

O'Rourke, Evelyn. "Coimisiún Na Meán Allocates €5.7 Million to News Outlets." RTE.ie, 6 Feb. 2025, https://wfblink.net/19XIDK.

Owen, David. Whiteness in Du Bois's The Souls of Black Folk. Philosophia Africana 10(2), 2007, (Pp.107-126).

PA News Agency. "Ashling Murphy's Partner 'Will Never Get to Marry Soulmate' as Killer Jailed." Irvine Times, 17 Nov. 2023, https://wfblink.net/9rJu9s.

Paul [Pseudonym]. "Trouble at Trudder's River Lodge." The Greystones Guide, 15 Mar. 2024, https://wfblink.net/cfPnQq.

Paul [Pseudonym]. "Speakers' Corner: Kellie McConnell." The Greystones Guide, 18 May 2024, https://wfblink.net/Vo3cgZ.

Pepper, Diarmuid. "President Says Israel Reducing Humanitarian Law 'To Tatters', Criticises EU Commission President." TheJournal.ie, 16 Oct. 2023, https://wfblink.net/OodYsg.

Pepper, Diarmuid. "Taoiseach Simon Harris Condemns 'Reprehensible' and 'Criminal' Actions in Coolock." TheJournal.ie, 15 July 2024, https://wfblink.net/ReOyol.

Perry, Patrick. "Development Programs in Ireland". IMF Staff Papers 1965.001 (1965).

Phelan, Shane. "FitzPatrick 'misled Auditors on Loans up to €100m', Court Told." Irish Independent, 4 Nov. 2016, https://wfblink.net/vWdtAH.

Pfeifer, Hans. "Why Germany's Far-right AfD Youth Wing Faces a Ban." dw.com, 27 Feb. 2024, https://wfblink.net/2jn7Sa.

Pluckrose, Helen and Lindsay, James. Cynical Theories. Swift Press, 2021.

Pollak, Sorcha. "Citywest Hotel in Dublin Was Paid €53.6m to Accommodate Asylum Seekers and Ukrainian Refugees in 2023." The Irish Times, 4 Apr. 2024, https://wfblink.net/lzwZUw.

Pollak, Sorcha. "Number of Palestinians Seeking Asylum in Ireland Rises Eight-fold." The Irish Times, 7 Feb. 2025, https://wfblink.net/SmJJxo.

Poulos, C. Essentials of Autoethnography, American Psychological Association, 2021, https://wfblink.net/FHRA3U.

Press, J. P. "Protectionism And The Irish Footwear Industry, 1932-39." Irish Economic and Social History, vol. 13, 1986, pp. 74–89.

Quinn, John. "The Rise and Fall of Repeal: Slavery and Irish Nationalism in Antebellum Philadelphia." The Pennsylvania Magazine of History and Biography, vol. 130, no. 1, 2006, pp. 45–78.

Quinnell, Sylvia. "Where Irish Settled in Australia." Hotham History Project, https://wfblink.net/HO4j2g.

Race Traitor. Wayback Machine. https://wfblink.net/hEzQu5.

Ray, William. "Unpacking Peggy McIntosh's Knapsack." Quillette, 20 June 2024, https://wfblink.net/fMzZ67.

Reuters Institute. "Interactive." Reuters Institute for the Study of Journalism, 2024, https://wfblink.net/JKxcY5.

Revenue. Conditions for Retaining Charitable Tax Exemption. https://wfblink.net/S6wNon.

Riach, Douglas. "Ireland and the campaign against American slavery 1830-1860." Ph.D. Thesis, University of Edinburgh, 1975.

RSF. "Ireland: RSF and Its Partners Urge Sinn Féin to Stop Taking Intimidating Legal Action Against the Media and Journalists." RSF, https://wfblink.net/yqjqu3.

RTÉ. Annual Report and Group Financial Statements 2022. 2022, https://wfblink.net/NfZ9pZ.

RTÉ. Annual Report 2023. Report, 2023, https://wfblink.net/8PHqTR.

RTÉ. "Investigation After Fire at Site Earmarked for IPAs." RTE.ie, 15 Apr. 2024, https://wfblink.net/ARW28q.

RTÉ. "Coolock Site Will Be Used to Accommodate IPAs—O'Gorman." 17 Jul. 2024, https://wfblink.net/pQD2rB.

RTÉ. "Clonmel Assault Condemned as 'Intolerable'—Smyth." RTE.ie, 18 May 2024, https://wfblink.net/2qASSt.

RTÉ. "Opening Night President's Address." RTÉ Archives, 1 Dec. 2011, https://wfblink.net/Ac2Trw.

Salido-Medina, José. (2025) Extremism and Places of Worship: Analysis of Strategies and Ideological Motivations. Peace Review 37:1, 2025, (Pp.118-133).

Sayers, Peig, et al. Peig: The Autobiography of Peig Sayers of the Great Blasket Island. Talbot Press, 1973.

Scally, Derek, and Burke-Kennedy, Eoin. "Taoiseach Blames Crash on 'mad Borrowing' Frenzy." The Irish Times, 26 Jan. 2012, https://wfblink.net/LEzlzy.

Senato della Repubblica. "Constitution of the Italian Republic." Constitution of the Italian Republic, 2019, https://wfblink.net/qm49A5.

Sherry, Alan. "Justin Barrett Is a 'Tout' for Going to Gardai About Gold Bars, New Party Chief Claims." SundayWorld.com, 7 Oct. 2023, https://wfblink.net/J3btO3.

Shiels, Damian. The Irish in the American Civil War. The History Press, 2013.

Simms, J. G. "The Bishops' Banishment Act of 1697 (9 Will. III, c. 1)." Irish Historical Studies, vol. 17, no. 66, 1970, (Pp.185–99).

Sinn Féin. International Protection: A Fair System That Works. https://wfblink.net/mGbbFC.

Sinn Féin. "Sinn Féin European Parliament Manifesto 2024", https://wfblink.net/nAZc3Y.

Sinn Féin Costing Budget, 2019. gov.ie, https://wfblink.net/NsvKmY.

Slattery, Laura. "News Publishers Welcome Zero VAT Rate as 'Tax on Information' Ends." The Irish Times, 27 Sept. 2022, https://wfblink.net/u5sLwu.

Slattery, Laura. "The Irish Times Group Posts Operating Profit of €2.9m." The Irish Times, 24 Nov. 2022, https://wfblink.net/cLkmDa.

Slattery, Laura. "Irish Times Group Returns to Profit as Revenues Climb 5%." The Irish Times, 8 Oct. 2024, https://wfblink.net/mzf8z9.

Table Media. "Alice Weidel Beendet Zusammenarbeit Mit Ihrem Referenten Roland Hartwig." Table.Media, 15 Jan. 2024, https://wfblink.net/j2wfgo.

Teagasc. 2020—CAP Provides Important Funds for Irish Farms—Teagasc | Agriculture and Food Development Authority. https://wfblink.net/IXlNMH.

The Heritage Council. Archaeology 2020. Repositioning Irish Archaeology in the Knowledge Society. By University College Dublin and The Heritage Council, University College Dublin, 2006, https://wfblink.net/weJ79h.

The High Court. "Between The Irish Human Rights And Equality Commission Applicant - and the Minister For Children, Equality, Disability, Integration And Youth, Ireland And The Attorney General Respondents", courts.ie, https://wfblink.net/7YAVPA.

The Irish Times. "TV3 Ordered to Pay Half of €140,000 Award to Solicitor Pending Appeal." The Irish Times, 27 Nov. 2015, https://wfblink.net/fiDAMh.

The Irish Times. "Net Emigration at Highest Since 1989." The Irish Times, 21 Sept. 2010, https://wfblink.net/5874Yo.

The Irish Times. "Nigerians Who Pose as Refugees Are Doing a Disservice to Themselves and Their Country." The Irish Times, 14 Aug. 2000, https://wfblink.net/bs2n1N.

The Irish Times. "Dublin Pensioner Opens Home to Traumatised Ukrainian Family." The Irish Times, 18 Mar. 2022, https://wfblink.net/zkSuDF.

Tighe, Mark. "News Media Applying for €1.8m State Grants Were Asked to Consider Focusing More on Climate Change and Rise of Populism" Irish Independent, 6 Oct. 2024, https://wfblink.net/MeD4Tj.

Tóibín, Peadar. [@Toibin1]. "The winks, guffaws & grins from FF & FG TDs to the Press Gallery in #Budget23 as the Minister announced a zero VAT rate for newspapers, was more than a little uncomfortable." X, 27 Sept. 2022, 5.43 p.m., https://wfblink.net/av3JEL.

Tóibín, Peadar. [@Toibin1]. "Long thread. I've completed a timeline of events relating to the bike shelter. A lot of people have been asking me if there were any political shenanigans at play. Here's the nuts and bolts of what I've uncovered." [Series of 12 Tweets] X, 26 Sept. 2024, 2.50 p.m., https://wfblink.net/UUZJVQ.

Treacy, Matt. "Who Are the Companies Who Regard Ballsbridge and Other Asylum Centres as Prime Investments?" Gript, 11 Jan. 2024, https://wfblink.net/OwEQRm.

Treacy, Matt. "22% of Population of Ireland Born Overseas, New Figures Show." Gript, 30 Mar. 2024, https://wfblink.net/aHbkIP.

Treacy, Matt. "State Loses Bid to Refuse €13billion Apple Windfall." Gript, 10 Sept. 2024, https://wfblink.net/taq431.

Treacy, Matt. "Amazon Recruits Almost All of Its Staff Here From Outside of the EU." Gript, 12 Sept. 2024, https://wfblink.net/ZgbELF.

Treacy, Matt. "More Than 70% of Google Jobs Don't Go to Irish People. Yet They're Crowding Dubs Out of the City." Gript, 1 Aug. 2021, https://wfblink.net/u4fTa7.

Trinity College Dublin. Black Studies—Trinity Electives— https://wfblink.net/Aosj8g.

Trinity College Dublin. Race, Ethnicity, Conflict (M.Phil.)—Trinity College Dublin—Courses, Trinity College Dublin. https://wfblink.net/ssk5Vh.

UCD. Black Studies and CRT—UCD Module—EDUC10210. https://wfblink.net/cu4qlT.

UCD. Gender, Sexuality and Culture.—UCD—https://wfblink.net/5VaQf9.

Uí Bhriain, Niamh. "Buncrana: Locals Block Migrant Bus, Say They Won't Accept Centre." Gript, 19 Oct. 2023, https://wfblink.net/1g8ky4.

Uí Bhriain, Niamh. "REVEALED: Asylum Seekers' Fingerprints NOT Checked Against Criminal Databases." Gript, 19 Jan. 2024, https://wfblink.net/k3asPD.

UNFCCC. Fund for Responding to Loss and Damage. https://wfblink.net/kqVZVj.

University College Cork. "Emigration Today, University College Cork." University College Cork, https://wfblink.net/AomSbG.

University of Galway. Killaguile House | Galway | Landed Estates | University of Galway. https://wfblink.net/YJyXzb.

Ventura, Luca. "Richest Countries in the World 2024." Global Finance Magazine, 16 Apr. 2025, https://wfblink.net/UbbGPa.

Webber, Jude. "Ireland's Luxury Problem: What to Do With Its €8.6bn Surplus." Financial Times, 2 Sept. 2024, https://wfblink.net/r7PfGF.

White, Jack. "CSO Records 'Strong Outward Flow' to Australia With 10,600 People Moving There From Ireland." The Irish Times, 27 Aug. 2024, https://wfblink.net/C92jZs.

Wilson, Jade. "Tributes Paid to Ashling Murphy at Vigils in Ireland, London and New York." The Irish Times, 15 Jan. 2022, https://wfblink.net/OgCoVr.

Woods, Keith. "Nationalism Doesn't Need National Socialism." Keith Woods, 5 Mar. 2025, https://wfblink.net/amug9L.

Woods, Keith. "Nationalism Vs. Neo-Nazism." Keith Woods, 23 Mar. 2025, https://wfblink.net/X94TzZ.

Whyte, Barry. "85% of Asylum Seekers Arrive at Dublin Airport Without Identity Documents." Newstalk, 29 Feb. 2024, https://wfblink.net/CSzjod.

ABOUT THE AUTHOR

Dr Eoin Lenihan is an independent journalist and researcher. Born in the west of Ireland, he grew up in the Celtic Tiger era which shaped his views on politics, culture, and national identity. He holds a B.A. in History and Archaeology as well as an M.A. in Archaeology from the National University of Ireland, Galway. He worked as a field archaeologist at the height of the Celtic Tiger. Witnessing the vandalisation of Ireland's archaeological landscapes, notably the Hill of Allen and the Hill of Tara to make way for economic 'progress', raised early concerns that Irish identity was in existential danger. Lenihan holds a doctorate in Pedagogy from the University of Augsburg. He worked as a teacher of Humanities at second level in Germany and taught student teachers at postgraduate level. After writing for education journals and magazines, he switched his attention to politics. His peer-reviewed empirical study of Antifa uncovered damning evidence of how Antifa in the US infiltrated the national media. It is the largest empirical study of the group to date. His work on violent extremism has appeared on Al Jazeera and Fox News among others. He has written for a wide range of international news outlets including The Federalist, The European Conservative, Gript, Daily Caller, Quillette and The Post Millennial. Lenihan maintains a presence on X at @EoinLenihan.

www.ingramcontent.com/pod-product-compliance
Lightning Source LLC
Chambersburg PA
CBHW061602120626
46550CB00004B/1590